Music Therapy and Neurological Rehabilitation

also by David Aldridge

Case Study Designs in Music Therapy
Edited by David Aldridge
ISBN 1 84310 140 8

Music Therapy Research and Practice in Medicine
From Out of the Silence
David Aldridge
ISBN 1 85302 296 9

Music Therapy in Dementia Care
Edited by David Aldridge
ISBN 1 85302 776 6

Music Therapy in Palliative Care
New Voices
Edited by David Aldridge
ISBN 1 85302 739 1

Spirituality, Healing and Medicine
Return to the Silence
David Aldridge
ISBN 1 85302 554 2

Health, the Individual, and Integrated Medicine
Revisiting an Aesthetic of Health Care
David Aldridge
ISBN 1 84310 232 3

of related interest

Constructing Musical Healing
The Wounds that Sing
June Boyce Tillman
Foreword by Paul Robertson
ISBN 1 85302 483 X

Music Therapy – Intimate Notes
Mercédès Pavlicevic
ISBN 1 85302 692 1

Music Therapy
and Neurological Rehabilitation
Performing Health

Edited by David Aldridge

Jessica Kingsley Publishers
London and Philadelphia

First published in 2005
by Jessica Kingsley Publishers
116 Pentonville Road
London N1 9JB, UK
and
400 Market Street, Suite 400
Philadelphia, PA 19106, USA

www.jkp.com

Library of Congress Cataloging in Publication Data
Music therapy and neurological rehabilitation : performing health / edited by David
    Aldridge.-- 1st American pbk. ed.
    p. cm.
Includes bibliographical references and index.
ISBN-13: 978-1-84310-302-8 (pbk. : alk. paper)
ISBN-10: 1-84310-302-8 (pbk. : alk. paper) 1. Music therapy. 2. Neurobehavioral
    disorders--Patients--Rehabilitation. I. Aldridge, David, 1947-
ML3920.M89763 2005
615.8'5154--dc22

2005009443

British Library Cataloguing in Publication Data
A CIP catalogue record for this book is available from the British Library

ISBN-13: 978 1 84310 302 8
ISBN-10: 1 84310 302 8

Printed and Bound in Great Britain by
Athenaeum Press, Gateshead, Tyne and Wear

*This book is dedicated to my father, Robert Aldridge,
who in his dying showed me the fragility of scientific knowledge
and returned me to the reality that is love.*

Acknowledgment

I would like to thank my colleagues in this book
who have so generously given their work.

Contents

List of tables

List of figures

List of boxes

CHAPTER 1

Looking for the Why, How and When

David Aldridge

There are often hidden motives for research and as research supervisors we will always ask why the researcher has chosen his or her topic. The motives will be various. Some wish to serve the community. Some will serve the profession. And sometimes we serve ourselves, not simply with the achievement of a qualification or a title, but in reaching a level of knowledge that reconciles a personal need. The same applies to editing books. We scrutinize particular problems because they raise questions and doubts within ourselves. Much of my early work with suicide and palliative care was a struggle with the angel of death, as was continuing work with spirituality and the meaning of dying. This volume is no different. It returns me to that nightmare of not being able to communicate, reconciled by the hope of song.

In my early contact with music therapy I saw how a music therapist communicated with a woman who, so we were told, could not communicate. But she did – or rather, they did. Therapist and patient sang together. The seemingly random screeches of a young handicapped woman were woven up into a tapestry of sounds. This was music and it was a clear denunciation of her non-communicativeness. And that touched a chord in me. Despite a career involving public speaking, a deluge of writing and a shower of singing, I still experience the horror of the thought that I will wake up not being able to communicate. Dumb. Voiceless. Inarticulate. Not being understood. But if we allow others to reach out to us, then we *can* be articulate. Communication is not resident in one person. Mutuality is central to our lives.

The authors in this book grapple with the same problem. Through them I have been able to see new perspectives on how we communicate with those who are deemed uncommunicative, or who are confronted with future failure. Through the work of my colleagues I see the potential in others. The 'other' is not separate. There is hope.

Many readers will be surprised that the chapters in this volume are restricted to such a small number of authors. The reason is that this is essentially a collection of doctoral studies from colleagues whose research I have supervised and with whom I have had a mutual understanding of music therapy. This is not to say that the therapeutic approach is the same throughout. Indeed, we may have to learn to speak of music *therapies* in that some therapeutic applications are quite specific, as revealed in the chapters from Monika Jungblut, Wolfgang Schmid and Hanne Mette Ridder. I did not supervise Gerhard Tucek, but we have a common understanding of the process of neurological rehabilitation and of musical influences, so it makes sense for his work to appear here. All the authors agreed to sing from the same hymn sheet, in that I asked them to consider my hypotheses that we are performed beings and that our performance is achieved through and with others as dialogue.

A performed niche

This book is about rehabilitation. The centre of the word constellation rehabilitation is from the Latin *habere*, which is a fit state or condition within which we can dwell. The process of neurological rehabilitation is concerned with returning us to those performances of our bodies within which we can dwell and recognize ourselves; where we feel at home within our bodies. The notion of 'fit' can also be extended. Fit need not be the sense of physically fit, but also as fitting into an ecology. Much is made of Darwin's notion of the survival of the fittest as if it will be the strongest and muscular who will triumph. This is a misreading of what fit is in a biological sense. We have to fit into an ecological niche that is performed. We play parts in an ecology in which we are important because we perform that ecology. 'Fit' is a process, perhaps better expressed as fitting. Rehabilitation is a process refitting us to a set of habits that make living sense – sense in a neurological way of feeling and sense as understanding. Fitting into an ecology is a continuing performance that we have with others; it is dynamic not fixed – like making music. The weak, the sick and the needy – the people we will read about in this book – also are part of that performance we have as a communal life. Not only are we challenged to help them fit into living life to the full, they challenge us to perform compassion.

We can also use 'fit' in the sense of being fitted for a new set of clothes. In this way, we fit our bodies and perform our habits to suit ourselves. Rehabilitation, as performed in this book, is a process whereby people are encouraged to dress themselves in the suits of their own making. These suits affect our performances.

We have identities that are performed and these are validated with others in performance (Aldridge 1989a).

Similarly, we can recall the notion of an ecology of communication – not simply a sender and receiver, a player and a listener, me and you, but a mutual performance; together we are.

What we have already

Two of the chapters in this book, by Hanne Mette Ridder and Simon Gilbertson, are concerned with structured reviews of the literature in music therapy. It is not simply enough to say any more that the literature exists, we need to begin to scrutinize that literature and see how that material can be used. We know that music therapy exists but we have to say what it achieves. Both authors are clinicians in practice and both conclude that the literature is wanting in terms of missing information. We need to bring some form of structure to our case reporting such that we achieve a commonality of basic data. Without evidence of specific effects we cannot offer any comparative studies. I am not talking here about pushing anyone into a straitjacket when reporting case study material, but simply making a plea for a commonality of data collection so that we can offer a sound basis for further studies. As Anke Scheel Sailer says in Chapter 10, the arts therapies were in use but nobody knew what they did specifically, why they were being used and when to implement them.

Ethics and the right to live

All the aforementioned chapters raise the question of what it is to be human and how we present ourselves in everyday life. They also challenge us to understand the meaning of human existence for those who have experienced trauma or are faced with degeneration. When I was young it was The Who who sang about 'my generation' and hoped to die before they got old. Well, many of us did get old. Forty years on, the same generation is fearful about de-generation. As music therapists will remind us, we have to be careful what we sing about.

Much is said about interdisciplinary studies in academic environments. All the researchers represented in this book raise issues that transcend their own disciplines. The right to live, the right to an equal existence, the right to be considered as a whole person, the demand to be seen of personal worth, and what it is to be fully human are not simply musical matters but the very stuff of philosophical anthropology. Furthermore, these chapters are not simply about functionality in health care. They challenge the poverty of functional thinking. The aesthetic is part of our culture and needs to be re-incorporated into health care discussions

(Aldridge 1991a, 1991b, 1997, 2004). The notion that all phenomena can be converted to quantitative terms is an impoverishment of our culture and essentially an anti-aesthetic stance.

Wolfgang Schmid's study of music therapy with multiple sclerosis patients in Chapter 7 reminds us that the people he plays with regard themselves as musicians, not predominantly as patients. This shift from my being a patient to considering myself a creative artist is itself a health-generating performance of self and closely related to the generation of personal identity (Aldridge 1989a). The people in Schmid's study are not denying the presence of a disease, simply stating that they are not the disease. Our identities are with our chosen performances, not pathological processes. We are more than a material change in our nerve cells. We are not the plaques in our brains. A consequence of this thinking is that as far as possible I have attempted to edit this book in terms of people suffering with an illness, not as aphasics, for example. I may have an illness but the illness does not have me.

A fragile consciousness

Ansgar Herkenrath, in Chapter 6, continues the wider debate about what life is and decisions that are made about the state of consciousness for people in 'coma vigile'. He reflects my concept of 'I perform therefore I am' with his 'I sound therefore I am'.

Several of the following authors comment upon singing, the importance of breath and the fragility of consciousness. Breath is an important binding factor herein because it can be used both as a subtle organizing property and as a material manifestation (Aldridge 2002, 2004). The reader will no doubt recognize here that I taught meditation in a previous career (Aldridge 1987). Singing is literally the intentional use of breath to heal, in a particular therapeutic form. A fundamental property of breathing is that it has rhythm. In musical terms, rhythm has to have the property of intention otherwise it would be simply cyclic repetition or pulse.

Life begins and ends with breath. Slight bodily changes are brought about by alteration in the mechanisms of breathing. In addition, mental changes are also influenced by breath. Our general condition of wellbeing is dependent upon the rhythmic cycles of breathing within us. Similarly, emotions change the rhythm of breathing – when we become overexcited we lose control over the breath. By gaining control of the breath we gain mastery of mind and body. Not only that, we also establish a connection with the world around us, of which we are part, through the breath. However, we forget this basic activity until the moment we become sick.

We can speculate that the various body rhythms have become disassociated in comatose states. The question remains then of how those behaviours can be integrated and where such integration is seated. My answer would be that it is breathing that provides the foundation of human communication upon which that coherence of being called health is built. Some people include music therapy as an energy medicine, but my contention is that energy alone is not enough, that energy has to be realized as form. We may need to consider music therapy as a performance medicine.

Central to the act of breathing is the concept of performance in the subjective 'now' (Aldridge 2004). The coordination of human activity that lends itself to the coherence that we experience of being healed is dependent upon a temporal concept. Time is structured and breath is the scaffolding of time in which the present is constructed. The construction in time that we call 'now', when extended, is the basis of cognition. That is how music therapy works – it offers a temporal structure for events that facilitates cognition: rhythm as the basis of consciousness. At the heart of this temporal coherence is the rhythm of breathing. Through the control of breathing we achieve coherence. For those disorientated in time, they then become oriented through that non-material activity of breathing, although the material necessity of gaseous exchange is present.

Says who?

I have written elsewhere that case study design encourages reflection by the researcher and by the participants. A central plank of this argument is trust rather than validity: can I trust what is being said by the researcher? The same thing goes for working in the field of neurological rehabilitation. Much of what we know about what has happened is through personal report. We have to ask the person. If the person cannot speak we have a potential problem. We can, however, as the music therapists show, perform with the individual and know something about how the person is through how he or she reacts. We are connected, not simply as an existential injunction, but also through our neurological make-up in terms of mirror neurons (Gallese 2003; Garbarini and Adenzato 2004).

In an early study (Aldridge 1996), I suggested that cognition occurs in developmentally delayed children when offered music therapy because their hand–eye coordination is encouraged through focused listening within a relationship that makes sense. The emphasis here is on sense being made. This is not a constructivist argument solely in a social science perspective but a literal constructivist argument in a biological sense. Sense is made. In my terms, sensing is performance. And this performance is mutual.

This is not a trivial argument, as I suggest in Chapter 2. Gestures are activities that we make in relationships and are the basis of communication. Not only do these have a cultural component, I argue that these cultural components are indeed embodied and that culture too is a performance and an extension of our biology. New developments in neurophysiology reinforce our clinical findings with developmentally delayed children. Exposure to language develops motor mirror neurons when an active sound is perceived (Westermann and Reck Miranda 2004), and language evolves from gestures (Corballis 2003) as we found through observation.

It is possible for us to know what is happening in the other person – intersubjectivity – as we resonate with the person. The activity of neurons is referred to as firing, and it is this mutual firing that we find in performance. On the basis of this we can reflect what is happening to the other person when we perform together. The significance of this understanding is that when we talk about consciousness we are essentially talking about intersubjectivity.

Consciousness is from the Latin *con* (with) and *scire* (to know). At the heart of the word is a concept of mutuality, knowing with others. Our consciousness is a mutual activity. We will see this over and over again in the accounts of music therapists here, and no stronger than in the chapters from Ansgar Herkenrath and Gerhard Tucek.

As humans we have to trust the reports of others. We can make physiological investigations and observe patterns of behaviour and kaleidoscopes of firings, but in the end these will provide us only with tangential evidence about mental processes. In the end we have to rely upon our common humanity, the brittle fineness of discernment and the richness of our expressive language. Introspection rules. As Jack and Roepstorff (2003) write: 'Personal level accounts help us to make sense of our experience, they inform our conscious strategies, they alter our interpersonal perceptions, and they help us to understand the implications of mechanistic accounts of our everyday lives' (p.xviii). The way that we perform our lives and reflect upon them reflects upon our wellbeing. We have to have understanding and that is based on our experiences. My thesis is that those experiences and understandings are performances.

What happens?

Chapters 7 to 10 of this book look at what happens when we do music therapy. A central plank of our research has been clinical application. This has had a mutual attraction to clinicians who want to see what their own work does. Wolfgang Schmid in Chapter 7 looks at how music therapy works with people suffering with multiple sclerosis. Not only does he make a clinical comparative; he extends this study into investigating what happens in music therapy over time as a qualitative study. He finds that there are phases to the therapy as both he and the patients become mutual music-makers.

Monika Jungblut in Chapter 8 makes a specific hypothesis about clinical change when working with people who have suffered over the years with aphasia. She identifies the elements of articulation and prosody in speech and singing and brings people to expressive language through her own form of specific music therapy. In an earlier book (Aldridge 1996), I referred to the biblical injunction that in the beginning was logos. While we as academics often take this as 'the Word', meaning the written word, it could just as easily be in the beginning was song. In pre-Socratic philosophy, logos is the active principle of the cosmos, the source of all activity and generation, and the power of reason residing in the human soul. In biblical Judaism, logos is the word of God, which itself has creative power and is God's medium of communication with the human race. My proposition is that music is prior to language, and to gain or regain speech we can call upon that logos of music to sing us into that performance we call health. Sung by the creator we achieve the performance that is our being.

Gerhard Tucek, too, calls upon an ancient knowledge of music healing. He uses ancient musical forms as a basis for his improvised work. There are many ancient and traditional music healing cultures. How these are transported into modern-day cultures and whether or not they transcend geographical location and temporal disruption is questionable, but it is important that we understand what treasures are available to us in terms of music healing.

We will see throughout this book that, just as there is no one music therapy, we also speak of various musics and the multiple forms of musicking.

Anke Scheel-Sailer is a medical practitioner. While working on a hospital ward she saw that the art therapies were being used as part of the team approach but no one really knew why or to what purposes. Intuitively she knew these were important. And the people paralysed after traumatic accidents certainly needed help that was beyond the medical. But what did the creative arts therapies, including music therapy, bring? It is not good enough simply to say that anything is better than nothing. We cannot afford such luxuries of thought in times of drastically limited resources. Nor can we ethically support such a perceptive when we do not really know that something is better than nothing. The whole concept of clinical trials is built upon challenging this premise. If we are to convince others that music therapy is worthwhile we have to begin to say exactly what music therapy brings for the sufferer, when, and if possible why. I fear too that we will also have to add how much it costs.

Researching neurological rehabilitation

We are faced with the challenge of providing evidence that music therapy brings results. While we cannot leap into the provision of systematic reviews and large-scale clinical trials, we can provide solid evidence of how efficacious music therapy is (see Chapters 6 and 7) and then how effective it is in practice.

In 1996 I made a plea that we establish common sets of data, or at least begin to use similar assessment tools (Aldridge 1996). Now I repeat the plea. We have a new generation of trained researchers. At the last European Congress in Jyväskylä in Finland, the majority of the keynote speakers had doctoral qualifications. Our literature, like this book, is a result of doctoral and post-doctoral studies. The major music therapy journal editors, and members of their editorial boards, are just as well qualified. We have the resources; what we now need is the political will to cooperate to bring the profession further.

If we begin to introduce rigorous case study designs then we can coordinate and compare our practices (Aldridge 2005). If we as authors and journal editors begin to offer guidelines for case reporting then we bring some structure to the relevant experiences that are emerging from practice. If we do not establish a common case study basis, then we are simply throwing away our hard-won experiences. This is a luxury we simply cannot afford, nor can the bigger endeavour of music therapy itself. Consider that if five practitioners in one country agreed to collect five case studies based on a common format with the same data structure in one year, then at the end of the year there would be twenty-five case studies. Over four years, this would be a hundred case studies. If three countries go together, then this would be three hundred studies at the end of a four-year period. Wouldn't that be a suitable basis for a meta-study? We have an organisation in the European Music Therapy Confederation that has recently gained recognition within the European Union, so it could coordinate such a programme. There exists the clinical and research experience to make such an undertaking. Some practitioners are represented here, but there are may others within the broader research field (Edwards 2002; Magee 1999a, 1999b; Magee and Davidson 2002).

One thing we have to establish is outcome research based on specific therapies with well-defined groups of clients. The initial phase of such research will be in carefully constructed case study designs. Then we shall need to determine what are relevant and successful outcomes, which patients respond, and what are appropriate forms of assessment that relate to other health initiatives. Monika Jungblut in her chapter uses an assessment of aphasia that is the gold-standard in speech therapy research in Germany. Neurologists and non-music therapists could immediately relate to her results as they were expressed in a form that was understandable to them. Similarly, Wolfgang Schmid has used a battery of tests that includes some common to other health care studies. These tests contextualize other less well-known tests. Central to these studies is a platform of data analysis using techniques that are understandable by other researchers and clinicians, some of whom may not be music therapists.

Supplementary statistical analyses: confirmatory and exploratory

Two of the studies in this book compare groups in a clinical trial. Monika Jungblut looks at her own method of treating aphasia in patients with a longstanding problem. As you will see, her method works, and we can demonstrate this through conventional statistical approaches including the effect size calculation described below. This is a confirmatory statistic that helps us to make sense of a small-scale trial and to suggest how it might be if we had had a larger population. Once we have done this, then we know it is worthwhile committing to a larger study.

However, we can also look at how the differing subscores of a composite test instrument relate to each other and perhaps find how these relate clinical improvement to what is done in therapy as a correlation between variables. Such an approach is exploratory. In an earlier study, I used a closer examination of a child development test instrument over time to ascertain how the music therapy could have had an influence on the improving abilities of the child (Aldridge 1996). In the child development study, it was scores on the relationship subscale that improved first, followed by improved hearing and then hand and eye coordination, leading to an eventual improved score on the cognitive subscale. This cognitive improvement could be directly related to an emergent therapeutic relationship that entailed focused listening, which included active playing on instruments by the children, which itself demanded hand–eye coordination. Such an in-depth understating is essential for us to relate practice and research together. Not only do we have evidence of significant statistical change, but these changes have also to be related to underlying theory. This understanding is what makes sense of the statistic. An analysis of correlation is also one way of seeing how scores relate to each other, as we will see below.

Statistical analysis is not simply the domain of quantitative researchers. As qualitative researchers, we can build our arguments upon observations and interpret statistics. Yes, interpret statistics. The major trap for novice researchers, particularly inexperienced doctoral candidates, is that they become so enamoured of the statistical process that they forget that a certain knowledge is necessary for interpretation. Statistic routines are one way of filtering a particular perspective on the observations that we have made.

Effect size and its implications

Effect size is a name given to a family of indices that measure the magnitude of a treatment effect. These indices are becoming the common currency of meta-analysis studies that summarize the findings from a specific area of research (Lipsey and Wilson 1993). Effect size measures display the magnitude of effects in terms of standard deviation units. While this approach does not supply a test of significance, it is useful in understanding how strong or meaningful the effect of the intervention is. It also allows a comparison across different clients or studies. That is, different clients or studies can be compared as to how many standard deviation units of change occur. Comparing effect sizes across studies is the basis of a field of research that is called meta-analysis. My suggestion is that we include effect size calculations so that we can offer a platform from which future studies can be assessed; but, more importantly, we can also see from small-scale studies whether future studies are worthwhile in terms of clinical significance (Schmid and Aldridge 2004). However, as with all statistical approaches, we need to know what we are doing. A common problem is that the statistic can be misleading if the studies are of different types of treatment or if the therapies are not described in enough detail (Pring 2004); and as we shall see (in the chapters from Hanne Mette Ridder and Simon Gilbertson) music therapy itself is not a homogeneous field nor are therapies described thoroughly enough for such comparison.

Effect sizes can be measured in two ways: as the standardized difference between two means, or as the correlation between the independent variable classification and the individual scores on the dependent variable. This correlation is called the 'effect size correlation' (Rosnow and Rosenthal 1996).

Effect size measures provide a standardized index of how much impact treatments actually have on the dependent variable. One of the most common effect size measures is the standardized mean difference, d, defined as $(M_t - M_c)/SD$, where M_t and M_c are the treatment and control group means, respectively, and SD is the pooled standard deviation. Cohen (1988) defines effect sizes as small with $d = 0.2$, medium with $d = 0.5$, and large with $d = 0.8$, stating that 'there is a certain risk inherent in offering conventional operational definitions for those terms for use in power analysis in as diverse a field of inquiry as behavioral science' (p.25). It is worth bearing this caution in mind, as we may begin to replace the questioned p value with d values as a ubiquitous measure without understanding what the statistic means. The evaluation of effect sizes requires that the researcher exercises judgement regarding the practical or clinical importance of the effects. If we mindlessly invoke Cohen's rules of thumb, contrary to his strong admonitions, in place of the equally unconsidered application of p value cutoffs such as 0.05 and 0.01, we are merely choosing to be thoughtless in a new metric.

Effect size can also be thought of as the average *percentile* standing of the average treated participant in the treatment group relative to the average participant in the untreated, or control, group. An effect size of 0.0 indicates that the mean of the treated group is at the 50th percentile of the untreated group. An effect size of 0.8 indicates that the mean of the treated group is at the 79th percentile of the untreated group. An effect size of 1.7 indicates that the mean of the treated group is at the 95th percentile of the untreated group.

Effect sizes can also be interpreted in terms of the percentage of non-overlap of the treated group's scores with those of the untreated group (Cohen 1988, pp.21–3). An effect size of 0.0 indicates that the distribution of scores for the treated group overlaps completely with the distribution of scores for the untreated group. An effect size of 0.8 indicates a non-overlap of 47.4 per cent in the two distributions. An effect size of 1.7 indicates a non-overlap of 75.4 per cent in the two distributions. In Monika Jungblut's study in Chapter 8, we see that there are clear differences between treatment and control groups from a comparison of the mean differences.

We are concerned not only with whether a null hypothesis is false or not, but also with how false it is. In other words, if the difference is not zero, how big is the difference that we should expect? By specifying an effect size that is the minimum difference that is worth our attention, we can design a study with optimal power rather than wasting resources on trivial effects. The larger the effect size – that is, the difference between the null and alternative means – the greater the power of the test.

The effect size statistic is not a magic formula that will solve all our problems. Some researchers have simply thrown all studies together – the so-called 'apple and pears' approach – in the hope of finding a statistic that will prove that music therapy works or that they have discovered the Holy Grail as heroic researcher. I must caution against this methodological irresponsibility. Statistical analyses are valuable if you understand how they work and the nature of the data. A large effect size *can* mean a poorly designed study.

One difficulty that we face in music therapy is a lack of resources. Research funding is scarce and it is difficult to find enough research support for data collection and skilled external assessors. (In Monika Jungblut's study, she was practically a lone researcher, paying for the external assessment herself.) In addition, by the very nature of the problems that we treat, it is not easy to recruit a lot of patients and offer them a comprehensive treatment package; hence, small-scale trials with a low number of participants.

Erdfelder (1984) has developed the concept of a *compromise power analysis* specifically for cases where pragmatic constraints prohibit *a priori* power analysis – in that the time required to recruit patients is not known beforehand or that the people recruited from self-help groups would respond slowly. The basic idea here is that two things are fixed, the maximum possible sample size and the effect we want to detect, but that we may still opt to choose alpha and beta error probabilities in accordance with the other two parameters. All we need to specify is the relative seriousness of the alpha and beta error probabilities. Sometimes, protecting against alpha errors will be more important, and sometimes beta errors are associated with a higher cost. Which error type is more serious depends on our research question. For instance, in proposing a new treatment of a current chronic disorder like aphasia, we would want to make sure that it is not worse than non-intervention. In this case, committing the beta error of accepting the treatment initiative and no treatment as equivalent, although the new treatment is worse, may be considered more serious than committing an alpha error.

In Wolfgang Schmid's study in Chapter 7, we shall see that music therapy has a modest impact as an intervention (see also below). The effect size statistic is moderate but is weakened by a power analysis, so there is the danger that we would accept the treatment when it really is no better than any other. Providing an effect size statistic with a power analysis offers a basis for further studies so that the new studies can improve upon what has already taken place. A larger-scale trial, with more patients and a specific assessment approach, will advance music therapy further as an intervention suitable for people suffering with multiple sclerosis and convince potential payers that music therapy is effective.

We can see from Table 1.1 that music therapy does bring changes, some of which are strong in terms of both effect and pragmatic power. These then will be a suitable basis from which we can make further comparison studies and refine specific hypotheses. Music therapy is shown to be efficacious in these small trials; that is, it works. What we need to know is whether it is effective. To judge effectiveness requires larger-scale studies located in everyday practice.

In another doctoral study (Kusatz 2002), a survey was made of a specialized form of music therapy within a comprehensive intervention for people suffering with tinnitus (a persistent ringing in the ear). By considering scores over time on a specialist tinnitus questionnaire, a standard measure within the German-speaking countries, we could calculate the effect of the intervention. Doing this offers a comparison statistic for other studies, and we can also compare this intervention with other clinical interventions.

Statistics of correlation

When we collect multiple variables in a study, we are interested in how one variable may influence another. As we shall see in Wolfgang Schmid's study, nine out of ten music therapy participants in a study described how important it was to become personally active in their own treatment (Schmid and Aldridge 2004; Schmid *et al.* 2003). All ten participants reported an immediate improvement in their wellbeing during sessions. In eight participants, this improved state continued for some time and was confirmed by partners or friends. This is also confirmed by improvements in the self-acceptance and depression scales, but not by quality-of-life scores.

Table 1.1 Effect size statistics from three therapy studies

Authors	Clinical problem	Measure	Cohen's d[1]	Error probabilities[2]
Jungblut and Aldridge 2004	Global aphasia	Aachen Aphasia Test	2.04	$\alpha < 0.05$ $1 - \beta < 0.95$
	Broca's aphasia	Aachen Aphasia Test	2.76	$\alpha < 0.05$ $1 - \beta < 0.99$
Schmid and Aldridge 2004	Multiple sclerosis	Hospital Anxiety and Depression Scale: Anxiety	0.65	$\alpha < 0.05$ $1 - \beta < 0.40$
	Multiple sclerosis	Hospital Anxiety and Depression Scale: Depression	0.65	$\alpha < 0.05$ $1 - \beta < 0.40$
	Multiple sclerosis	Hamburg Quality of Life Scale: MS	0.74	$\alpha < 0.05$ $1 - \beta < 0.40$
Kusatz 2002	Tinnitus	Tinnitus Questionnaire		
		total scores	1.37	Not applicable
		psychological distress	1.37	Not applicable
		emotional distress	1.17	Not applicable
		cognitive stress	1.25	Not applicable

Effects size conventions: *d* small 0.20, medium 0.50, large 0.80
[1] Calculated from www.uccs.edu/~1becker/psy590/escalc3.htm
[2] Calculated with G*Power: www.psycho.uni-duesseldorf.de/aap/projects/gpower/

To investigate this further we can see how variables are related to one another using a *correlation statistic*. Differences over time in the depression scores and self-acceptance scores are correlated with each other (see Table 1.2), and this may reflect their common conceptual background. We also see that a relief of depression is correlated with a lessening of anxiety, with ramifications for feelings of self-acceptance.

These are not causal arguments, simply indicators that the changes in the variables are somehow related to one another. However, relief of depression and changes in self-acceptance are not correlated with changes in quality of life. The quality-of-life scale is measuring something quite different. While we can argue that music therapy relieves depression and improves self-acceptance, we cannot say that these are related to improvements in quality of life. The quality-of-life scale, when we look at it closely, is predominantly concerned with functional approaches like being able to dress oneself. So the theoretical backgrounds of the instruments can be validated in the results that we find and related to the clinical arguments that we make. The correlation statistic provides us with a basis from which we can argue what is happening; the statistic is used for an interpretation of what we have found (Aldridge 2005).

Table 1.2 Correlation between domain score changes in the MS study using Spearman's *rho*

	SESA	BDI	HAD-A	HAD-D	HAQUAMS
SESA	1.00	-0.367	-0.332	-0.611**	0.033
BDI		1.00	0.566**	0.493*	0.127
HAD-A		**	1.00	0.411	0.118
HAD-D	**	*		1.00	0.011
HAQUAMS					1.00

SESA: Self-esteem and self-acceptance scale
BDI: Beck's Depression Inventory
HAD-A: Hospital Anxiety and Depression Scale: Anxiety
HAD-D: Hospital Anxiety and Depression Scale: Depression
HAQAMS: Hamburg Quality of Life Assessment: Multiple Sclerosis
** Correlation is significant at the level 0.01 (2-tailed)
* Correlation is significant at the level 0.05 (2-tailed)

When we argue about how music therapy works as an intervention for people suffering with multiple sclerosis, then we can propose – on the basis of this evidence – that people feel less depressed and less anxious and have a different self-perception of their own self-esteem. Indeed, seven participants described an enhanced perception of themselves with an increasing self-confidence over the course of the therapy. They were increasingly able to let themselves be surprised by the music as it emerged and by their own previously undiscovered musical skills. Music and music therapy are experienced by patients as 'something moving' that shifts negative thoughts about the disease into the background and offers a means of expression for feelings of security, freedom and pleasure. One partici-pant related how she met a friend in the university that she had not seen in a long time, after treatment. They talked for a while and it was only on parting that she told her friend that she has multiple sclerosis. This was a shift in her perception of herself as first and foremost 'a sick person' to a normal person with other priorities in life.

The correlation statistic does not prove anything here; it offers us the basis for an exploratory understanding of how the therapy works. Just as I saw in the child-development study, a statistical analysis helped me relate the data to an underlying theory. In Monika Jungblut's study, we shall see how direct changes in the test scores for repetition and articulation and prosody are related to overall improvements in the total test profile. We can relate these to musical elements in the therapy, which were also included in the hypotheses generated from underlying theory. This is not searching haphazardly for any connections, but rather looking for relevant correlations that suggest how the music therapy relates to therapeutic change.

In conclusion

Effect sizes tell us that something has happened, music therapy works. Correlations help us to determine what happened, why music therapy works.

A consequence of these comparative approaches is that we have to accept that subsequent studies will be better than those we have already made. This is how research works, for the betterment of the profession but principally for the improvement of patient care. Just as we as teachers have to accept that our students will be better than we are, so it is with research results. We stand on the shoulders of those who have gone before us to reach higher. Now is the time for research in music therapy to accept this situation. It is not a competition to see who is the best artist; it is a communal challenge to see how we can best serve those who come to us for help.

CHAPTER 2

Gesture and Dialogue: Music Therapy as Praxis Aesthetic and Embodied Hermeneutic

David Aldridge

When we consider people with neurodegenerative diseases we are essentially thinking of people confronted by minds and bodies that are failing to *perform* as they have previously expected. This situation is for them and their families a tragedy. Futures are damaged and hopes challenged.

More about performance

I chose the word 'perform' carefully as it is at the centre of my argument here. Indeed, as I have written in my other books about music therapy, my contention is that we are performed beings; that is, we realize ourselves in the world – mentally, physically and socially – as performances. And what we see in the process of the neurodegenerative diseases is a restriction in performance of movement, of communication, of thinking and, for some, a sense of becoming lessened as a whole person. The reason why I use the performance metaphor is that it is active and dynamic, lending itself readily to an artistic activity. Furthermore it is a temporal activity, not necessarily a permanent product. All too often we concentrate on art *products*, the material that has been made, when it is the actual *doing* of the art that is important. Music therapy reminds us of this very activity. We bring ourselves into form continually throughout each day. And we commit these per-*form*-ances with others.

Form naturally decays: the whole notion of entropy is that the world is falling apart. But contrary to this is negentropy, the bringing together. We are part of that forming the world together and that is why the arts are important. We have the ability to recreate forms. When this ability fails then we experience an existential loss. Performing ourselves back into the world, a world of others, is a vital activity of being alive and being human. Yet form is fleeting, so we must be continually present for a new performance. The reason behind this is simple. A fixed form is a fossil: it no longer has life. We are continuously forming (as living) and losing form (as dying) and the challenge is to see the bigger gestalt.

Health too is a performance (Aldridge 2000c). It is a state that has to be continually achieved through shifting according to the challenges from without and from developmental needs within. The health performance of a two-year-old is a lot different from that of a sixty-year-old. Our very biology is a creative performance, not a mechanical act. The same goes for the wholeness of being that we are as human beings – physical, mental, social and spiritual. We are works of art, peripatetic performances perpetually in progress on shifting stages. To put the 'being' into human being we have to perform.

Communication and dialogue

The body also has an aesthetic that influences our identity: how we present ourselves in the world, and how we are recognized. It is through our bodies that we are in the world. What our bodies express is an important part of communication, so I refer to gesture and dialogue as an 'embodied hermeneutic'. My intention is to place this hermeneutic, as the interpretation of experience, within the location of the body, and a moved body at that. This hermeneutic, as the art of understanding, is not solely speech dependent but action dependent within dialogue that interprets human actions, gestures and utterances. One person may gesture but it is the other person who gives meaning by completing the gesture. Indeed, I will argue that rather than using the term neurodegenerative diseases, what we are really faced with are dialogic-degenerative diseases, an argument that Hanne Mette Ridder continues in Chapter 4.

Meaning and understanding are embedded in living. We have to be engaged in the play of understanding, and that is performance – understanding achieves form that can then be recognized and completed by the self and others. This also moves the centre of responsibility away from the other person alone, the non-communicator, and places the emphasis on us as communicators. Rather than label the other solely as unable or disabled, we must take a part in how we fail them in their communicative needs or how we disable them from their contact with us.

Essentially I argue that the basis of human communication is musical, and the authors in this book take that basic hypothesis further and ground it in observational studies. We know that the essential properties of human understanding regarding verbal communication are speech prosodics – tempo, timbre, volume and pitch (Aldridge 1996). Through these we interpret the meaning of what people say to us, particularly in regard to emotional content. They are also elements that fail in some patients suffering with Parkinson's disease, and their failure is considered to be a general problem of timing (Kremer and Starkstein 2000). Timing, I hardly need to add, is a central feature of musical performance (Aldridge 1994). Monika Jungblut in Chapter 8 shows us convincingly how people suffering with aphasia (from the Greek, literally speechless: *a* – not, *phatos* – speakable) improve their ability to communicate, including by speech, through improvising with the musical parameters of the voice – literally embodying language within music (what we know, in other words, as singing).

We do not live our lives alone, and that means we have to enter into dialogue with others around us. That is what communication is for, to establish and maintain relationships. Music therapy is a prime example of how, when speech fails, we can establish meaningful communication. We can interpret what the needs of the other are through musical communication, as we will see in Chapter 6 from Ansgar Herkenrath. This is essentially a hermeneutic – the interpretation of meaning – and is *not* restricted to a verbal competence. For those who appear to be failing in their communicative capacities, we can retain significant communication. Wolfgang Schmid illustrates in Chapter 7 how people express themselves and demand understanding through improvised mutual music-making.

A problem remains: how do we know that the other person is communicating or attempting to communicate? In our work with children, the coordination of hand and eye movements as gesture, in a listening environment of musical performance, were central to achieving communication. We also know from studies in child development and the study of communication in primates that gesture is a foundation of communicative ability. Gesture as a communicative essential brings, however, a dilemma. While we can see and hear what others do, and this is important for understanding, it is precisely the elements necessary for gesturing that begin to fail in neurodegenerative diseases. Timing is lost and movements fail to be coordinated, so communication begins to fail. Music therapy has the potential to promote coordination such that communication is achieved (Aldridge 2000b). We come together in mutual time; indeed mutuality is all about timing.

Communication is based upon linking behaviours together, our own and those of others. This dialogue, which constitutes a sense of coherence to what we are as 'selves', is narrative in nature. It is personal and social. If this breaks down then we lose a sense of meaning for ourselves, and we lose meaning as a person in a social context. We lose the meaning of what we do and what we do with others. What we do literally makes no sense; this is the process of de-mentation.

The maintenance of meaning on an everyday level demands a sense of coherence between events (Crossley 2000). When disorder happens, then coherence must be rebuilt. Music therapy is one way of establishing a short-term coherence and thereby of re-establishing identity (Aldridge 1989a). Meaning is an activity demanding a temporal structure of connectivity and relationship between those events that we call 'consciousness' (Aldridge 2000c). Trauma, whatever its sources – as we will see in Chapter 5 by Simon Gilbertson – disrupts this coherence and the horizon of time is limited.

A subjective sense of self is dynamic and multifaceted, being composed of interactions within the individual and with others (Lysaker and Lysaker 2001). Thus, the existence of self is dependent upon a rich context of dialogical interaction. Other people degenerate when we fail to interact with them. This is true not only of those starving in Africa, or those incarcerated in prisons; it is what fails in dementia, and it fails progressively. That is why I refer to dialogic-degenerative diseases as much as neurodegenerative disease. The restricted communicative environments in which people find themselves further compound the stigma of dementia, and indeed of chronic illness. A therapeutic environment will necessarily promote a rich diversity of dialogic possibilities sensitive to a broad range of communicative possibilities; hence the range of creative arts therapies including music therapy, art therapy and dance/movement therapy.

We are differing minds with multiple voices. The challenge is to communicate with one another, and that is to promote a performance in which the other achieves understanding in us. Through dialogue, we achieve the social. While many authors predicate dialogue on language, my argument is that dialogue is performance like music. It is common play together that overcomes our differences and promotes plurality. Gurevitch (2000) emphasizes that when dialogue breaks down, it does so in silence. However, for musical communication, the very core of performance is the tension between sound and silence. Gurevitch writes of 'the possibility of dialogue as poetics where the plurality of sociality is informed by the breaks of conversation' (p.247). I would reinterpret this as: 'the possibility of dialogue as performance where the plurality of sociality is informed by the pauses of musical play'.

Silence is the basis for the meaning of what becomes evident. What makes sound and silence coherent is a sense of time. When timing fails, then we lose coherence. What music therapy offers for the patient is a performance from out of this silence. I am using performance in a broad sense here – as utterance, as gesture, as beat on an instrument, as tone. It is through performing ourselves that we achieve recognition by others and that we recognize the presence of others. I use 're-cognize' deliberately here as pointing to the achievement of cognition. But we need a site for these performances to occur; these are dialogues in the context that we call 'relationship'. When we limit the sites of these performances then we impoverish the possible dialogues and restrict the ability of patients to achieve their 'selves'. Dialogue, then, is existential and necessary for the achievement of health in the sense of becoming whole (Aldridge 2000c).

Dialogue is not simply given, it has to be achieved and negotiated. And meanings within this dialogue are never forced. We are constantly involved in interpreting the meaning of what others are doing. We do this constantly in clinical practice, first in diagnosis as understanding what the problem is, and then in understanding what is happening through the course of the therapy. These negotiated meanings are fragile, and performance has to be maintained in its mutuality. While we talk of degenerative disease, we must also be aware of the adequacy of our own performative abilities in the context of our therapeutic dialogues. Can we be adequate in our performance to meet the needs of others? This performance is based upon what we as practitioners bring to the dialogue as an ability to exist in time – the expressions on our faces, the postures of our bodies, the repertoire of our utterances, and the prosodics of speech.

When dialogue fails then we have alienation and despair (Aldridge 1989a, 2000c). The maintenance of the self degenerates through isolation. As I mentioned earlier, we have the potential for dialogic-degenerative disease. Patients may be forced into a silence so that they cannot transform nor structure; they are banished from the social to an isolated and degenerated self. We become part of that degeneration through our neglect.

To resume dialogue, however, is to achieve reciprocal recognition (Gurevitch 2001). We invite communication and require the 'yes' of participation. We complete the gesture of the other that is mutual understanding. This is exactly what can happen in music therapy. There is an invitation to participate. It is in the performance of both parties that we have the dynamics of interaction. To achieve plurality, we need two voices (Gurevitch 2001).

We have then a shift from the self to the other, the act of mutual recognition. Achieving cognition is not simply a personal act; it is social. We make our understandings of the world through others and so are performed by them.

Utterances

If we lose the means of producing language, then we become aware of how restricted we are in presenting ourselves. Music therapy is a means of producing communication and it is based on gesture, which is the basis of communication in a variety of species. We know that communication without language is possible in primates (e.g. Bond and Corner 2001). An essential feature of gesture is the concept of 'utterance'. We do make sounds outside the range of lexical language, as any parent of a teenage son will tell you. Utterances can be linked together in a grammatical form such that meaning is understood. This linking together as grammatical form in time is the basis of song and we are able to understand the general meanings of songs sung in other languages.

Structure, as form, is a way of schematizing experience, and this is how we learn to think. We achieve cognition through linking together events in time; it is the achievement of memory. We link sounds together into phrases, and this is the basis of musical meaning in that sounds begin to function as music when we discern a structure between the tones. Utterances, then, are a positive sign of the producer attempting to regain cognition, to mentate out of de-mentation by providing an expressive cue to an underlying temporal dynamic. Rather than dismissing utterances as meaningless, we need to offer a performed context that catches such utterances in time and thereby makes them meaningful. The task that we have as music therapists is to recognize this temporal dynamic and structure a mutual participatory performance.

A quality of utterances, and many gestures, is that they are spontaneously expressive. With demented patients, the challenge of therapy is to move from the spontaneously expressive sound to the performatively reflexive utterance that is intentional. It is a shared temporal dynamic that offers a structure for spontaneity, which allows repetition within musical form, and thereby focuses attention and the possibility of regulation. As with all acts there is a constitutional aspect (what this event means) and a regulative aspect (what is to be done next as a meaningful response). Thus utterances become articulate when we offer a context of understanding. This context is that of a performed relationship and it exists in time.

A fundamental property of mental ability is that it is explicated in verbal and musical expressions, gestures and bodily expressions. As we have seen earlier, understanding is achieved through performance. The body is active in the world to open up the world and belongs to the world. Illness becomes a restriction of this bodily presence and thus restricts both presence in the world and understanding (Svenaeus 2000). The challenge of music therapy is the challenge that we all face: how to establish the pattern of meaning.

At the heart of this understanding is *time*. Time is the 'how' of events being organized and is the attribution of meaning to change (Tabboni 2001). How we perceive time is multifaceted, it is part of our personality and part of our culture and achieved in our relationships. We have various modes of understanding time, but in neurodegenerative diseases these are restricted. In Parkinson's disease there is a disruption of time and its expression in emotion (Kremer and Starkstein 2000) and movement (Thaut and McIntosh 1999); in Alzheimer's disease there is a loss of memory and of fluency (Aldridge and Aldridge 1992; Aldridge and Brandt 1991). The phenomenon of 'sundowning' in dementia patients is a physiological change whereby the time structure that coordinates activity and temperature is lost (Volicer et al. 2001).

The coupling of the neural system, the musculoskeletal system and the environment demands a coordination of temporal dynamics. There are scale relationships of time dependent upon biological events – muscular, cellular, planetary and galactic. Behaviour is temporally structured and it is in the organization of time that we synchronize our communication. Anticipation of events and coordinating responses demands a temporal dynamics based upon attention (Keijzer 1998). Anticipation of events is central to playing rhythm with another person, and we see this in the mutual playing of improvised music where even severely disabled patients have the ability to anticipate events and coordinate their behaviour within a context of a flexible temporal dynamic. We are speaking here of musical time that itself is flexible as performed, not the chronological time of a machine.

Gesture

In therapy we have a performed dialogue. The body is central for interaction. We perform most of our actions in daily life without reflecting on how we do them. Everyday skills are the basis of the knowledge that we need to perform our lives. Knowledge is done. It is based on interaction with others and is the background from which we achieve understanding of what others are doing. Therefore, the performance possibilities that we offer others will enhance the abilities that they have. Relationship in this sense is not going to be based upon what we say, but what we do.

Gesture is a central feature of a communicative setting for the ecology that we call understanding. If there is a breakdown in the background, when relationship fails, then the mutuality of time is lost, events lose their context and we become isolated. We literally fall out with each other: fall out of time and, thereby, understanding. This is the process of becoming isolated. To repair performance, we have to offer a structure in time. Structured time is precisely what music is in all its myriad of styles and possibilities for performance. For those losing cognition, or struggling to regain cognition, the achievement of musical form is the basis of an enhanced cognitive ability. In coma patients, this is the regaining of levels of consciousness (Aldridge 2000c). Within our varying cultures we have repertoires of performance suitable for promoting understanding; the challenge for us as practitioners is to expand the repertoires of treatment necessary to achieve competent performance for those suffering with neurodegenerative diseases.

We know that non-verbal behaviours like hand gestures convey important information and are a rich source of unspoken knowledge (Breckinridge Church 1999; Goldin-Meadow 1997, 1999, 2000; Mayberry and Jacques 2000; Mayberry and Nicoladis 2000). They are robust across cultures and are used by people of various ages. Not only do they reflect understanding, they also shape understanding. Like utterances, they are an attempt to regain cognition; they are used to inform the listener of the state of the expresser. We judge intentions by gestures. In children, gestures signal that a particular notion is available in the repertoire of understanding but not necessarily accessible to speech. However, for the elderly, we can see that a concept is retained in the repertoire but no longer accessible to speech or conscious reflection. Gestures also allow expressions that do not easily fit into a categorical system but still reflect aspects of the performer's state. This eases the cognitive burden and, for the understanding of emotions, allows the performer to achieve emotional expression without prematurely labelling that emotion, in giving the emotion a particular valence.

Setting and performance

How we perceive sounds as music or noise is dependent upon culture. Art productions are a ritualized form of performance, as are some clinical encounters. Yet, the everyday stuff of life is improvised. How we participate in these performances, and understand what is happening, is a matter of culture. Culture too is performed.

One of those influential cultural aspects will be the setting within which the performance takes place. Thus the setting of the home, the clinic, the day-centre or the hospice will be important for understanding of the performance.

The nature of this performance, too, will be dependent upon the engagement between the performers, and this is inevitably emotional and sensual (Smith 2000). The emotional relationship is a way of understanding the world and this is absolutely central for the sufferers of neurodegenerative disease. We have the massive problem of agitation in demented patients, and the confounding problem of depression throughout the broad spectrum of disorders. Music therapy, with the cultural aspects of emotion and sensuality related to music, has an important role to play in relieving the suffering of these patients.

Musical performance does not cause feelings but is the embodiment of feelings given form. Music therapy is important for demented patients because it offers a form for interaction. Feelings regain their shape such that they can be initiated, formed and resolved. The idea of emotions achieving closure is important because it emphasizes performances that are bodily satisfying, if not intellectually satisfying. What cannot be articulated in speech can be expressed through music, primarily because the medium of musical performance is that of organized perceptions and related actions. The basis of human intimacy is the coordination of understanding between self and other. For infant and mother, it begins as a mutual dialogue. Such dialogues also occur for adults and we simply have to extend our repertoires of caring such that these can be achieved. Music therapy is one form of acceptable intimate dialogue.

If our bodies are the source of musical performance, then disruptions in kinesis, rhythm and hearing will disturb that performance. The goal of therapy will be to restore the organizational property that binds these sources of performance together, such that coherence of the whole person can be achieved once more. This binding, organizational property is time experienced as musical form.

Gestures also boost activation levels and are involved in the temporal structure of thinking (Alibali, Heath and Myers 2001; Alibali, Kita and Young 2000). We see this in the simple beat movements when people listen to music. Even when people are talking on the telephone they gesture. The use of gesture also modulates responses to sensory input. Where agitation is a problem then gesture is an attempt to regulate arousal, either as an oversensitivity or, as mentioned earlier, to boost activity. Sensory integration, including proprioception, demands an adaptive response if communication is to take place. Integration requires arousal (maintaining alertness), attention (ability to remain focused on a desired stimulus or task), affect (emotional regulation) and action (goal-directed behaviour as praxis in planning behaviour). For patients suffering with a neurodegenerative disease it is imperative that sensory integration be maintained as long as possible and that this integration can be practised, maintained and achieved through active musical play. For the active synchrony of neural events a pattern of strong signals has to be established, and this demands orientation with focused attention with a conscious discrimination of auditory events (Engel and Singer 2001).

Movement and experience

> ...understanding is pre-eminently a practical thing. Understanding is embedded in life, in relationships and experiences, in 'the totality of human existence'. (Carr 1996, p.44)

How experience is unified and organized is a central question. Behavioural integration is the key to experiential unity that opens the lock of mutual performance. The experiencing person is not simply a set of brain activities but an embodied mind actively engaged with an environment; that is, the ecology of events and ideas that we call consciousness (Aldridge 2000c).

Disorders that interfere with the generation of voluntary actions have dramatic psychological consequences (Haggard 2001). Movements are generative of complete sequences of interactions that promote cognition. Perception and action are interwoven as activities. In the network of pre-motor actions there is a repertoire of possible actions, and one action must be selected. Attention is therefore necessary to perform an action. Similarly, performance will focus attention – thus the emphasis on music therapy as performance. Again referring to the work with children, it was a setting of musical activity that promoted attention from which meaningful coordinated sounds could be performed.

Mood regulation

> It is not the affect that regulates people rather than people regulating their affect. (Erber and Erber 2000, p.210)

A central feature of our emotional lives is the ability to regulate our emotions (Larsen 2000). Indeed, when such regulation fails we take it as a sign that something is going wrong and, in the extreme, we suspect a psychological disturbance. Affective states also influence attention, alter the way in which we perceive the world and influence our social relationships. Emotions are expressive, and we achieve this expression through gesture, postural changes, facial expression and the use of voice. It is not what we say, but the way that we say it, that indicates our emotional state and intentions. The musical parameters of communication indicate emotional valence.

Emotions are bodily events that have shape and duration. How these events are regulated on a daily basis is also a matter of ecology balancing our personal environment and the social world. Although we consider our emotional life to be personal, it takes little persuasion to convince us that it is our life with others that has an influence on those emotional reactions. When we fail to interact satisfactorily with others, then a source of emotional regulation may also fail. If we lose attention with both external and internal events then there is loss of feedback and the potential for emotional disregulation. We need to know, for example, the difference between a current state and a desired state. This is a cognitive activity. The linking of emotional events to understand the profile of an emotion is a matter of time. While the ability to express emotions is important, the facility to inhibit emotions forms the profile of our everyday life. Choosing the form of an emotion, in terms of expression and inhibition, is necessary for appropriate emotional articulation. In dementia of the Alzheimer's type, agitation is a problem of emotional expression – agitation being a state of emotional arousal that fails to achieve a satisfactory emotional form, that appears to have no potential for inhibition and thus no closure as an emotional form.

Motor mimicry is an essential feature of empathy and understanding the other person (Neumann and Strack 2000). Facial and postural expression influence emotional expression. Thus the perceptions of another person's behaviour may activate the same action codes within the observer that generate that behaviour. Thus, how we approach the demented is important in the way in which they will respond. Imitation is a feature of musical play and used in improvisation.

We also judge the expressive behaviour of others to know something about ourselves. The vocal expression of emotion embedded in the speaking voice is a powerful indicator of relationship and promotes a response. Expressed emotions promote congruent mood states in the listener; therefore we have to be as careful about *how* we say what we do as *what* we say. In music therapy, the use of timbre is central to emotion expression, as it is in the performance of operatic arias.

Cohen-Mansfield (2000) writes of the need to recognize the unmet needs of patients where symptoms may be an attempt to alleviate need (pacing provides stimulation), agitation may be an overexpression of emotional arousal, symptoms may be an attempt to communicate needs, and behaviour may represent the outcome of an unmet need (crying from pain).

Patients with Parkinson's disease have speech that is flat and unemotional. Although they understand emotions and can express emotions linguistically, what fails are the musical elements of speech. At the core of the problem is the processing of temporal information, particularly regarding temporal change as a cue to vocal emotion.

In conclusion

As Cohen-Mansfield (2000) suggests, therapeutic interventions need to be tailored to meet the needs of individual patients and their characteristics. Music therapy recognizes individual needs and adapts to meet them (see Box 2.1). In various social and treatment settings, music therapy can promote dialogue. The implication of such dialogues is that the sufferer can maintain, or even recover, an identity that has a broad repertoire of possibilities. When we enter into such dialogues, then the caregivers are also offered a broader potential of identities. The sufferer is reintegrated within a communicative ecology and this prevents isolation. Hanne Mette Ridder develops this further in Chapter 4 and she has also written extensively about how communicative abilities remain through singing (Ridder 2003, 2005a).

Music therapy offers a flexible temporal structure for processing temporal information. If timing is an ability that is failing, then musical form offers an alternative form within which timing can be temporarily recovered and practised. The expression of timing in communication will utilize gestural abilities, including utterance, that spontaneously bind events together and are indicative of performed ability. Gestures are seen within this context as attempts to regain cognition, not solely as failed abilities.

As emotional regulation is a common core problem within neurodegenerative diseases, attempts to regulate emotion positively will have benefits for both sufferers and carers. Emotional arousal is located within a context of attention and

Box 2.1 Benefits of music therapy for the neurodegenerative diseases

- Meets the needs of individual patients and their characteristics
- Promotes dialogue and the maintenance of an identity that has a broad repertoire of possibilities
- Reintegrates the person within a communicative ecology and prevents isolation
- Offers a flexible temporal structure for processing temporal information where timing can be temporarily recovered and practised
- Utilizes gestural abilities, including utterance, binding events together that are indicative of ability
- Gestures seen as attempts to regain cognition, not seen as failed abilities
- Encourages rhythmical movement
- Regulates emotional arousal in terms of expression and inhibition with implications for sufferers and caregivers
- Needs can be expressed
- Motivates communication and participation without being speech dependent
- Attention, arousal, affect and action embodied in musical form.

action whereas needs may be unmet, are unable to be expressed or fail to be recognized. The expression of emotion, and similarly the ability to inhibit arousal, will contribute to communicating needs effectively.

Communicative abilities are essential. This mutual need is usually achieved through speech. When speech fails, then it is important to utilize those properties of human communication that are not speech dependent. Attention, arousal, affect and action all occur in musical per-form-ance. Music therapy has the potential to promote communication, stimulate cognitive abilities and alert us to residual communicative abilities.

CHAPTER 3

Dialogic-Degenerative Diseases and Health as a Performed Aesthetic

David Aldridge

Neurodegenerative diseases are, and will remain, an enormous public health problem. Interventions that could delay disease onset even modestly will have a major impact. These diseases are disabling to the sufferers because there is a loss of normal motor functioning, a change in mood, and a gradual loss of cognitive abilities. Furthermore, they do not suffer alone: these losses have an impact upon family and social life. While there are numerous projects aimed at finding medical relief for suffering and the treatment of disease, we are reminded that these problems are also illnesses. Behaviour is influenced. We are challenged as a society that people within our midst are suffering and it is our responsibility within the delivery of health care to meet that challenge with appropriate responses. A major confrontation for those offering treatment, as it is for the patient, is that the problem itself is degenerative – there is no cure. Furthermore, the problems facing patients confront the deepest fears of a success-oriented society. Decline, physical and mental, is not readily faced within communities that expect youthful appearance, worldly success and physical ability as the outer sign of acceptable personhood (Aldridge 2000c).

Epidemiology and features of disease

In 1997, the number of individuals in the United States with Alzheimer's disease was estimated at 2.32 million (range: 1.09 to 4.58 million). Of these individuals, 68 per cent were female. The number of newly diagnosed cases that could be expected over the next 50 years was estimated from a model that used age-specific incidence rates summarized from several epidemiological studies. It was projected that the prevalence will nearly quadruple in the next 50 years, by which time approximately 1 in 45 people in the United States will be afflicted with the disease (Brookmeyer, Gray and Kawas 1998).

The prevalence of dementia in subjects 65 years and older in North America is 6 to 10 per cent, with Alzheimer's disease (AD) accounting for two-thirds of these cases (Hendrie 1998). If milder cases are included, the prevalence rate doubles. While a genetic basis for Alzheimer's disease has been identified, the search for non-genetic risk factors has been less conclusive. Only age and family history of dementia are consistently associated with AD in all studies.

Dementia is a source of chronic disability leading to both spiralling health care expenditure among the elderly and a progressive disturbance of life quality for the patient and his or her family. In the United States the cost of institutional care for patients with dementia is estimated at over $25 billion a year. If 4 to 5 per cent of the elderly population there suffer from dementia, then 1.25 per cent of the total population are suffering with the problems of severe dementia. Other estimates of the same population suggest that 15 per cent of those over the age of 65 will have moderate to severe dementia, with projection to 45 per cent by the age of 90 years (Aldridge and Aldridge 1992; Aldridge and Brandt 1991). As the prevalence of dementia increases dramatically with age, the elderly represent the largest population manifesting dementia (Brotons, Koger and Pickett-Cooper 1997). With projected increases in the population of the elderly in Europe (23–25 per cent of the national populations aged over 65 by the year 2040; Aldridge (1993b)), it is timely to identify treatment initiatives in the Western world that will ameliorate the impact of this problem.

It is in a primary care setting where dementia is mostly recognized, and early recognition is important for initiating treatment interventions before a person becomes permanently or semi-permanently institutionalized, and to minimize disability (Larson 1998). The challenge that we face is how to handle such a progressive degenerating disability over time.

Parkinson's disease (PD) is another common neurodegenerative disease affecting approximately 1 per cent of the elderly population. The disease is defined by motor abnormalities, the signs of which are bradykinesia, rigidity and tremor when the body is at rest. The clinical picture is, however, much more complex, and patients with PD, like those with Alzheimer's disease, are prone to affective disturbances, anxiety syndromes and possibly psychosis (Marsh 2000b).

Multiple sclerosis (MS) is a progressive disease resulting in motor disturbances, sensory disturbances and changes in cognition. Although treatments are continually being sought, those available are orientated to the relief of symptoms and to palliation. As in the other diseases, we see a picture of cognitive dysfunction and sometimes dementia (Mahler and Benson 1990). When combined with the severest possible symptoms of ataxia or paralysis impairing nearly all voluntary and functional movements, loss of speech, the inability to swallow, and extreme fatigue, the individual can experience doubt, anxiety and reduced self-esteem (Randall 1982).

Huntington's disease (HD) is a chronic progressive hereditary disease affecting the central nervous system. Here too we see large involuntary movements accompanied by gradual cognitive deterioration. Emotional disorders, behavioural problems and personality change may be experienced, leading to psychiatric symptoms (Folstein, Folstein and McHugh 1975; Morris 1991). Speech is increasingly challenged as the disease progresses. In terms of communication and movement, initiation, spontaneity and rate of speech are influenced. However, insight may remain into the most advanced stages of the illness (Shoulson 1990). The average age of onset is 36 to 45 years and, like the other degenerative diseases, it appears to follow stages (Folstein 1989). Studies examining the duration of the illness have yielded widely varying results – 10 to 40 years following onset (Harper 1991).

In all the above diseases we see a common core of progressive deterioration: a loss of bodily integrity, failing cognitive competence and the demise of emotional coherence. To this we must add the potential for social isolation that this deterioration brings, and isolation is the road to despair (Aldridge 1998a) – see Figure 3.1. Any adjuvant therapies that address these factors will form a significant part of a modern treatment strategy for the neurodegenerative diseases. The expressive arts therapies are to be considered as a part of this strategy.

We can see in Figure 3.1 that it is possible to intervene at various levels – from self-help group or family interventions at level I, to practitioner and specialist referrals at levels II and III. The interventions in this book are made at level III, and mostly as hospital or specialist referrals.

Clinical features of dementia

The clinical syndrome of dementia is characterized by a decline of cognitive function, which is represented by memory and language impairments. While the term 'dementia' itself is used widely throughout the medical literature, and in common usage, to describe cognitive impairment it is generally applied to two conditions: dementia of the Alzheimer's type (DAT) and multi-infarct dementia.

The course of Alzheimer's disease is one of progressive deterioration associated with degenerative changes in the brain. Such deterioration is presented in a clinical picture of episodic changes and a pattern of particular cognitive failings that are variable (Drachman *et al.* 1990). Mental status testing is one of the primary forms of assessing the cognitive failings which include short- and long-term memory changes; impairment of abstract thinking and judgement; disorders of

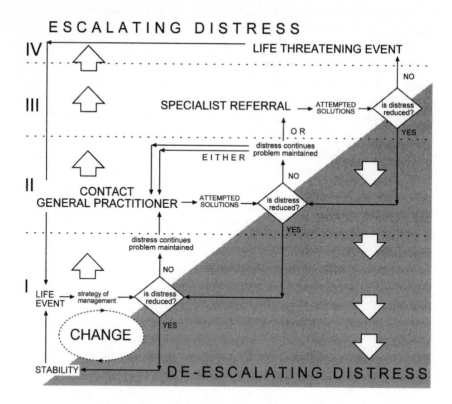

Figure 3.1 Cycles of distress escalation and de-escalation (from Aldridge 1998a)

language (aphasia), and difficulty in finding the names of words (anomia); the loss of ability to interpret what is heard, said and felt (agnosia); and an inability to carry out motor activities, such as manipulating a pen or toothbrush, despite intact motor function (apraxia). When such clinical findings are present then a probable diagnosis can be made, while a more definite diagnosis depends upon tissue diagnosis.

I have suggested elsewhere that music therapy provides a sensitive ecological method of assessment for determining cognitive abilities that are residual when speech is being lost, and communicative abilities, within an ecological context that makes sense to the patient (Aldridge 1993b, 1993c, 1994; Aldridge and Aldridge 1992; Aldridge and Brandt 1991). Indeed, the music therapy setting can be experienced as less challenging than cognitive testing, and therefore uncon-founded by patient anxiety.

While dementia of the Alzheimer's type begins after the age of 40, and is considered to be a disease of the elderly, the influence of age on prognosis is not as significant as the initial degree of severity of the problem when recognized (Drachman *et al.* 1990). Disease severity, as assessed by intellectual function, appears to be the most consistent predictor of the subsequent course of the disease, particularly when accompanied by a combination of wandering and falling, and behavioural problems (Walsh, Welch and Larson 1990). However, the rate of decline between subgroups of patients is variable, so a patient's rate of progression in year 1 may bear little relationship to the future rate of decline (Salmon *et al.* 1990). Cooper, Mungas and Weiler (1990) suggest that an as yet unproven factor, other than declining cognitive ability, may also play a part in the associated abnormal behaviours of anger, agitation, personality change, wandering, insomnia and depression which occur in later stages of the disease.

A performed identity

There is a profound level of understanding that lies beyond, or before, verbal communication. Underlying the concept of a performed identity is the notion that we 'do' who we are. We perform our very selves in the world as activities. This is as basic as our physiology and provides the ground of immunology, a performance of the self to maintain its identity. Over and above this, we have the performance of a personality, not separate from the body, for which the body serves as an interface to the social world. We also perform that self amongst other performers: we have a social world in which we 'do' our lives with others. This is the social self that is recognized and acknowledged by our friends, lovers and colleagues. This performed identity is not solely dependent upon language but is composed rather like a piece of jazz. We are improvised each day to meet the contingencies of that day – and improvised *with others*, who may prove to be the very contingencies that day has to offer!

We perform our identities and they have to have form for communication to occur. Such form is like musical form. Language provides the content for those per-*form*-ances. Thus we need an authored identity to express any distress in a coherent way with others to generate intelligible accounts (Aldridge 2000c). We have a network of coherent symbols as performed narratives. If language fails then the opportunity for us to accord our form, as selves, with others, appears to fail.

Narratives are constructed and interpreted. They lend meaning to what happens in daily life. We all have our biographies. What happens to our bodies is related to our identities as persons. These narratives are not simply personal stories, but sagas negotiated in the contexts of our intimate relationships. These understandings are also constructed within a cultural context that lends legitimacy to those narratives. Thus meanings are nested within a hierarchy of contexts. The same process applies to the history of our bodies, to the biography of our selves, to the narratives used by clinicians, or to the tales told by the elders of a tribe (Aldridge 2000a).

The patient and his or her family have a story about the problems they face, and this story has to be told. It is in the telling that we understand what the needs are. It is also in this act of telling that they have the opportunity to express themselves. The expression of needs is a performative activity. A patient's narrative about his or her illness does not always point out the meaning directly; rather, it demonstrates meaning by recreating pattern in metaphorical shape or form in the telling that is interpreted within a relationship. Symptoms in an illness narrative are a symbolic communication as they are told and confessed. Symptoms are signs that have to be both observed and interpreted in their performance. For example, we know that many elderly people visit their general practitioner expressing pain and expect a physical examination. Very few say directly that it is painful being lonely and that they are rarely touched. In a culture where one is not allowed to express such emotional needs of suffering and touch directly, then the narrative becomes a medical story of pain. Suffering is embodied as pain. While we may temporarily relieve pain with analgesics, our task is also to understand, and thereby relieve, suffering. In this way the ecology of ideas, that some call knowledge, is explicated within the body as a correspondence between mental representations and the material world. The setting in which we express ourselves will have an influence upon what we express. An extension of this will be that we, as caregivers, are open to the expression of other narratives. Creative arts therapists then will be only too aware of the possibilities of symbolic communication. We are the setting in which narratives may be creatively expressed.

The nature of communication breakdown – how it is signalled, how it is repaired, and the outcome of the repair process – appears to be dependent upon the stage of the disease. What is unknown, however, is the nature of the longitudinal changes in the resolution of communication breakdown over the progression of the disease. In the early and middle stages of a progressive disability, it is possible to achieve some success in resolving communication breakdowns despite declining cognitive, linguistic and conversational abilities of the sufferer. We may need to consider not just the patient but the caregivers too in training programmes (Orange *et al.* 1998).

Meanings are linked to actions, and those actions have consequences that are performed. What our patients think about the causes of their illnesses will influence what they do in terms of treatment, which in turn will influence what they do in the future. As practitioners, we lend meaning to the events that are related to us by our patients, weaving them into the fabric of our treatment strategies. We must learn to understand each other's language for expressing and resolving distress, and act accordingly. In a series of studies by Pennebaker (Dienstfrey 1999; Pennebaker, Kiecolt-Glaser and Glaser 1988), writing as means of disclosing distressing experiences is seen to have health care benefits. These expressions are non-verbal and predicated upon bodily expressions, which can be seen in movement; or vocal, that is sung; or visual, that is painted. In this way the creative arts offer not only contexts for expression, but also contexts for resolution, congruent to the mode in which the patient chooses to perform himself or herself.

For the verbally inarticulate person, this has an important ramification, as he or she is offered understanding and the potential for resolution of distress. For the elderly suffering with dementia, although verbal communication fails, we can offer contexts of expression and understanding where gesture, movement and vocalization make communicative sense.

For those struggling with verbal articulation, the structuring of narratives offers a meaningful context in which expression can occur. Remembering a story offers an overarching framework that links events together. We shall see later that when a piece of favourite music is played then there is a cascade of memories from an initial prompting, even if the name of the composer or lyricist cannot be remembered. As individuals we are stories: we are composed and those compositions remain.

Health as performance in a praxis aesthetic

Performed health is dependent upon a variety of negotiated meanings, and how those meanings are transcended. As human beings we continue to develop. Body and self are narrative constructions, stories that are related to intimates at chosen moments. Meanings are linked to actions, and those actions have consequences that are performed. The maintenance and promotion of health, or becoming healthy, is an activity. As such it will be expressed bodily, a praxis aesthetic. Thus we would expect to see people not only having sets of beliefs about health but also actions related to those beliefs. Some of these may be dietary, some involve exercise, some prayer or meditation, some medication and others artistic.

The social is incorporated, literally 'in the body', and that incorporation is transcended through changes in consciousness, which become themselves incarnate. Through the body we have articulations of distress and health. While health may be concerned with the relief of distress, and can also be performed for its own sake, sickness is a separate phenomenon. It is possible to have a disease but not be distressed. Indeed, it is possible to be dying and not be distressed. Yet for those who are described as being demented, there is a schism between the social and the body. When communication fails, we literally 'fall out' with other people – we fall out of relationship. We lose our consciousness when connections fail: these connections are literally organic in the context of dementia and the implications are far-reaching when our body falls out with our self.

If we take my earlier metaphor of composition, when bodily function fails, then we are literally de-composed. Yet, as human beings we know that despite our physical failings, something remains within us. There is a self that responds. Despite all that medical science will have to offer us regarding the decomposition of the physical body, it is the composition of the self that we must address in our therapeutic endeavours. It is to the psychological and humanistic sciences that we must direct our attention if we are to gain the knowledge necessary that will aid us in working with those who come to us for help.

The coherent body and the subjective now

The body becomes an interface for the expression of identity that is personal and social. In a metaphysical tradition, the human being is considered as a self-contained consciousness, *homo clauses*; yet Smith (1999) argues for an alternative model, *homo aperti*, the idea that human beings gain identity through participation in social groups. My argument is that this identity is performed. Both personal and social are necessary. The interaction of personal and social is circular, and the difference between them constructed. Bodies express themselves at the interface of the personal and the social. Using the body communicates to others. Using the body achieves perception of the environment, and that includes those with whom we live. But the performance of the body requires a biological system that is intact, a system that remains coherent over time. Memory is the coherence of events in time. When memory fails then a sequence of events lose their coherence. Not only that, if we fail to respond to events that demand a return performance, we are perceived as unresponsive. And the coherence of events is a rudimentary narrative. Our perception of self is dependent upon coherence in time.

I have used, in earlier books, the concept of a human being like a piece of improvised jazz (Aldridge 1999a, 2000c). For the piece to work as music it has to maintain coherence. We could just as well have taken a raga form where a theme is improvised to its limits, the tension lying in the variation and its relationship to the original theme. To achieve coherence, we have to engage in a form that exists in time. A piece of music achieves coherence in its maintenance of form. The same goes for our personal identity: we have to maintain an identifiable personal form in social life. If we lose time, then we lose our sense of coherence, and we lose our cognitive abilities too. Just as children gain cognitive skills with their increasing ability to hold events together coherently in time, we see the reverse process in the performance of the demented – demented being literally without mental form (de-mentia). This may occur as a performance difficulty because connections have been lost. However, there remains within that person a self, with its continuing story that has a developmental need to be realized each day and fulfil its purpose. How is that story then to be expressed? How does the narrative continue such that the saga is told to its end? To do this the person needs to reconnect. As we see in recovering coma patients described by Simon Gilbertson in Chapter 5 and by Ansgar Herkenrath in Chapter 6, it is the connection of existing capacities in a context of joint attention that leads to an improvement in consciousness (Aldridge 1996; Aldridge, Gustorff and Hannich 1990). With elderly patients who are demented, therapy must be directed to connecting what intrinsic abilities remain. While these may not be verbal, there are other possibilities.

The body has perhaps been neglected in communication studies as we emphasize language, yet it is gesture that is pre-verbal and promotes thought. Posture, movement and prosodics in relationship provide the bases for communication. Through the medium of an active performed body, health is expressed and maintained. Here is the bodily form that guides communication and by which the other may be understood and has an ambiguous content – it is social. Language provides a specific content – it is cultural. We know that someone is suffering by their appearance, but what the specific nature of that suffering is they need to tell us. We know someone is happy by what they do, but what exactly makes them so happy they need to tell us. In addition, by moving as if we are happy, we may promote happiness. By moving as if we are sad, we may promote sadness. Thus the body, and a moved body at that, is central to a life amongst others.

Understanding each other

Our stories are our identities. How we relate them to each other constructively, so that we mutually understand each other, is the basis of communication. What we do, or persuade others to do, as a consequence of those communicated stories is an exercise of power. How narratives are interpreted is important for understanding the ensuing possibilities of treatment. If a person is seen as being illegitimate in her demands for treatment, then she may be seen as a social case not needing medical help, and this is critical at a time of stretched medical resources. If a person is seen as being aggressive in his demands by the way he expresses himself, then he may be sedated rather than have the setting changed in which he finds himself. This process of problem resolution has consequences for the continuing narration of a patient biography that becomes dislocated from a healthy personal biography. If we become dislocated from our personal biographies then we suffer. Either we are labelled as deviant and become stigmatized, or we become isolated.

In the elderly who become demented, we see people dislocated from their biographies socially (by entering into caring institutions) and personally. Memory fails, and with it self fails to achieve a performance in daily life that integrates varying faculties. The very 'I' that is myself fails to perform as the 'me' that we all know. Thus the interface that is self in performance loses its narrative form. Fortunately, the fundamental basis of communication on which that performance is based, our inherent musicality, remains. In the following chapters we shall see how skilled practitioners invoke what is still there. The 'I' finds its 'me'. All is not lost. There is hope, and with that hope then healing is possible (Aldridge 2000c).

Creative arts approaches and the promotion of identity

The maintenance of an intact identity is a central therapeutic principle in working with those suffering from neurodegenerative diseases (Aldridge 2000b; Harlan 1993; Johnson, Lahey and Shore 1992; Magee 1999a; Ridder 2003, 2005a). At the same time, we also see that coping with emotions and finding a suitable form for their expression is necessary and is facilitated by the expressive arts therapies. Furthermore, we also find that the arts therapies motivate sufferers to communicate and this itself is a way out of what is often an increasing isolation. Expressive arts offer a challenging and stimulating experience within the capabilities of the sufferer (Harlan 1993).

Magee (1998) alerts us to working with individuals who have advanced neurological disabilities. She writes that one of the many challenges for the therapist is that of finding instruments that are appropriate to meet a diverse range of needs – particularly those that are safe for the uncontrolled nature of ataxic or choreic movements, and which are sensitive to very small, weak or fatigued movements (Magee 1999a). In a process of 'illness monitoring', through the involvement in music therapy, patients are aware of cognitive, vocal and physical changes (Magee 1998). Through playing instruments within clinical improvisations, individuals monitored their physical abilities to manipulate instruments and control the sounds they produced. Aldridge and Aldridge (1992) found a similar situation when playing with a female patient who became aware of her failing capabilities as well as the benefits of music playing. Ridder (2005a) documents how it is possible to demonstrate the communicative abilities of the demented elderly through physiological parameters when speech fails and through their response to singing in music therapy.

It is, however, the maintenance of ability – and in some cases even the promotion of potentials – that is a valuable therapeutic resource for such patients despite a prevailing sense of loss. Music therapy challenges a stigmatized and changed identity (Aldridge 2000b). Through actively playing, people have the opportunity to experience themselves as both creative and beautiful in the midst of deterioration and a severely curtailed future.

Research approaches to new treatments

In the next chapter, Hanne Mette Ridder surveys the literature published so far on the neurodegenerative diseases and offers recommendations for future work on precise indications of type and stage of dementia, the identification of needs and type of intervention, and of the exact purpose of the music initiative. Research outcomes are categorized and summarized to outline recommendations that may be used in clinical practice as well as in future research. In general, music therapy seems to be an effective intervention to maintain and improve active involvement as well as social, emotional and cognitive skills, and to decrease behavioural problems of individuals with a dementia. What has been lacking is an effective clinical trial of music therapy, but this situation is gradually being improved as we see in the clinical studies of Monika Jungblut (Jungblut and Aldridge 2004) and Wolfgang Schmid (Schmid and Aldridge 2004; Schmid et al. 2003).

Until recently, psychotherapy and counselling techniques had rarely been used with people with dementia. However, the change in emphasis within dementia care towards a person-centred, often non-pharmacological, approach has meant that there is a growing clinical interest in their use (Beck 1998; Bender and Cheston 1997; Bonder 1994; Cheston 1998; Johnson et al. 1992; Richarz 1997). This has also meant an increase in studies using creative arts therapies (Bonder 1994; Harlan 1993; Johnson et al. 1992; Kamar 1997; Mango 1992) and overviews of music therapy as a treatment approach to Alzheimer's disease have already been written (Aldridge and Brandt 1991; Brotons 2000; Brotons et al. 1997; Ridder 2003, 2005a; Smeijsters 1997; Vink 2000).

Individuals with AD often experience depression, anger and other psychological symptoms. Various forms of psychotherapy have been attempted with these individuals, including insight-oriented therapy and less verbal therapies such as music therapy and art therapy. Although there are few data-based outcome studies that support the effectiveness of these interventions, case studies and descriptive information suggest that they can be helpful in alleviating negative emotions and minimizing problematic behaviours (Bonder 1994).

Although there is a developing clinical literature on intervention techniques drawn from all the main psychotherapeutic approaches, there has been little research into the effectiveness of this work, and such research as does exist often uses methodologies that are inappropriate for such an early stage of clinical development. While some authors (e.g. Cheston 1998) argue that clinical research should adopt case-study or single-case designs, some researchers are also planning group designs for evaluating new clinical developments. My argument is for a broad spectrum of research designs that will satisfy differing needs, but for music therapy to be accepted within a framework of health care delivery. Then we will need to commit ourselves to a series of clinical trials.

The caregivers

In the absence of definitive treatments for Alzheimer's disease and related dementias, researchers in a variety of disciplines are developing psychosocial and behavioural intervention strategies to help patients and caregivers better manage and cope with the troublesome symptoms common in these conditions. These strategies include cognitive interventions, functional performance interventions, environmental interventions, integration of self-interventions, and pleasure-inducing interventions. More research is needed to develop these strategies further and establish their best use, but psychosocial and behavioural interventions hold great promise for improving the quality of life and wellbeing of dementia patients and their family caregivers (Beck 1998; Orange et al. 1998).

We know that people who are suffering do not suffer alone (Aldridge 1998a, 1999a). There is an increasing expectation that the community will care for its elderly infirm members, although this expectation is rarely matched by financial resources – placing the carers under stress, while relieving a community budget in the short term. Recent research on caregiver stress focuses extensively on its predictors and health consequences, especially for family members. Gwyther and Strulowitz (1998) suggest four areas of caregiver stress research: caregiver health outcomes; differential impacts of social support; caregiving for family members with dementia; and balancing work and caregiving responsibilities.

In a study by Harris (1998), in-depth interviews were conducted with 30 sons actively involved in caring for a parent with dementia. Common themes that emerge from their narratives are a sense of duty, acceptance of the situation and having to take charge, as well as issues regarding loss, a change in relationships with other brothers and sisters, the reversal of roles, and the need to develop coping strategies.

The psychological wellbeing of carers of demented elderly people has been investigated also by Pot, Deeg and VanDyck (1997). Three groups of carers were distinguished: those providing care for two years after baseline; those whose care-recipient died within the first year after baseline; and those whose care-recipient was institutionalized within the first year. All groups of carers showed a great amount of psychological distress compared to a general population sample, with an overall deterioration of psychological wellbeing. As the elderly patient declined, and the caregiving at home continued, then psychological distress increased. For carers whose demented care-recipient had died or was institutionalized in the first year after baseline there was no measurable deterioration. There is, then, a high level of psychological distress and deterioration among informal carers of dementia patients, so we may have to reconsider the personal and social costs of demented older people living on their own as long as possible if we are not able to release adequate resources to support the caregivers.

Part of this support will include sharing information and developing methods of counselling appropriate to caregivers. Increasing public awareness, coupled with the wider availability of drug therapies for some dementing conditions, means that carers are often informed of the diagnosis of dementia. However, it is unclear how much sufferers themselves are told about their diagnosis. In a study of how sufferers of dementia were given diagnostic information, Heal and Husband (1998) reported that half of the sufferers had gleaned their diagnosis more from their carers than from their doctors. The age of the patients was related to whether or not doctors told them their diagnosis, which supports a suspicion that there is a prejudice regarding the elderly about what they can understand. Only 21 per cent of carers were given an opportunity to discuss the issues involved, and younger carers were significantly more likely to feel that such an opportunity would have been useful. Most of the carers who had informed the patient said that the person had wanted to know, or needed a meaningful explanation for his or her difficulties, rather than giving more practical legal or financial reasons. Carers who had not disclosed feared that diagnostic information would cause too much distress, or that the sufferer's cognitive impairments were too great an obstacle. The process of 'informing' is a political act and demands the sharing of knowledge. While this is indeed a specialist medical task, the consequences of that task are explicated in a social nexus. Caregivers need to be informed that they can inform.

In the broadest sense of the term, knowledge as *diagnosis* is based not solely upon physiology but also upon the deep needs of the patient and carers. Neither of these knowledges excludes the other; both can be reconciled. From such mutual knowledge, a *prognosis* can be made. The diagnosis of a medical complaint is also a statement about personal identity and the stigma that may be attached to such an identity. Understandings are the loci of power whereby illness is explained and controlled. In the demand for caregiver information, such loci are shifting from the educated health professionals to increasingly better-educated caregivers as consumers.

Distress and the neurodegenerative diseases

Clearly, a neurodegenerative disease causes distress for the patient. The loss of memory and the accompanying loss of language, before the onset of motor impairment, mean that the daily lives of patients are disturbed. Communication, the fabric of social contact, is disordered. The threat of progressive deterioration and behavioural disturbance has ramifications for the family who must take some of the social responsibility for care of the patient, and the emotional burden of seeing a loved one becoming confused and isolated. Furthermore, we see a massive impact on the way in which the patient views his or her future, as radically curtailed, confounded by an identity that is severely impaired.

In a patient suffering with Parkinson's disease, it is often the patient's perception of the handicap that influences his or her emotional state as much as the actual disability (Schrag, Jahanshahi and Quinn 2001). While motor problems are an important feature of these diseases, from a patient's perspective it is 'difficulties in communication and maintaining independence; feelings of anxiety, foreboding, and depression; lowered self-esteem; limitations in social interaction, and the loss of accustomed activities' that are just as debilitating (Brod, Mendelsohn and Roberts 1998, p.214). Indeed, it is mastery of these varying problems that is considered to be important in improving the quality of life of sufferers (Koplas *et al.* 1999).

Emotional context and ability

It is important to consider the internal world of the sufferer. In this context, Bender and Cheston (1997) present a stage model of the subjective world of dementia sufferers drawing on ideas from both clinical and social psychology. The first stage involves feelings engendered by the process of dementia and includes four discrete states of anxiety, depression, grief and despair. The second stage of the model concerns the behaviours provoked by the process of decline. Finally, a continuum of emotions is considered, wherein the ability of an individual with dementia to engage in emotional behaviour depends upon the extent of his or her cognitive impairment and the social context in which the person is located.

In another study, Vasterling *et al.* (1997) examine unawareness of social interaction and emotional control competency. Impaired awareness of social interaction and emotional control deficits are positively correlated with dementia severity.

As the disease progresses there is a degeneration of the ability to comprehend and express emotion that is linked with mental impairment (Benke, Bosch and Andree 1998). Creative arts therapists have based some of their interventions on the possibility of promoting emotional expression and retaining expressive abilities.

Emotional changes

A source of error in diagnosing Alzheimer's disease is that it is masked by other conditions. Principal among these is depression, which itself can cause cognitive and behavioural disorders. In addition, it is estimated that 20 to 30 per cent of patients with AD will have an accompanying depression (Kalayam and Shamoian 1990), thereby compounding diagnostic problems.

We see a similar picture in other neurodegenerative diseases. At the very onset of Parkinson's disease, a group of our patients were so demoralized by the diagnosis that they refused treatment, and an association between depression and PD is considered to be a part of the clinical picture. Anxiety syndromes, too, are increasingly recognized in the neurodegenerative diseases (Kremer and Starkstein 2000). Marsh emphasizes that while the focus has been on depressive syndromes in PD, anxiety syndromes are being recognized as a common problem (Marsh 2000a). Similarly, in multiple sclerosis, major depression is considered to be an important clinical problem that diminishes quality of life, and when untreated, worsens (Mohr and Goodkin 1999). The prevalence of depression in MS sufferers is estimated to be 36 to 50 per cent (Wang *et al.* 2000). In another study, 52 per cent of MS patients reported a depressive episode before the onset of the disease, compared to 17 per cent of patients suffering with low back pain (Sullivan *et al.* 1995).

In all these disease profiles mentioned so far, we can see that an affective disorder has a significant influence in patients' lives, and it may also have an influence on the way that treatment for the disease is delivered. Music therapy, with its known anxiolytic effect and its potential for influencing mood, offers a potential for direct therapeutic intervention and as an adjuvant therapy.

Depression

Depression is a common disorder in the elderly (Forsell, Jorm and Winblad 1998). The rate of treatment of depression in the very elderly is low, especially amongst dementia sufferers, and the course is chronic or relapsing in almost half of the cases. The interface between depression and dementia is complex and has been studied primarily in Alzheimer's disease (Aldridge 1993b) where depression may be a risk factor for the expression of AD in later life (Raskind 1998). A contributory factor to this depression is the patient's perception of his or her own deficits, although this may be ill-founded (Tierney *et al.* 1996). Emotional context is an important factor, linked to the way in which the patient sees his or her current life situation and an understanding of what life holds in the near future.

Hope will be a major component in a coping strategy, but depression will work against this. Conversely, hope combats depression. Life aims can be redefined and refocused. With the progression of physical deterioration the future becomes less defined in terms of the body and time, and in relationships with family and friends. Hope is a replacement for therapeutic nihilism, enabling us to offer constructive effort and sound expectations.

Hearing impairment

Hearing impairment is another confounding factor in recognizing cognitive degeneration. Central auditory test abnormalities may predict the onset of clinical dementia or cognitive decline. Hearing loss significantly lowers performance on the verbal parts of the Mini-Mental State Examination, a standard test for the presence of dementia (Gates *et al.* 1996). Central auditory dysfunction precedes senile dementia in a significant number of cases and may be an early marker for the condition. Gates *et al.* recommend that hearing tests should be included in the evaluation of persons older than 60 years and in those suspected of having cognitive dysfunction. Thus we may have to include this consideration in designs of research studies of music therapy, because the patients might not be actually hearing what is being played but instead responding to social contact and gestures.

Gesture

Gesture is a part of language. When spontaneous communicative hand/arm gestures were evaluated in elderly patients with probable Alzheimer's disease and compared to those of healthy controls, patients with AD produced proportionately more referentially ambiguous gestures, fewer gestures referring to metaphoric as opposed to concrete contents, and fewer conceptually complex bimanual gestures. Impaired clarity while gesturing correlated with severity of linguistic impairment and disturbed production of pantomimic movements on a test of ideomotor limb apraxia (Glosser, Wiley and Barnoski 1998). This ties into results that we found with developmentally retarded children. When children developed better hand–eye coordination, and improved gesturing, they began to score better on the cognitive subscale of the Griffith's test of child development. Gesturing is an important part of meta-communication, and it is gesturing that can be fostered by the expressive and creative arts when verbal language fails (Aldridge 1996).

In our study of developmentally challenged children, where hearing disability was ever present, it was the joint attention involved in making music that brought about an improvement in listening that appeared as an improvement in hearing. This listening feature of active music therapy is something that needs to be further investigated in its connection with gesture. A combination of focused awareness necessary for listening, and the companion visual modality of gesture, promoted coherent expressive communication. Indeed, task-orientated therapies focus perception and action, thus enabling competence, and are a step to regaining some integrity.

What happens

Most music therapists have concentrated on the pragmatic effects of music therapy. As we shall see, practitioners and researchers alike are concerned with demonstrating the benefits of music therapy for dementia sufferers. How music therapy actually achieves its effects is relatively unresearched, although Thaut and colleagues have made significant investigations into the role of rhythm in gait analysis (Thaut and McIntosh 1999; Thaut et al. 1996; Thaut et al. 1999). Pacchetti and colleagues have made a study of active music therapy in Parkinson's disease as an integrative method for motor and emotional rehabilitation bringing about an improvement in quality of life (Pacchetti et al. 2000). Grün and colleagues, too, have studied the impact of music therapy for the rehabilitation of patients with PD (Grün, Dill-Schmölders and Greulich 1999).

Rhythm constitutes one of the most essential structural and organizational elements of music. When considering the effect of music on human adaptation, the profound effect of rhythm on the motor system strongly suggests that the time structure of music is the essential element relating music specifically to motor behaviour (Aldridge 1996). It is the coupling of rhythm and motor action that is central to active music-making, and this is the feature of several therapeutic interventions. Grün et al. (1999) found that patients with PD had difficulty in maintaining a stable musical tempo, that they had a reduced ability in freely forming rhythms, and that in improvised playing there was a monotony of speech tone and emotional flatness reflecting the inflexibility of rhythmic form. Pacchetti et al. (2000) hypothesize that it is external rhythmic cues that stabilize the internal formation of rhythm in the patient.

Structured time

My hypothesis is that music offers an alternative form for structuring time that fails in working memory. Just as developmentally delayed children achieve a working memory that enhances their cognitive ability, the reverse process occurs in dementia sufferers. The inability to maintain, and freely form, rhythm is an expression of this deficit.

An 82-year-old musician with Alzheimer's disease showed a preserved ability to play previously learned piano compositions from memory while being unable to identify the composer or titles of each work (Crystal, Grober and Masur 1989). He also showed a preserved ability to learn the new skill of mirror reading while being unable to recall or recognize new information. Both anterograde and retrograde procedural memory appeared to be spared in AD.

While several components of working memory may be affected, not all aspects of the central executive mechanism are necessarily influenced (Collette *et al.* 1998). White and Murphy (1998) suggest that tone perception remains intact, but there is a progressive decline in working memory for auditory non-verbal information with advancing Alzheimer's disease. A similar decline was noted on a task assessing working memory for spoken verbal information. This ties in with what we know about hearing impairment and again encourages a test of hearing capabilities before music therapy is used as a treatment modality.

Temporal coherence

I have argued that music therapy is indicated because it offers an external sense of temporal coherence that is failing in the patient. Ellis (1996) reported on the linguistic features and patterns of coherence in the discourse of mild and advanced Alzheimer's patients. As the disease progresses, the discourse of AD patients becomes pre-grammatical in that it is vocabulary-driven and reliant on meaning-based features of discourse rather than grammatically based features. Temporal coherence fails. Knott, Patterson and Hodges (1997), considering the short-term memory performance of patients with semantic dementia, suggested that impaired semantic processing reduces the 'glue' or 'binding' that helps to maintain a structured sequence of phonemes in short-term memory. I argue that this temporal coherence, the metaphoric glue or binding, is replaced by musical form.

No loss of semantic memory

Several lines of evidence suggest that in Alzheimer's disease there is a progressive degradation of the hierarchical organization of semantic memory. The structure of semantic memory in AD is probably degraded, but there is no evidence that this process is progressive. Instead, progressive worsening of verbal fluency in AD seems to be associated with the deterioration of mechanisms that govern initiation of search for appropriate subcategories (Beatty *et al.* 1997a). This pattern can be interpreted as reflecting significantly impaired procedural routines in Alzheimer's disease, with relative sparing of the structure of semantic memory (Chenery 1996).

No loss of source memory

A source memory task, using everyday objects in actions performed by either the participant or the experimenter, was given to probable Alzheimer's disease and elderly normal individuals (Brustrom and Ober 1996). When the overall recognition performance of the two groups was made equivalent by increasing the test delay intervals for the control group, both groups of participants showed similar patterns of correct and incorrect responses. For a given level of event memory, memory for the source of the events is comparable between elderly normals and individuals with AD.

Contextual cues

Two experiments examined whether impairments in recognition memory in early-stage Alzheimer's disease were due to deficits in encoding contextual information (Rickert *et al.* 1998). Normal elderly people and patients diagnosed with mild AD learned one of two tasks. In an initial experiment, correct recognition memory required participants to remember not only what items they had experienced on a given trial but also when they had experienced them. A second experiment required that participants remember only what they had seen, not when they had seen it. Large recognition memory differences were found between the AD and the normal elderly groups in the experiment where time tagging was crucial for successful performance. In the second experiment where the only requisite for successful recognition was remembering what one had experienced, memory of the temporal record was not necessary for successful performance; in this instance, recognition memory for both groups was identical. Memory deficits found in early-stage Alzheimer's disease may be partly due to impaired processing of contextual cues that provide crucial information about when events occur.

Foster (1998a, 1998b, 1998c) carried out a series of studies of background auditory conditions that provided such a context, and their influence upon autobiographical memory. While the use of background music had no effect on word-list recall in the normal elderly, there was a constant beneficial effect of music for autobiographical memory in patients with Alzheimer's disease. This music did not have to be familiar to the sufferer, nor did it reduce anxiety. The effect of music is stronger in cognitively impaired participants, thus promoting another reason for using music-based interventions in treatment initiatives. Foster, like myself (Aldridge 1993b), argues for the use of music in assessment procedures.

As part of a programme of studies investigating memory for everyday tasks, Rusted *et al.* (1997) examined the potential of auditory and olfactory sensory cues to improve free recall of an action event (cooking an omelette) by individuals with dementia of the Alzheimer's type. Both healthy elderly and volunteers with AD recalled more of the individual actions which comprised the event when they listened, prior to recall, to a tape of sounds associated with the event. Olfactory cues that accompanied auditory cues did not produce additional benefits over auditory cues alone. The pattern of recall suggests that the auditory cues improved recall of the whole event, and were not merely increasing recall of the specific actions associated with the sound cues. Individuals with AD continue to encode experiences using a combination of senses, and they can subsequently use this sensory information to aid memory. These findings have practical implications for accessing residual memory for a wide range of therapeutic activities using the creative arts that emphasize sensory abilities.

Reminiscence

We know that people with Alzheimer's disease experience progressive memory and language losses. When people suffering with AD tell their own stories, those narratives are chronologically disorganized, include repetitions and often omit salient events; they also contain less detail in description than narratives by participants in a comparison group (Usita, Hyman and Herman 1998). In addition, most members of the AD group in the study by Usita *et al.* sought assistance during the narrative task. Nevertheless, these persons were willing and able to complete their narrative assignment despite limitations, mirroring a situation in music therapy (Aldridge 1999a).

In Mills' (1997) study of eight demented elderly people in a psychogeriatric day service setting, emotions associated with past experiences provided a strong cue to recall and formed a significant feature of their accounts as well as providing all informants with narrative identity. This sense of narrative identity began to dissolve as their illness progressed and stories faded from memory. The active participation in story-telling may be a crucial feature of maintaining a social identity and is available to several forms of therapeutic activity involving the expressive arts therapies.

Silber and Hes (1995) investigated the value of song/poetry writing with patients diagnosed with Alzheimer's disease. A music therapist facilitated the writing exercise by proposing the themes, choosing music, writing the patients' dictated text, suggesting the use of metaphors and/or analogies, and deciding when the concluding sentence had to be written. Patients wrote songs based on descriptions and images of seasons and the themes of love and stages of life. Results suggest that, based on the preservation of memory for tunes and melodies, patients were able to write songs and poetry when assisted by appropriate stimuli and provided with encouragement. The activity of song writing not only provides pleasure to the participants but also improves group cohesion and social interaction.

Magee has used song writing extensively in her music therapy practice (Magee 1998, 1999a), as has O'Callaghan (1999). Traditionally music offers a valid form of emotional expression, and using songs allows people to find an appropriate social form for the expression of strong emotions. Furthermore, some emotions need to be expressed before they achieve recognition for what they are.

It is in the act of expressing that we understand ourselves and are similarly understood by others. The expressive arts can thus play a vital role in stimulating fulfilling emotional expression, particularly in the treatment of those conditions where depression is seen as a confounding factor that worsens the clinical picture.

Taking this argument further, we should investigate how music therapy can offer an appropriate form for emotional expression so that patients suffering from intense labile emotions, or the severe agitation of later-stage dementias, can be offered a non-pharmacological therapy by which emotions can be regulated.

In conclusion

Music therapy offers a broad potential for addressing the problems encountered by patients suffering with neurodegenerative diseases.

Facilitating communication

Gesture is a part of language and promotes thought. Posture, movement and prosodics provide the bases for communication. The moved body is important for expressing and articulating emotion. The creative arts therapies involving music and dance are grounded in movement.

Retaining identity and promoting memory

For those struggling to articulate themselves, the structuring of narratives offers a meaningful context in which expression can occur. Remembering a story offers an overarching framework that links events together. When a piece of favourite music is played then memories are evoked.

Encouraging rhythmic movement

When bodily integrity begins to fail, sufferers literally fall out of time. If this is, as speculated, because an internal timekeeper fails to function, then an external source of time appears to resynchronize movements. What we do not know is how long the benefits of such rhythmic facilitation last. Certainly music and dance promote fluency in movement and speech. What we do know is that tasks are central to the whole process of perception and action, and music therapy provides a coherent sensory world of time and space that is the ecology of movement.

Emotional expression and relief

Depression and anxiety are increasingly being mentioned as major debilitating factors of neurodegenerative diseases. Music therapy is a known anxiolytic and also improves mood. Furthermore, emotions can be expressed in satisfactory forms that need not be brought into words. For the verbally inarticulate, and those challenged by language when it is failing, other expressive forms are potentially of great value for the sufferer and his or her caregivers.

Quality of life

An improved communicative ability, coupled to a regained identity, where some movement is retained or even regained, and a possibility of satisfactory positive emotional expression, will promote an improved quality of life. If isolation is a major contributory component of emotional distress, music therapy offers methods by which sufferers can achieve their remaining potentials and communicate with others.

CHAPTER 4

An Overview of Therapeutic Initiatives when Working with People Suffering from Dementia

Hanne Mette Ridder

When I see Lasse for the first time, he sits in his wheelchair. He is very small, pale and skinny. His face is crinkled with fine lines and I am not surprised when the nurse, who helps him drink his coffee, tells me that he will celebrate his 100 years' birthday next year. My impression is that life is gradually seeping out of old Lasse who is almost blind and suffers from severe dementia. Lasse is referred to music therapy as he is often very agitated during the afternoon. My first impression of Lasse changes dramatically in our first music therapy session. I have sung a couple of songs, and then start singing an old harvest song. He joins in the song at the very beginning. It is astonishing to hear his voice. This small, wasted man has a strong and powerful voice. He only joins in the first verse, where he sings every word accurately. Then he stops again. But I have a clear feeling that I have met Lasse, a strong-minded and proud farmer.

In this example, music was the first key for me to communicate with Lasse. Later I saw other glimpses of Lasse's person, mediated through other songs that he was closely related to. In this chapter I will describe how music is used in a wide range of initiatives with persons suffering from dementia. There are various ways of implementing music: in groups or individually, by singing songs, listening to music, dancing, or improvising on instruments. I hope to give an introduction to these initiatives and the general idea behind them, based on a systematic qualitative literature review. The first section of the chapter starts with some information about dementia as a dialogic-degenerative disease and sums up the various treatment initiatives. The overall results from a large number of research studies are then considered.

Dementia as a dialogic-degenerative disease

Dementia is a progressive degenerative disease with a prevalence that increases with age. It can be described as a syndrome, representing 100 different diseases, and within the Western population about 2 per cent are estimated to have one of these. Alzheimer's disease (AD) represents the majority of diagnosed dementia cases. Others are Lewy-body dementia, multi-infarct (vascular) dementia, AIDS dementia, alcoholic dementia, herpes encephalitis, dementia pugilistica (boxer's syndrome), heavy metal poisoning, and diseases named after Pick, Creutzfeldt–Jakob, Huntington, Parkinson, Wilson and Binswanger.

Dementia is normally categorized as either cortical, subcortical or mixed, but it may also result from other conditions, such as vascular, infectious or toxic. In cortical dementias it is primarily the grey matter that is affected, as in Alzheimer's disease, where massive cell loss and brain shrinkage are seen. But even if AD is termed a cortical dementia, changes in subcortical areas (e.g. hippocampus and amygdala) are seen. The neural changes (some may not be registered until post-mortem inspection) show atrophy, deterioration of the large neurons, missing neurotransmitter activity, cell death, accumulation of neurofibrillary tangles or beta-amyloid, and clumps of neuritic plaques between the cells.

As a very general rule of thumb there are five main symptoms of dementia, the five A's: amnesia, aphasia, agnosia, apraxia and agitation. *Amnesia* means loss of memory – loss of old memories (retrograde amnesia), or loss of the ability to encode and learn new information (anterograde amnesia). *Aphasia* is a partial or complete loss of language abilities. *Agnosia* is an inability to recognize the form and/or function of objects and people. *Apraxia* is impaired cortical motor processing and an inability to perform voluntary actions, despite an adequate amount of motor strength and control (Zillmer and Spiers 2001). *Agitation*, although not the only behavioural and psychological symptom associated with dementia, is a symptom that reduces quality of life for the sufferer, and makes dementia care very demanding and challenging. Here a distinction is made between primary symptoms that are related to neurological changes, and secondary symptoms originating in causes not directly related to the dementia disease. The secondary symptoms might be treatable by pharmacological as well as non-pharmacological means. Agitation is just one symptom of dementia, embraced by the term BPSD (behavioural and psychological symptoms of dementia; see www.ipa-online.org) that has replaced the term 'behavioural disturbances'. BPSD also includes symptoms of psychosis, delusions, paranoia, hallucinations, aggression, hyperactivity and depression. The term is increasingly used, at least in the Nordic countries, but is not (yet) classified as a subtype in the dementia diagnoses in DSM-IV or ICD-10 – showing that psychological symptoms are underestimated as a health problem in official registration.

Dialogic-degenerative disease

The various clinical symptoms of dementia occur very differently according to type of dementia. Alzheimer's disease is often associated with anomic aphasia, characterized by word-finding and naming difficulties. The way the person talks can be viewed as 'word salad'; there seems to be no meaning in what is said, but the way things are said sounds quite 'normal'. In these cases semantic meaning has disappeared, but phonological and syntactical aspects of language seem to be preserved. Other types of dementia (e.g. vascular) may show either very small signs of aphasia or, according to which parts of the brain are most affected, signs of global aphasia. Some sufferers may show signs of non-fluent aphasia, where they clearly know what they want to say but can't find the word, even though it is 'just on the tip of the tongue'.

In general, loss of conversational skill is likely to be an early marker of dementia syndrome (Orange *et al.* 1998). In the later stages of the different dementia diseases it seems very troublesome or even impossible to maintain conversation or dialogue. Language deterioration is a serious problem and might cause secondary consequences of dementia.

> Studies that consider communication-related stress show that communication breakdown is perceived by caregivers to be a primary problem in coping with the disease, and that communication problems increase the risk of early institutionalisation of the individual with DAT [Dementia of Alzheimer type]. (Orange and Colton-Hudson 1998, p. 57)

Considering the severe implications of communication breakdown, David Aldridge calls dementia a dialogic-degenerative disease:

> ...rather than neuro-degenerative diseases, we are faced with dialogic-degenerative diseases... (Aldridge 2001a)

In dialogic-degenerative diseases, the following symptoms of dementia mainly disturb communication:

- semantic anomic aphasia
- expressive speech deficits
- speech comprehension deficits
- attention and orientation disturbances
- response latencies.

Orange and Colton-Hudson suggest that caregivers must pay attention to the communication breakdown that might lead to isolation, depression and agitation:

...caregivers will need to learn that they may be able to overcome these progressive declines in communicative performance if they adjust their language, speech, and nonverbal components of their communication, the environments in which communication takes place, and their attitudes, perceptions, and expectations of performance. (Orange and Colton-Hudson 1998, p.136)

Lacking abilities to communicate might cause secondary symptoms that are not primarily caused by the neurological deficits. Roberts and Algase (1988, p.89) set up three types of behaviour that indicates a disordered person–environment interaction:

1.   *Repetitive behaviour* (wandering, trailing, rubbing, etc.) may indicate that the person is unable to access adequate physical and/or social environmental information.

2.   *Catastrophic reactions* (emotional outbursts, aggressive acts) may indicate that environmental demands exceed the capacity of the person to respond adaptively.

3.   *Situationally inappropriate behaviour* (hiding and wrapping things, fiddling, making noises, eating non-food) suggests that the person is misinterpreting environmental or personal information.

To catastrophic reactions I want to add reactions when the person is not only in a more or less constant state of stress caused by excessive environmental demands, but also is in social isolation so that it is not possible to fulfil psychosocial needs. Aldridge (1998a) suggests that when dialogue fails then we have alienation and despair. The maintenance of the self degenerates through isolation. Patients may be forced into a silence in which they have no possibilities to either transform or structure – they are banished from the social to an isolated and degenerated self.

Only through social contact and communication is it possible to understand and validate psychosocial needs. To have these needs met might be hindered by the damage of abilities to enter dialogue. This emphasizes the importance of adjusting one's communication with the person, bringing into focus the establishment of a communicative relationship. In Chapter 2 of this book Aldridge points out that dialogue is not simply given, it has to be achieved and negotiated. In music therapy there is a possibility for negotiating reciprocal communication; that is, dia-logue. If we focus on performing health through basic communicative elements – such as attention, timing, utterance and gesture – we can establish a meaningful dialogue where psychosocial needs are met.

The use of music with people with dementia

Music appears to have the relevant potential for entering into meaningful relationships with people suffering with dementia. But what are the concrete therapeutic initiatives that can be offered? An answer to this question might be found in the literature about music therapy in dementia care and in research reports with a focus on music and dementia. In the following pages I give an overview of therapeutic initiatives that have been described in published clinical articles or research documents.

The first hurdle was to find out whether there is, in fact, any material that describes the topic in question. In a meta-analysis concerning music therapy for dementia symptoms in the Cochrane Database, Koger and Brotons (2000) found no randomised controlled trials, or trials with quantitative data suitable for analysis. This was confirmed by Vink *et al.* (2004) in a recent review where only five studies could be included. They concluded that the methodological quality of these studies was generally poor, and that the study results could not be validated or pooled for further analysis – a finding reinforced by Simon Gilbertson in Chapter 5 of this book.

Nevertheless, in spite of these discouraging conclusions showing that music therapy research does not fulfil the required standards, I carried out a literature review – but with a focus on clinical strategies. I shall refer to this review, which was published initially in Denmark in 2002 and in a second updated edition in 2005 (Ridder 2005b). I shall give an overview of the findings, including short descriptions of the different approaches that integrate music in dementia care.

Literature review

The focus of this literature review is clinical music therapeutic initiatives with persons having dementia. The purpose is to give an overview of different ways of implementing music in health care settings, including *both* music therapeutic strategies *and* activities that health care personnel might implement. The inclusion criteria for material are the following:

- studies concerning music and dementia
- studies or reports published in scientific journals, specific music therapy journals, journals concerning dementia care, geriatrics, psychology, psychiatry, medicine, etc.
- books or book chapters from the music therapy literature
- material from the period 1980 to August 2004
- research articles or studies with documented descriptions of clinical practice

- anecdotal case descriptions if they contain a clear description of clinical practice
- studies in the English, German, Norwegian, Swedish and Danish languages.

Some studies did not have a clear definition of participant population – Riegler (1980) for example – but are included if the target group is described as elderly residents in general care settings with distinct cognitive deficits. Other studies, like that of Moore, Staum and Brotons (1992), mix healthy elderly and persons with dementia without differentiation and are excluded as the focus here is on specific initiatives for dementia.

Also excluded are background material, handbooks, literature of theoretical or philosophical character, as well as non-published material, master theses and material from before 1980. This means that comprehensive material from, for example, Aldridge (2000a), Bright (1986), Bunne (1986) and Friis (1987), or systematic literature reviews by Brotons (2000), Lou (2001), Sherratt, Thornton and Hatton (2004a) and Smeijsters (1997) are not included in the analysed studies.

Two search strategies have been used: either continuous search in reference lists in incoming material, or search in electronic databases (e.g. www.music-therapyworld.net, ingenta.com, Medline, PsycLit, PubMed, RILM, CAIRSS, www.musik.aau.dk). In relation to the first strategy, Brotons' overview of the music therapy literature relating to elderly people (Brotons 2000), and the music therapy article collection at University of Witten-Herdecke, as well as the music therapy library at Aalborg University, gave a good basis for further search.

As a result of the search I identified 92 studies concerning music and dementia, as listed in Box 4.1.

Data analysis

The 92 studies deal with very different strategies of how to implement music in dementia care, such as background music, active improvisation with instruments, singing, or folk dancing. Various kinds of settings are described: group or individual settings, in common areas or at home where the participant lives. In order to get an overview and define general characteristics, the studies were analysed with a qualitative research strategy making use of data displaying (Miles and Huberman 1994). Coded information from the studies was set up in tables giving information about: authors, year of publication, country, research design, music initiative/method, techniques, number of sessions, participants, stage of dementia, dependent variables, short abstracts, comments, conclusions/results.

Box 4.1 Studies concerning music and dementia

Abad (2002)

Aldridge, G. (2000)

Ansdell (1995)

Ashida (2000)

Baumgartner (1997)

Beatty *et al.* (1988)

Beatty *et al.* (1994)

Berger *et al.* (2004)

Bolger and Judson (1984)

Braben (1992)

Bright (1986)

Brotons and Koger (2000)

Brotons and Marti (2003)

Brotons and Pickett-Cooper (1994)

Brotons and Pickett-Cooper (1996)

Brown *et al.* (2001)

Brust (1980)

Carruth (1997)

Casby and Holm (1994)

Christie (1992)

Christie (1995)

Clair (1991)

Clair (1996a, b)

Clair (2002)

Clair and Bernstein (1990a, b)

Clair and Bernstein (1993)

Clair and Bernstein (1994)

Clair and Ebberts (1997)

Clair *et al.* 1995

Clark *et al.* (1998)

Crystal *et al.* (1989)

Denney (1997)

Eeg (2001)

Fitzgerald-Cloutier (1993)

Foster (1998a, b, c)

Foster and Valentine (2001)

Gaertner (1999)

Gardiner (2000)

Gerdner (1997)

Gerdner (2000)

Gerdner and Swanson (1993)

Glynn (1992)

Goddaer and Abraham (1994)

Götell *et al.* (2000)

Groene (1993)

Groene (2001)

Groene *et al.* (1998)

Hanser and Clair (1996)

Hanson *et al.* (1996)

Hintz (2000)

Johnson *et al.* (1998)

Korb (1997a, b)

Kydd (2001)

Lindenmuth *et al.* (1992)

Lipe (1991)

Lipe (1995)

Lord and Garner (1993)

Mathews *et al.* (2000)

Mathews *et al.* (2001)

Munk-Madsen (2001a, b)

Newman and Ward (1993)

Norberg *et al.* (1986)

Odell-Miller (1996)

Olderog-Millard and Smith (1989)

Palo-Bengtsson *et al.* (1998)

Polk and Kertesz (1993)

Pollack and Namazi (1992)

Prickett and Moore (1991)

Ragneskog and Kihlgren (1997)

Ragneskog *et al.* (1996)

Remington (2002)

Ridder (2001)

Ridder (2003)

Riegler (1980)

Rolvsjord (1998)

Sambandham and Schirm (1995)

Sherratt *et al.* (2004b)

Silber (1999)

Simpson (2000)

Smith-Marchese (1994)

Suzuki *et al.* (2004)

Swartz *et al.* (1992)

Tabloski *et al.* (1995)

Thomas *et al.* (1997)

Tomaino (2000)

Van de Winckel *et al.* (2004)

Wellendorf (1991)

York (1994)

General results from data analysis

The main results deal with the therapeutic initiatives. Before I go through these, I shall give a summary of general results that give an idea of studies in music therapy in dementia care.

First of all, 1090 people with dementia participated in these studies. They took part in various settings where music was involved, and they were either video-recorded, observed directly in the setting, tested before and after, or described in logs. A big majority were women, and in all stages of dementia. Unfortunately, especially in the earliest studies, information was not given about stage of dementia or precise diagnosis. This information seems to be included in newer studies, generally reflecting a better standard for precise medical accounts and comprehensive knowledge about dementia. Most studies are from the United States (64%), with a single study from Canada. The Nordic countries represent 12 per cent of the studies, and Great Britain 10 per cent (with Foster's doctoral thesis from 1998 counting as three different studies). There are a few from Germany, Belgium, France, Spain, Israel, Australia and Japan.

In the 1990s there was a boom in studies in the United States with more than 40 studies, as can be seen in Figure 4.1. This productivity might be related to the Senate hearing in 1991 about older adults, when Oliver Sacks and Connie Tomaino among others gave information about music therapy. In Europe only a few studies were carried out before 1995; but between 1995 and August 2004, 23 studies were published, showing a marked growing interest in music interventions with persons having dementia.

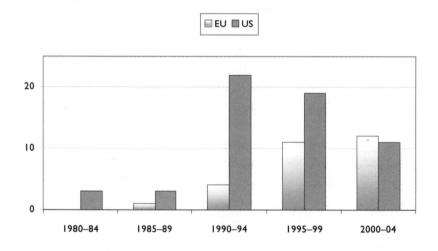

Figure 4.1 Number of studies about music and dementia in the period 1980 to August 2004

In both Europe and the United States the use of active techniques, where participants either sing, play instruments or dance, were employed in two-thirds of the
studies, whereas receptive techniques with the use of, for example, music CDs
were employed in almost one-third. A few studies used a 'reactive' technique, a
mixture of active and receptive techniques, where participants play instruments to
CD music or listen to live music.

Most of the 1090 participants participated in groups with from 3 to 12
people. Notwithstanding this, most studies were investigating the use of *individual*
initiatives. Especially in Europe there was a tendency to investigate individual
settings. It is also interesting to look at the number of sessions a person participated in. In Europe there was a slight tendency to investigate initiatives with more
than 10 sessions, whereas there were fewer sessions in the United States. This
might reflect differences in therapeutic strategies – with a tendency towards
long-term intervention in a European psychoanalytic orientated tradition, and
short-term interventions in an American behaviouristic or cognitive tradition.
Other differences are reflected in the number of participants included in the
studies: as shown in Figure 4.2, the average number of participants is increasing.
There has been a tendency in the United States to carry out fewer studies in the last
ten years, but at the same time to increase the number of participants. This trend is
seen in Europe as well, but with pronounced smaller samples.

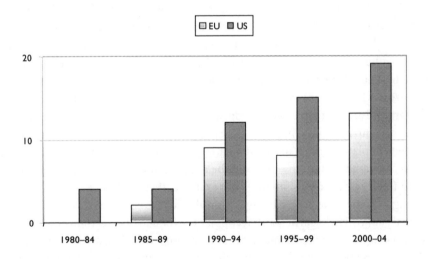

Figure 4.2 Participant average in five-year periods in Europe and the USA

With regard to research strategies, there is a clear preference for controlled trials in
the United States, with 67 per cent being controlled. These designs are here
defined as: experimental designs with a control group, within-subject designs

where each participant serves as his or her own control, or within-subject pre-test/post-test designs. In Europe there were the same number of experimental designs (14 studies) and case designs (13 studies). The case studies represent two groups of almost equal size, documented case studies and anecdotal case descriptions.

In the United States a small group of studies investigated possibilities for using music in assessment procedures. Studies having a main focus investigation of the use of assessment procedures are not seen in Europe.

Therapeutic initiatives

Apart from these comparative data, the literature gives information about various therapeutic initiatives. Based on descriptions of how music was implemented in diverse settings, 17 different therapeutic initiatives were identified. The purposes and objectives for these different initiatives were very different. Some initiatives were clearly economy measures whereby staff's use of taped music or the possibility to entertain big groups with as few staff as possible is emphasized, allowing easy administration that did not demand specially educated staff, whereas other initiatives stressed one-to-one interaction and built on several individual sessions with highly skilled professionals.

In Figure 4.3, fifteen of these initiatives are listed with some very general characteristics that are meant to point to the most specific qualities. The solid symbols indicate that the approach is used in the initiative, while the open symbols indicate that it *might* be used. Initiatives with the purpose of integrating relatives or participants without dementia, or initiatives related to assessment procedures, are not included in the list, as they are already related to one of the 15 other initiatives.

We can look at 'sing-along' as an example. In sing-along initiatives live music is characteristic. Participants or therapist will sing with piano, guitar, accordion or other accompaniment. They will not sing to taped music and there will be no instrument playing, as in 'music stimulation' for example. If no therapist or others are accompanying, the singing might be a capella singing. There will be a structured framework for the initiative. For example, there will be a planned weekly setting with the same person being responsible for the course of sessions. Environmental cues will help participants recognize the framework – certain objects in the room (songbooks, piano); and a certain structure will define the framework – music that marks the beginning and the ending of the setting. There will be no structured programme deciding which songs to sing and in which order, as in 'music and movement' where a planned programme ensures that the group works through specific exercises. 'Sing-along' might be planned with a defined group with the same members coming every time, but typically sing-along initiatives are

	Live music/accomp	Taped music	Instrument playing	A capella singing	Structured programme	Structured framework	Defined group	Open group	Individual setting
Background music		■						■	
Folk dancing, social dancing	■	□			■	■	■	□	
MTC: Music therapeutic care				■			■		■
Music and movement	■	□			□	■	■	■	
Music listening		■							■
Music reminiscence		■			■	□	■	■	
Music stimulation	■	□	■			■	■	■	
Play-along			■	■				■	
Sing-along	■				□		■	□	■
Song writing	■	□			□		■		
Stress reduction			■	□	□	■	■	■	
Therapeutic improvisation	■		■		□		■		■
Therapeutic singing				■			■		■
Vibroacoustic therapy		■					■		■
Vibrotactile stimulation	■		■			□	□	□	□

Figure 4.3 Characteristics for music initiatives in dementia care (see text)

for larger groups of people with an open invitation to participate, which means that the group changes from setting to setting.

This is an attempt to generalize the way the initiatives are carried out. In real life there are variations, nuances and mixtures, as well as other names to describe the initiatives.

Implicitly certain ideas and philosophies rule these very different initiatives. What is the purpose to singing old personal songs with Lasse, or to inviting Mr K to participate in square dance, or to playing soft classical CDs at dinnertime in unit M? In order to give an overview of *why* these initiatives are implemented, I have again used qualitative strategies of coding and categorizing. By looking at the dependent variables and the conclusions of the studies, the data material has been sorted into categories, inspired by strategies in grounded theory (Glaser and

Table 4.1 Seven groups of general purposes, describing four overall functions of music

Function of music	Purpose
Evaluative	Assessment
Regulative	Sedative/relaxing adaptation
	Behavioural adaptation
Stimulative	Bodily stimulation
	Cognitive stimulation
	Social interaction
Communicative	Personal interaction

Strauss 1967; see www.ATLASti.de). These categories are displayed in Table 4.1 and give a general idea of the purpose of the initiative, and which function the music had. The four general categories that describe the function of the music are evaluative, regulative, stimulative and communicative.

In our everyday understanding, music as art may mostly be considered for its aesthetic function. This overall category is not a focus in the 92 studies concerning music therapy work with persons suffering from dementia. In the following I shall try to clarify the overall categories that are represented in this material.

When music is used with the function to *evaluate*, singing, playing together or reactions to the music therapy are observed and used for assessment procedures in order to obtain evidence or information (Wigram, Nygaard Pedersen and Bonde 2002, p.246). The way the participant responds to or interacts in the music therapy session is used for assessment purposes, observing either cognitive or motor functioning such as language abilities, concentration and attention, or expressive and psychosocial conditions.

With a *regulative* function, musical elements are used to change behaviour or mood – not to be confused with 'regulative Musiktherapie' developed by Christoph Schwabe in Germany (Decker-Voigt, Knill and Weymann 1996, p.317). Music played at dinnertime might regulate agitation or time spent on eating. Techniques used for receptive or active music therapy, such as the iso-principle defined by Ira Altschuler (1948), as well as entrainment (Rider 1997), might make it possible for the therapist to 'provoke' a change in the participant.

Music might also be used to *stimulate* the participants to be active in various ways. Music is used to motivate and engage, with a focus on language functioning, cognitive abilities or physical movements, with the view to either 'use it, or lose it'.

Finally, music is described as a way to *communicate* with a person. Focus is on interaction at a social–pragmatic level where the 'whole' person is considered – a person with emotions, cultural identity, psychosocial needs and a personal biography.

The various approaches to music in the studies reflect different music therapeutic traditions and especially reflect the different needs of the client group. In only about 20 studies is there a precise description of the participants' stage of dementia. Knowing the precise stage of dementia or precise descriptions of needs makes it possible to search information on music implementations targeted at a specific group. This is difficult with the small number of studies giving this precise information.

The way an activity is carried out is strongly dependent on the social, cognitive and functional abilities of the participants. When the demands in the activity are adjusted to participants' capacities, the consequence seems to be a wide range of therapeutic initiatives. The music can be used actively or receptively, in groups or individually, with or without instruments, with accompaniment or a cappella, with live or taped music, in structured activities or in activities of daily living (ADL), including other participants (staff, relatives, children) in open groups, where participants are free to come and go, or in closed groups where the constellation of group members is carefully composed.

I shall now correlate the categories set out in Table 4.1 and Figure 4.3 with the main results concluded from the 92 studies.

Evaluative approach: music as an assessment tool

Hintz (2000), Lipe (1995) and York (1994) suggest assessment tools using active music activities and/or improvised music, and Glynn (1992) suggests an assessment tool where taped music is used. The clinical assessment tools are seen as supplements to the Mini-Mental State Examination (MMSE) or other tests.

Munk-Madsen (2001b) describes an initial period of clinical assessment in individual music therapy and presents a protocol to be used after the first 3 to 4 music therapy sessions. Gudrun Aldridge (2000) concludes that music therapy offers a very sensitive assessment tool that gives nuanced information about participants – information that is very difficult to obtain from traditional test batteries:

> Improvised music therapy appears to offer the opportunity to supplement mental state examinations in areas where those examinations are lacking. ...
> It tests those prosodic elements of speech production, which are not lexically dependent. Furthermore, it can be used to assess those areas of functioning, both receptive and productive, not covered adequately by other test instruments, that is fluency, perseverance in context, attention, concentration and intentionality. (G. Aldridge 2000, p.162).

This use of musical assessment tools is still in its initial phase. The studies are more recent, and there seems to be a growing interest in the evaluative function of music.

Regulative approach: music with sedative function

Hanser and Clair (1996) implement direct stress reduction techniques with early-stage Alzheimer's disease in settings together with caregivers or family members. Body movement, self-massage of facial muscles, muscle relaxation, guided imagery experience, tips for sleep induction, etc., are included in the settings, showing that 'music therapy is a viable approach' for persons with AD and for their caregivers.

Music listening, using cassettes intended specifically for relaxation and played whenever nurses found the patients restless, made persons with AD in an experimental group ($n = 9$) sleep significantly longer than persons with AD in a control group ($n = 9$) (Lindenmuth, Patel and Chang 1992).

Up to now only two studies have examined the sedating regulative function of music and how music can function to enhance relaxation with persons suffering from dementia.

Regulative approach: music leading to behavioural adaptation

Reduction of agitated behaviour, such as ambulation or aggressive and disturbing behaviour, is seen in a great number of studies. Music stimulation is a group initiative wherein participants take part in a programme including different musical activities and instrument playing. It reduces agitation (Brotons and Pickett-Cooper 1996; Groene 1993) – also when implemented individually (Gardiner *et al.* 2000) – and increases social interaction after sessions (Brotons and Marti 2003). Music therapeutical singing reduces ambulation (Fitzgerald-Cloutier 1993; Olderog-Millard and Smith 1989), and singing used in music therapeutic care (MTC) reduces agitation during bathing episodes (Brown, Götell and Ekman 2001).

The use of tapes with familiar music reduces agitation during bathing episodes too, and even reduces aggressive behaviour (Clark, Lipe and Bilbrey 1998; Thomas, Heitman and Alexander 1997). During dinnertime, which might be noisy and turbulent if food is served in canteen-like surroundings, the use of background music reduces aggressive behaviour (Denney 1997; Goddaer and Abraham 1994) and increases the time spent on eating (Ragneskog *et al.* 1996). Remington (2002) shows that the use of background music and of hand-massage (implemented separately or together) significantly reduces physically non-aggressive agitated behaviour. Clair and Bernstein (1994) and Sherratt, Thornton and

Hatton (2004b) were not able to establish an effect on agitation of stimulating or sedating background music played during dinnertime and in the dayroom of the unit.

Individual music listening, where the person with dementia might sit in his or her own room listening to familiar tapes, reduces symptoms of agitation (Casby and Holm 1994; Gerdner 1997, 2000; Gerdner and Swanson 1993; Korb 1997b; Tabloski, McKinnon-Howe and Remington 1995; Sambandham and Schirm 1995).

Nearly a quarter of the studies deal with a regulative effect of music on behavioural adaptation. Two of these studies are from Sweden, the rest from the US, where there is a stronger tradition for behavioural research.

Stimulative approach: music as bodily stimulation

Music and movement, a group activity where moving, dancing or exercises to taped or live music is part of the programme, shows increased response, increased quality of life, reality orientation, active participation and sociability (Götell, Brown and Ekman 2000; Groene et al. 1998; Hanson et al. 1996; Mathews, Clair and Kosloski 2001; Newman and Ward 1993; Smith-Marchese 1994). In Newman and Ward's (1993) study the presence of preschool children was a stimulus to responsiveness and involvement. Suzuki, Kanamori and Watanabe (2004) found that sixteen music stimulation sessions in eight weeks with ten Japanese participants showed decreases in saliva CgA levels, indicating a reduction in stress levels.

Social dancing (Palo-Bengtsson, Winblad and Ekman 1998) is concluded to preserve and support patients' intellectual, emotional and motor functions; and group activities where dancing is part of the programme are concluded to elicit adequate positive behaviour, engagement, reminiscence, and improving social interactions between patients and caregivers, and between patients and peers, and to increase relatives' satisfaction with visits (Baumgartner 1997; Clair and Ebberts 1997; Götell et al. 2000; Newman and Ward 1993; Pollack and Namazi 1992).

Clair and Bernstein's (1990b) study of vibrotactile stimulation shows increased participation, and their study of vibroacoustic therapy (1993) shows that the participants do not choose between different sorts of stimulation. Bolger and Judson (1984) give a medical report about a patient with chronic obstructive pulmonary disease, making her unable to follow verbal commands to cough or to take a deep breath. But the patient would repeat words, and repeat singing too. When singing, the patient was noted to be taking deep breaths and to cough. 'Her clinical status, arterial blood gas levels, and emotional status all improved greatly during this therapy' (Bolger and Judson 1984, p.1704).

Close to 20 per cent of the studies listed in Box 4.1 focus on the stimulative effect of music by implementing activities with dance and movement. No studies directly examine the physiological effect of music with this target group.

Stimulative approach: music as cognitive and attentional stimulation

Music stimulation groups positively influence speech ability and fluency of speech (Brotons and Koger 2000; Suzuki et al. 2004), improve active participation and engagement (Brotons and Pickett-Cooper 1994; Christie 1992; Hanson et al. 1996; Odell-Miller 1996), affective responses (Korb 1997a), and reality orientation (Riegler 1980). The degree of active participation increases when a music therapist has instructed staff how to carry out the activity (Mathews, Clair and Kosloski 2000), or when the music therapist structures the session, and gives adequate instructions to participants about the use of the instruments (Clair, Bernstein and Johnson 1995). Individual music stimulation increases face–name recognition (Carruth 1997) and number of words recalled correctly (Prickett and Moore 1991).

Music and movement using a music-based exercise programme shows significant improvement in cognition, examined, among other tests, with the use of MMSE.

In play-along improvement in recall, mood and active participation is seen (Lord and Garner 1993). Lord and Garner had 20 participants sit around a big table supplied with instruments to play, while they were listening to big band music. Therapeutic singing increases alert responses (Clair 1996a, b), and when a person with dementia hears personal significant songs images and recollections are stimulated (Tomaino 2000).

Background music improves autobiographical recall with no difference between familiar and novel music (Foster 1998b; Foster and Valentine 2001), and music listening improves spatial–temporal skills (Johnson et al. 1998), reality orientation (Lipe 1991), and active response (Norberg, Melin and Asplund 1986). Persons with dementia show ability to learn new song material even though they are not able to learn new verbal material (Prickett and Moore 1991). Silber finds no influence of background music on MMSE, compared to conditions without music (Silber 1999).

Including the studies of Beatty et al. (1988, 1997a), Crystal et al. (1989), Polk and Kertesz (1993), and Swartz et al. (1992), about a third of the 92 studies examine the stimulative effect of music on cognition and attention. Most of the studies are from the United States, but with studies from Britain, Sweden and Israel represented.

Stimulative approach: music to increase social interaction at the interpersonal level

When staff participate in music stimulation, dance and movement or MTC, social interaction between participant and caregiver changes to a deeper level, where 'the personnel experienced bonding with the patients, who seemed easier to care for' (Götell *et al.* 2000, 2002, 2003). The participation of relatives in music-stimulation increases the personal bonding between the couples (Brotons and Marti 2003; Clair 2002). When preschool children participate in music and movement activities, increased social interaction is seen with persons suffering from severe dementia – an increased social interaction that is not seen when the children are not there (Newman and Ward 1993).

Sing-along groups have a significant effect on the amount of social behaviour (Olderog-Millard and Smith 1989), and *after* sessions with music stimulation or music listening increased social interaction between peers is seen (Abad 2002; Kydd 2001; Pollack and Namazi 1992; Sambandham and Schirm 1995). Compared to listening to background music, listening to *live* music increases emotional and behavioural responses (Sherratt *et al.* 2004b).

Individual therapeutical improvisation, where the music is improvised not *for* but *with* the client, increases active involvement and confirms that persons with the darkening isolation of dementia 'are, indeed, alive, and that relatedness with other people is still possible' (Simpson 2000, p.177). After 20 individual sessions with Jack who suffers from AD, Ansdell states that the music therapy shows 'the restoration of some quality in Jack's life: his sustained attention and positive engagement in his playing, his ability to share an activity with another person, and a decrease of the frustration, confusion and delusions that dogged his everyday life' (Ansdell 1995, p.132). Fewer than 10 per cent of the studies register the stimulative effect of music on social interaction; three in four of these studies are from Europe.

Communicative approach: music to increase personal interaction at the intrapersonal level

Music therapy, with a purpose to increase personal interaction in the direction of intrapersonal matters, approaches psychotherapy. None of the studies mentioned here directly labels the work as psychotherapeutic, but they present or directly work with aspects of communication, personhood, contact, confidence, interrelations, emotional needs, psychosocial needs and therapeutic change.

Implementing *individual therapeutical improvisation* is an approach in which intrapsychic matter might be part of the interpersonal exchange. Eeg (2001) and Munk-Madsen (2001a) work with long-term therapy with more than 30 sessions where they integrate improvisation in an individual approach. The long therapeutic courses help to break isolation, decrease anxiety, and elicit autobiographical memory and means of expressing own identity. Gudrun Aldridge states that active 'music-making' promotes interaction, thereby promoting initiatives in communication (G. Aldridge 2000, p.161), and states that the music therapy might influence underlying depressions.

Even though creative music therapy (Nordoff and Robbins 1977) deals with 'the creation of something which is at once both communicative and expressive' (Simpson 2000, p.177), and integrates an understanding of psychosocial needs defined by Tom Kitwood (1997), Ansdell would not call his work psycho-therapeutic, because:

> Psychotherapy's use of words to explore the past, to ask 'why?' questions of motive and significance is quite different from Creative Music Therapy's use of music to create a musical experience of the present. Its questions are rather 'what?' questions – What is happening now? (Ansdell 1995, p.31)

The 'why?' questions in a psychotherapeutically orientated approach deal with the understanding of intrapsychic matter. The 'why?' questions are not asked directly to the participant suffering from dementia, but are questions that influence the work and the thinking of the therapist. Working or exploring the past and the cultural background is here understood as working with integrating 'the whole person', even though the person suffering from dementia is often *dis*-integrated from past, present and future. Working with personal songs, or therapeutic singing, is seen as a way of integrating the past and aspects of identity: 'a single song can encapsulate an entire period of one's life, and hearing it can restore the essence of that reality' (Tomaino 1998, p.21).

Therapeutic singing, using personal songs with persons with dementia, is described and accentuated in the background literature dealing with this client group (Aldridge 2000a; Bright 1997; Bunne 1986; Friis 1987; Tomaino 1998) and is integrated as part of the therapeutic approach in a large number of studies and articles that are listed here:

Bolger and Judson 1984; Braben 1992; Brotons and Pickett-Cooper 1994, 1996; Brown *et al.* 2001; Carruth 1997; Christie 1992, 1995; Clair 1991, 1996a; Clair and Bernstein 1990a, 1990b; Eeg 2001; Fitzgerald-Cloutier 1993; Gaertner 1999; Gardiner *et al.* 2000; Groene 1993; Groene *et al.* 1998; Götell *et al.* 2000; Hanser and Clair 1996; Hanson *et al.* 1996; Hatfield and McClune 2002; Korb 1997a; Lipe 1995; McCloskey 1990; Munk-Madsen 2001a; Newman and Ward 1993; Olderog-Millard and Smith 1989; Pollack and Namazi 1992; Prickett and Moore 1991; Ridder 2001, 2003; Riegler 1980; Rolvsjord 1998; Silber and Hes 1995; Simpson 2000; Smith-Marchese 1994; Tomaino 2000; Wellendorf 1991.

Individual therapeutic singing increases interactions with another human being at an intimate, personal level, allowing the participant to express him or herself – for example in a very positive manner as here with the participant Claire: 'Many times while Claire and the therapist were singing, Claire would lean her head very close to the therapist, move her head to the beat and smile, then lean her head back and laugh' (Fitzgerald-Cloutier 1993, p.35). The choice of personal songs might stimulate recognition, and 'the more emotionally charged the song is, the more likely a person will respond' (Tomaino 1998, p.26). The songs might serve as a means of expressing and containing intense feelings and make it possible to share these feelings with another person (Hatfield and McClune 2002; Ridder 2003).

The Norwegian music therapist Randi Rolvsjord describes musical interaction with focus on reminiscence as an important way to cope with 'stress of ageing, death or physic and psychic failures' (Rolvsjord 1998, p.4). She states that dementia leads to an increased need for reminiscing, but at the same time reduces the ability to reminisce. By referring to the Swedish culture researcher Johan Fornäs, she defines three levels of identity – subjective, social and cultural – and connects these different aspects of identity with the memory-work: 'The musical interaction engages the old person to act, feel, reminisce, sense, and communicate, and may in this way remind him/her of the most basic aspects of the old person's identity' (Rolvsjord 1998, p.7, my translation).

Gaertner (1999) implies both improvisation and music listening, but also contacts her clients, here Monsieur F, by *improvised singing*:

> I took his hands and sat quietly beside him. After a little while I imitated his cries, then, by slightly modifying the pitch and the volume, we eventually changed to sighing and singing in the style of Maurice Ohana. With our vocal expression we moaned, we complained, we sighed, we questioned life's injustices, then changed into expressions of hope and partial acceptance. When Monsieur F was spent and peaceful, we returned to *Unité de Vie I* (the unit where Monsieur F lives). (Gaertner 1999, p.255)

For those with dementia, some memories and episodes from the past fade away, whereas other memories push themselves forward and overshadow reality. Working with reminiscences from the past and feelings in the present by means of songs is described in the literature as a valuable approach. Only a smaller number of studies, mostly European, explore the communicative function of music focusing on intrapersonal aspects, but it seems to be broadly agreed that the use of familiar and personal songs is meaningful to those with dementia.

The various approaches

We have seen that it is possible to divide the literature included here into four main categories pointing to different approaches: evaluative, regulative, stimulative and communicative. Most of the studies examine regulative and stimulative effects of music using controlled experimental designs or 'within-subjects designs', stressing statistical proofs, measuring agitation, ambulation, engagement, social interactions, number of recalled items, etc. A big part of these studies is rooted in behavioural music therapy.

A smaller number of studies examine the communicative function of music by describing the interpersonal interaction with focus on intrapsychic aspects. These studies are from Europe, and there is a tendency to use case design strategies. They are of a recent date, and are rooted in psychotherapeutically orientated approaches.

In the music therapy literature covering other client groups, additional approaches might be taken into account. With clients suffering from dementia the music therapy work seems to be concentrated mainly on two approaches: regulative or stimulative. Traditionally the classic music therapy models focus on *one* approach, not mixing the approaches. This especially comes to the fore when research is formulated and carried out. In eclectic models, approaches are mixed according to what works, and the music is thought to have several functions. When this eclectic approach is theoretically founded and the various 'ingredients' sorted out and described, it might be called an *integrative model*.

Dividing the literature into categories according to function is a process by which the differences of the studies are stressed. Instead of concentrating the music therapy work on one single approach, it might be an enrichment to integrate usable techniques and theories from different approaches, although such eclectic methods might conflict with deep-rooted understandings of which approaches belong to which classic music therapy models.

The evaluative function is very important to evidence-based practice and research, as well as for clinical work. In the literature most of the evaluative tools deal with the regulative and stimulative functions of music. Standardized measures and scales are used to assess behaviour or participation, and few tools deal with the communicative function. One reason is that a major part of the research in dementia care is influenced by behavioural theory. Another reason is that evaluative tools assessing music and communication in persons suffering from a dialogic-degenerative disease are not developed. In order to develop such tools that facilitate evaluative procedures of the music therapy process, or establish effects of the therapy, the phenomenon 'communication' in relation to people with dementia needs to be clarified.

In conclusion

In the 'typical' decline of Alzheimer's disease some skills (or resources) seem to be spared longer, such as the prosodic aspects of language, abilities related to procedural memory, and skills related to music. AD is the most common dementia disease, and the 'typical' deterioration in AD might be very different from that in other dementia. Generally, people with dementia suffer a dialogic-degenerative disease, and adjustment of the communication process seems to be essential in order to fulfil psychosocial needs.

The literature on music and dementia points to an increasing interest in music therapy in dementia care. Here different assessment tools using music and musical interaction are described, a few studies examine the sedative adaptation of music, and several studies describe how different approaches might decrease symptoms of agitation. Music in connection with techniques to stimulate the body, such as dance or movements, or stimulation and motivation to active participation, are described in a considerable part of the literature. A great number of studies show positive effects on cognition and on social interaction. Personal interaction with focus on emotional or intrapsychic material is referred to in a smaller number of studies. The use of familiar songs as a way to express feelings and identity and to enable reminiscing processes is integrated at different levels in a considerable number of studies. This shows that the literature covering music and dementia reflects evaluative, regulative, stimulative and communicative approaches, especially with a focus on stimulative and regulative approaches.

In each of the 92 studies and case descriptions, music is described as representing a resource to the individual person. The music is used in very different ways and settings, with a range of different diagnoses, mostly AD, and at different stages of the disease. From the literature it is clear that the use of music in dementia is administered mostly in order to regulate behaviour (e.g. agitation) or to stimulate active participation, and may generally be concluded to increase quality of life. A growing interest in the communicative function of music might show the way to new fields of research.

In music therapy work with people with cognitive deficits it makes sense to work with regulation and stimulation in order to enhance communication and prevent the vicious circle due to a dialogic-degenerative disease. The regulation serves as a means to lead the participant to a state where it is possible to enter into communication in order to meet psychosocial needs and perform health. The stimulation and regulation serve as ways of establishing a communicative relationship. Instead of dividing the approaches in different directions, it might be profitable to use results and clinical instructions from these different directions in integrated methods. Music seems to have the potential for entering into a meaningful relationship, and without being aware of regulative and stimulative functions of music it is difficult to evoke situations where interaction at a deeper or more intensive level is possible with a person suffering from dementia.

Recommendations for future work in music therapy are that we be precise about the types and stages of dementia, identification of specific needs, of the type of intervention that is used, and of the exact purpose of the music initiative. These observations will provide the basis of a thorough evaluation and documentation. Only when we have this basis can we begin to make comparative studies, as we will see in the next chapter.

CHAPTER 5

Music Therapy in Neurorehabilitation After Traumatic Brain Injury: A Literature Review

Simon K. Gilbertson

The consequences of traumatic brain injury (TBI) are sudden and disastrous. The effect on the life of the individual is immense. To meet the needs of these individuals, we are challenged to find adequate responses and to develop relevant and effective therapy strategies (Aldridge 2001b). Music therapy has increasingly been applied in rehabilitation, particularly during the past decade, as a response to these challenges. This chapter provides a comprehensive overview of the literature about music therapy with people who have experienced traumatic brain injury.

Epidemiology of traumatic brain injury

Traumatic brain injury is a form of acquired brain injury and is defined as 'damage to living brain tissue caused by an external, mechanical force' (Lemkuhl 1992). TBI has both accidental and non-accidental causes. The most common cause is road traffic accidents (Murray *et al.* 1999) which are currently the sixth most common cause for life years spent with disability (Disability Adjusted Life Years or DALYs) for males and the fifteenth most common cause for females (World Health Organization 2004). In a European study of the treatment of head injured individuals, 52 per cent of the 1005 involved patients had been involved in a road traffic accident (Murray *et al.* 1999). The other head injuries were related to work accidents (6%), assault (5%), domestic accidents (12%), sport (3%), a fall under the influence of alcohol (12%), and others (10%) (Murray *et al.* 1999).

In 1997, the Global Burden of Disease Study (Murray and Lopez 1997) calculated baseline, optimistic and pessimistic projections for the causes of death and disability globally for the year 2020. Globally, road traffic accidents are projected in the baseline scenario to become the third largest cause for Disability Adjusted Life Years with an increase of 107.6 per cent, although this figure will be subject to regional differences. Road traffic accidents are projected to become the fourth most common cause of disability in the developed regions (WHO categorization) and will be responsible for 6.9 million DALYs or 4.3 per cent of all causes. In developing regions, road traffic accidents are projected to become the second most common cause of disability and will be responsible for 64.4 million DALYs or 5.24 per cent of all causes.

In 2004, the World Health Organization focused upon road traffic accident prevention and published its first report on the subject (World Health Organization 2004). In this report, it is stated: 'The term "accident", in particular, can give the impression of inevitability and unpredictability – an event that cannot be managed. This is not the case. Road traffic crashes are events that are amenable to rational analysis and remedial action' (p.3). This point emphasizes the tragic nature of these possibly avoidable injurious events and the significance of the implementation of effective prevention strategies in the future. We will have to wait to see whether the magnitude of the projections for 2020 become reality. What seems to be certain is that the number of individuals requiring care and support after sustaining traumatic brain injury related to severe road traffic accidents will increase.

Sequelae of traumatic brain injury

Diagnosis of the sequelae of traumatic brain injury occurs over a span of time. Directly after TBI the immediate clinical signs can include alterations in autonomic function, consciousness, motor function, pupillary responses, ocular movement and other brainstem reflexes (Synder Smith and Winkler 1990). The most common sequelae include changes in consciousness, motor disturbances, memory impairments, speech/language disorders, disorders of cognition, behavioural changes, and disorders of bodily functions.

The consequences of traumatic brain injury can be understood along 'a continuum from altered physiological functions of cells through neurological and psychological impairments, to medical problems and disabilities that affect the individual with TBI, as well as the family, friends, community, and society in general' (NIH Consensus Development Panel 1999, p.976).

Traumatic brain injury is caused by an event of dramatic nature. This type of injury, often occurring within seconds or less, may influence the whole remaining life of the person and, 'in many cases, the consequences of TBI endure in original or altered forms across the lifespan, with new problems likely to occur as the result of new challenges and the ageing process' (NIH Consensus Development Panel 1999, p.976).

The term 'rehabilitation' is commonly used in the literature in two ways: to describe a specific phase of health care systems, and to determine a specific form of treatment in health care.

Rehabilitation as a form of health care treatment

The word rehabilitation derives from the Latin term, *rehabilitare*, meaning 'to restore to a previous condition; to set up again in proper condition' (Shorter Oxford English Dictionary). An alternative definition is 'restore to health or normal life by training and therapy after imprisonment, addiction, or illness' (Oxford Dictionary of English). Both of these definitions express the expectation that rehabilitation is concerned with the process in which an individual returns to a previous, earlier and 'normal' state. In neurorehabilitation, it is misleading to consider rehabilitation simply from this restorative perspective. The World Health Organization (WHO) defines the term rehabilitation as 'the combined and coordinated use of medical, social, educational and vocational measures for training or retraining the individual to the highest possible level of functional ability' (WHO 1969; cited in Glanville 1982, p.7).

The neuropsychologist Barbara Wilson describes rehabilitation as a two-way process (Wilson 1999, p.13). She states:

> Unlike treatment, which is given *to* a patient, rehabilitation is a process in which the patient, client or disabled person takes an active part. Professional staff work together with the disabled person to achieve an optimum level of physical, social, psychological, and vocational functioning. The ultimate goal of rehabilitation is to enable the person with a disability to function as adequately as possible in his or her most appropriate environment.

From this perspective, we can understand rehabilitation as a collection of activities that rely on the recognition of the patient's needs, wishes and environmental context.

The National Institutes of Health Consensus Development Panel on Rehabilitation of Persons with Traumatic Brain Injury (1999) published the results of a conference in which reviews of expert opinion and a comprehensive literature review were used 'to provide biomedical researchers and clinicians with information regarding and recommendations for effective rehabilitation measures for persons who have experienced a traumatic brain injury' (p.974). In this report, the Panel states, 'the goals of cognitive and behavioral rehabilitation are to enhance the person's capacity to process and interpret information and to improve the person's ability to function in all aspects of family and community life' (p.978).

The review identified restorative and compensatory approaches in rehabilitation: 'restorative training focuses on improving a specific cognitive function, whereas compensatory training focuses on adapting to the presence of a cognitive deficit' (p.978). The modalities of therapies described in this report include cognitive exercises, psychotherapy, pharmacological agents, behavior modification, vocational rehabilitation, and comprehensive interdisciplinary rehabilitation. In referring to music therapy, the panel states:

> Other therapies, such as structured adult education, nutritional support, art and music therapy, therapeutic recreation, acupuncture, and other alternative approaches, are used to treat persons with Traumatic Brain Injury. These methods are commonly used, but their efficacy has not been studied. (p.979)

Welter and Schönle (1997) highlight the significance of four central considerations expressed by the WHO about rehabilitation:

- rehabilitation does not generally lead to a profit
- the aims of rehabilitation should not be directed to economic factors
- rehabilitation should be a social strategy aimed at a fair and equal society
- rehabilitation can be seen as a measure of our willingness to cooperate with the most dependent in our society.

Here, rehabilitation is understood as a necessary element of our society that is based on participation and equality, regardless of health situation. In his discussion of music therapy in neurological rehabilitation, Aldridge (2001b) asserts: 'We are challenged as a society that people within our midst are suffering and it is our responsibility within the delivery of health care to meet that challenge with appropriate responses.'

A note on terminology

The subject of this review is the therapeutic use of music in therapy with people who have experienced traumatic brain injury. The diversity in terminology and differing practices in describing patients make the comprehensive identification of reports relevant to this review a difficult target. 'Traumatic brain injury', 'craniocerebral injury', 'cerebral trauma', 'head injury', 'traumatic head injury' and 'severe brain damage' are only some of the terms used to describe damage to the brain caused by external forces. Some authors solely refer to the clinical symptoms presented by people who have experienced TBI, and others provide vague descriptions of the traumatic event. Not only do these factors make identification difficult, they also compound difficulties in evaluating and comparing the identified material. Solutions for these difficulties exist and will be mentioned at appropriate points in this review.

Literature review methodology

Search strategy

A search strategy was developed to identify literature about music therapy with people who have experienced traumatic brain injury using guidelines presented elsewhere (Gilbertson and Aldridge 2003a). Electronic databases known to index journals that publish music therapy and music therapy-related material were searched.

An initial assessment of the state of indexing of music therapy journals highlighted the poor quality and very limited coverage of articles (Gilbertson and Aldridge 2003b). As a consequence, a new bibliographic database called the Music Therapy World Journal Index was created (Aldridge, Gilbertson and Wentz 2004; also available via www.musictherapyworld.net). This holds references to all articles published in twelve music therapy journals and is the first freely available and comprehensive electronic database of music therapy journal articles (see Table 5.1).

The scope of coverage of all the databases searched in this review is shown in Table 5.2. The databases were searched in May 2003 and January 2004.

Table 5.1 Music therapy journals indexed in the Music Therapy World Journal Index

Journal	Coverage
Australian Journal of Music Therapy	1990–2002
British Journal of Music Therapy	1987–2002
Canadian Journal of Music Therapy	1973–1979; 1993–2002
Journal of Music Therapy	1964–2002
Music Therapy	1981–1996
Music Therapy Perspectives	1982–2002
Music Therapy Today (online)	2001–2003
Musik-, Tanz- und Kunsttherapie	1990–2002
Musiktherapeutische Umschau	1980–2003
New Zealand Society for Music Therapy Annual Journal	1987–2002
Nordic Journal of Music Therapy	1992–2003
Voices: A World Forum for Music Therapy	2001–2003

Some journals are not indexed in electronic databases and so must be searched by hand. The identification of relevant books and book sections must also be carried out by hand. Some conference proceedings and books of abstracts of congress papers have been scanned to help identify work related to this review. A small amount of the material reviewed in this study has been identified through personal communication with the primary authors. Some authors have kindly provided material for review purposes that is unobtainable using usual recovery methods.

A search of reference lists should be an integral part of a literature review and has been referred to as 'pearling, the ancestry approach, or citation chasing' (Clarke and Oxman 2002, p.29) or ancestry searching (Conn *et al.* 2003). By doing this, reviewers avoid omitting material that has been cited in previously reviewed articles and are encouraged to consider the relevance of the path of thought of the original author. To support these two practices, a database of the bibliographic references cited in the articles identified in this review is being created. This resource will provide the ability to search through the cited material of other authors, and by doing so, we will be better able to judge where missing research exists and become more aware of the efforts of others.

Inclusion criteria

The targeted literature was required to report the use of music in therapy with people who had experienced traumatic brain injury. Experimental studies without direct relevance to therapeutic application of music were excluded from the review. All full texts of the identified references were retrieved so that the material could be assessed on the contents and not solely on the basis of the article's abstract. Only literature published before January 2004 is included in this review.

Exclusion criteria

No exclusion criteria were applied based on language, date of publication or type of report by the reviewer. Restrictions in the identification of relevant material cannot be completely avoided because of limitations in journal selection and the range of journal coverage in electronic bibliographic databases.

Search terms

The terms used in the search procedure were 'music', 'brain', 'craniocerebral', 'lesion' and 'head injury'. The terms were combined for electronic searches using Boolean operator commands to increase the relevance of the identified material.

Table 5.2 Names, abbreviations and scope of coverage of the electronic databases included in the search strategy

Database name	Database abbreviation	Scope of coverage
Allied and Complementary Medicine	AMED	Complementary medicine, physiotherapy, occupational therapy, rehabilitation, podiatry, palliative care, speech and language therapy
American College of Physicians Club	ACP Club	Evidence-based medicine
BIOSIS Previews	BIOSIS	Preclinical research in life sciences, biomedicine
CAIRSS	CAIRSS	Music and music therapy
CINAHL	–	Nursing and allied health, alternative therapies
Cochrane Central Register of Controlled Trials	CCRCT	Cochrane database of randomized controlled trials
Cochrane Database of Systematic reviews	CDSR	Database of systematic reviews of health care interventions
Database of Abstracts of Reviews of Effects	DARE	Database of evaluations of published systematic reviews of the effectiveness of health care interventions
Dissertation Abstracts	DISSABS	Database of masters and doctoral dissertations
EMBASE	–	Biomedicine and pharmacology
INGENTA	–	Wide-range including: medicine, business, humanities, life sciences, and complementary medicine
Music Therapy DATA 5	MTDATA5	Music therapy and related literature
Music Therapy World Journal Index	MTWJI	Music therapy journals
PREMEDLINE	–	In-process database for MEDLINE, containing details of very recently published articles
PsycINFO	–	Behavioural science and mental health and related fields (psychiatry, management, business, education, social science, neuroscience, law, medicine, and social work)
PSYNDEX	–	Psychology (English and German language)
PubMed/MEDLINE	–	Medicine, nursing, dentistry, veterinary medicine, the health care system, and the preclinical sciences
SOCSCI	–	Social sciences
System for Information on Grey Literature	SIGLE	System for information on unpublished, or grey, literature
Temple University Music Therapy Database	–	Music Therapy

The final search string used was ('music' AND ('brain' OR 'craniocerebral' OR 'lesion' OR 'head injury')). The search strategy used was intentionally wide-ranging to reach a maximum level of comprehensiveness.

Results of the search strategy

After removing duplicated or inaccurate references from the initially identified 1170, 939 references were stored in a central electronic database created using the Endnote™ bibliographic software produced by Thomson ISI ResearchSoft. All references to texts identified by hand were added to the database. Using this search strategy, 62 references to texts related to the use of music therapy with people who had experienced traumatic brain injury were identified.

Eight of the identified references were excluded, as inclusion criteria were not fulfilled. The article by Oepen and Berthold (1983) reports test procedures and not therapeutic intervention. Ojankangas (1984) mentions only the existence of music therapy in a brain injury rehabilitation programme. Glentzer (1995) presents a list of clinical symptoms for which music therapy (individual and group therapy) is indicated (coma, coma remission, aphasia, amusia, frontal brain syndrome, and neuropsychological disorders) but does not provide specific information about the clinical application of therapy. Wingruber (1995) mentions the use of music therapy in an organisation providing home treatment for people with acquired brain damage but does not provide any information about music therapy. One article was excluded (Jochims 1995) as it is a translation of an earlier published article (Jochims 1992). Three further papers were excluded as they were identified through misleading data or were not related to music therapy treatment (Usher 1998; Vertes 1996; Widmer 1997). Two dissertations could not be retrieved and information was extracted from study reports and abstracts (Carlisle 2000; Robinson 2001).

Three doctoral studies relate to the field of rehabilitation (Cohen 1992; Jungblut 2003; Magee 1998). These studies do not focus primarily on the treatment of people who have experienced traumatic brain injury. Nicki Cohen investigated the effect of music and singing on verbal ability of people with aphasia. Wendy Magee completed her doctoral research in 1998 on the use of familiar pre-composed music and improvisation with people with chronic neurological disease. Monika Jungblut completed her research on music therapy in late-rehabilitation with people with aphasia in 2003 – see Chapter 8.

Two doctoral studies specifically concerned with traumatic brain injury and music therapy were in progress at the time of writing. Felicity Baker is currently in the final stages of completing her research on the effects of music therapy on the vocal intonation of people who have experienced TBI. My own doctoral research investigates the use of music improvisation in individual music therapy with people who have experienced TBI.

There are existing reviews of the literature related to music therapy with people who have experienced TBI. Aldridge (1993a) reviewed literature related to the application of music therapy in medical settings. In the overview, music therapy is described in the rehabilitation of aphasia, a speech/language disorder that commonly, but not exclusively, is related to brain damage. Positive effects upon articulation, fluency, breath control and capacity, and spontaneous speech, were identified in the reports of music therapy reviewed.

Purdie's (1997) review of the literature published between 1981 and 1996 includes the use of music in the treatment of people in neurorehabilitation. The review identifies publications related to the use of music therapy and people with stroke (25), Parkinson's disease (14), traumatic brain injury (13), Huntington's chorea (6), multiple sclerosis (3), coma (2), spinal cord injury (1), brain disorders (general) (16). Though Purdie's review provides a general overview of the use of music in therapy in the context of neurological rehabilitation, the particular search strategy was restricted and included only the Medline and PsychLit electronic databases. Hand searches of British and American music therapy journals were included, but unfortunately Purdie does not state which of the British and American music therapy journals were hand-searched, so the scope of the review is unclear.

However, in Purdie's review the search terms used were 'music therapy', 'rehabilitation', 'neurological disorders', 'aphasia' and 'gait'. Rehabilitation aims, as described in the identified papers, were psychological adjustment (27), motor skills (25), speech revalidation (10), general rehabilitation (10), cognition (5) and other (3). These findings are predetermined by the search terms used. By selecting the search terms 'aphasia' and 'gait', a certain pre-selection of references occurs. Purdie identified positive reports of change in music therapy in the areas of vocal/verbal ability, regaining musical skills, attention and memory, mood, initiation and motor planning, coping, social interaction, emotional empathy and reduction of depression. No specific information is provided about the reports related to traumatic brain injury.

In the same study, thirteen texts related to traumatic brain injury and music therapy published between 1981 and 1996 are identified and reviewed. In this chapter, I have identified 33 texts related to TBI and music therapy published during the same period. Because material had been missed, some of the conclusions made in Purdie's previous review are inaccurate, particularly those regarding the numbers of publications per year, statistics concerning geographical source, and areas of clinical application. Purdie's review highlights the difficulties in selecting appropriate search terms in a literature review. It is a feature of literature searches that the reviewer is forced to choose between using primary illnesses, or clinical symptoms, or identifying characteristics of the targeted population or topic, as search terms. In principle, decisions about the inclusion of search terms determine the results of the search. For this reason, authors should explicitly report the search terms and the scope of the search used in any review of the literature.

Paul and Ramsey (2000) reviewed the literature on the use of music and physical therapy in the areas of neurology, rehabilitation, orthopaedics and paediatrics. In their review the authors do not make the applied selection criteria explicit. The authors identify suggestions in the literature that physiotherapy and occupational therapy integrated with music therapy may lead to positive changes in increased participation, ease discomfort and bring improvements in quality of life, strength, range of motion, balance, communication and cognition. It is further suggested that such a therapeutic strategy may lead to an increase in functional independence. As Paul and Ramsey's article provides a general overview, without explicit detail, the original articles must be consulted for further information. What I shall attempt here is to provide an overview but also specific details about what works.

After the removal of the excluded material, doctoral studies and existing reviews, 46 references about music therapy with people who had experienced traumatic brain injury were analysed and reviewed.

Since the 1980s, there has been an increase in the frequency of publications relating to music therapy with people who have experienced traumatic brain injury (Figure 5.1).

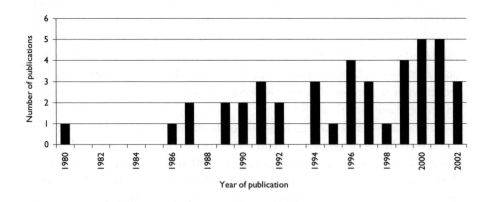

Figure 5.1. Publications related to music therapy and traumatic brain injury between 1980 and 2003

The 46 reports have been categorized according to the type of material, music therapy technique, primary diagnosis, and age groups of any individuals described (Table 5.3). Some of the articles are reports of clinical work in which the therapists applied a variety of music therapy techniques. Because of this, some reports may appear more than once in the ensuing tables. The categorization of some clinical reports is complex as they are not extensive or comprehensive enough to be considered as case studies. Therefore, a large number of case reports have been given the label 'practice reports with case vignette'. It is hoped this reflects the intentions of the authors to portray particular aspects of clinical practice and to highlight these issues or topics with vignettes taken from therapeutic practice.

Of the 46 reports, 24 are practice reports with case vignettes. Ten of the publications are quantitative studies and there are six case studies. Two experimental quantitative studies exist and two of the texts are reviews of the literature. Three reports are descriptions of practice without case vignettes. One of the reports is a multimedia case report in which audio and video recordings taken from therapy are presented (Gilbertson 2002).

The number of subjects in the reports varies between 1 and 20. For those reports providing information about gender, there is a female to male ratio of 40:55. The age of the subjects ranges from 3 years to 84 years.

My analysis of the reports has highlighted the large diversity in comprehensiveness of the reporting of case material, both in formal studies and case reports. Nonetheless, data about age, gender, traumatic event, primary diagnosis, neurodiagnostic information, clinical symptoms, timescale of treatment, assessment strategies, music therapy technique, concurrent therapies, musical biography of the patient, and the reported results of the therapy have been extracted from the identified reports and tabulated. This information is required to compare and identify cases and is necessary to provide the reader with information about the context of the therapeutic endeavours and results.

As clinicians, we need information about a range of facets of the patients we are treating and about the circumstances of therapy. Most clinicians will need to know the age and gender of the patient. Information about primary diagnosis and clinical symptoms will determine the initial paths of intervention. Specific to neurological rehabilitation, we will need to be informed about the traumatic events leading to the injuries and any neurodiagnostic information. We will need to know the time point and duration of therapy along with the type of intervention applied. The results of the therapy can be best understood if we are aware of the influences of other therapies that the individual is receiving. Researchers too require this information, and if it is missing, the definition of the 'case' will remain unclear.

Table 5.3 Reports of music therapy included in this review

Name	Year	Type of material	Music therapy technique	Population	Age group
Emich	1980	Practice report with case vignette	Intonation exercises	TBI	Children and adolescents
Gadomski and Jochims	1986	Practice report with case vignette	Improvisation	Post-coma, related to TBI	Adults
Hohmann	1987	Practice report with case vignette	Auditive music therapy	TBI, non-traumatic brain injury	Adults
Lucia	1987	Practice report with case vignette	Vocalization, song singing, rhythmic speech exercises	Head trauma	Adults
Claeys et al.	1989	Practice report	Improvisation	Long-term care, brain damage	Adults
Hiller	1989	Case study	Song story	TBI	Adolescents
Jochims	1990	Practice report with case vignette	Improvisation	TBI	Adolescents and adults
Jones	1990	Practice report with case vignette	No formal method: music reception	Persisting vegetative state	Adults
Barker and Brunk	1991	Practice report with case vignette	Improvisation	TBI, spinal cord injury, stroke	Adults
Gervin	1991	Practice report with case vignette	Song lyrics during dressing	TBI	Adolescents and adults
Glassman	1991	Practice report with case vignette	Song reminiscing and song text writing, alongside bibliotherapy	TBI	Adolescents
Cohen	1992	Quantitative study	Singing instruction, vocal exercise, physical exercise, breathing exercise, song singing	TBI, stroke	Adults
Jochims	1992	Practice report with case vignette	Improvisation	TBI	Adults

Table 5.3 continued

Jochims	1994	Practice report with case vignette	Improvisation	TBI	Adults
Jones *et al.*	1994	Controlled trial	Music reception, non-musical acoustic stimuli	TBI, coma	Adults
Wit *et al.*	1994	Practice report with case vignette	Electro-acoustic music for training attention	TBI, non-traumatic brain damage	Adolescents
Schinner *et al.*	1995	Controlled trial	Auditory stimulation	TBI	Adults
Knox and Jutai	1996	Literature review	Music reception	TBI, non-traumatic brain damage	All age groups
Livingston	1996	Practice report with case vignette	Singing, song composition, breathing techniques, melodic exercises, playing instruments	TBI	Adults
Price-Lackey and Cashman	1996	Narrative analysis of life history interviews	'Playing music' (alongside various other activities)	TBI	Adults
Robb	1996	Practice report with case vignette	Fill in the blank song writing, group song writing, improvisational song writing, songs used for discharge from hospital	TBI	Children and adolescents
Kennelly and Edwards	1997	Practice report with case vignette	Song singing, song creation, improvised song, improvisation	TBI	Children
Lee and Baker	1997	Practice report with case vignette	Song composition, creation of 'song-portfolio', instructional song	Closed head injury	Adults

Continued on next page

Table 5.3 Reports of music therapy included in this review continued

Author	Year	Type of material	Music therapy technique	Population	Age group
Purdie	1997	Literature review	Active, receptive	TBI, stroke, neurological disease	All age groups
Hurt et al.	1998	Quantitative study	Rhythmic auditory stimulation	TBI	Adults
Bright and Signorelli	1999	Case study	Improvisation	TBI, non-traumatic brain damage	Adults
Gilbertson	1999	Practice report with case vignette	Improvisation	TBI	Children and adults
Magee	1999b	Practice report with case vignette	Modified melodic intonation therapy, improvisation mentioned	TBI	Adults
Rosenfeld and Dun	1999	Practice report with case vignette	Song listening, song singing alongside instrumental improvisation, physical stimulation	TBI	Children
Burke et al.	2000	Case study	Song writing, song listening, song quizzes, instrument playing	TBI	Adolescent
Carlisle	2000	Quantitative study	Music and relaxation therapy versus verbal relation therapy	Brain injury	Adults
Nayak et al.	2000	Quantitative study	Improvisation	TBI, or stroke	Adults
Paul and Ramsey	2000	Theoretical paper	Accompaniment of physical or occupational therapy	Neurology, rehab.	Adults
Tamplin	2000	Practice report with case vignette	Improvisation	TBI, coma	Children

Table 5.3 continued

Baker	2001	Crossover study	Music reception	Post-traumatic amnesia	Adults
Bischof	2001	Practice report with case vignette	Improvisation	TBI	Children
Kennelly, Hamilton, and Cross	2001	Practice report with case vignette	Joint treatment with speech pathologist, song singing, song creation, and improvised song	TBI	Children
Robinson	2001	Quantitative comparison study	Improvisation	Brain injury	Adults
Tucek et al.	2001	Practice report with case vignette	Traditional oriental music therapy	TBI	Adults
Gilbertson	2002	Multimedia case study	Improvisation	TBI	Adults
Herkenrath	2002	Practice report with case vignette	Improvised singing	TBI	Adults
Magee and Davidson	2002	Quantitative study	Improvisation, song singing	TBI, MS, stroke, anoxia	Adults
Noda et al.	2003	Quantitative study (conference proceedings)	Musico-kinetic therapy	TBI	–
Oyama et al.	2003	Quantitative study (conference proceedings)	Musico-kinetic therapy	TBI	Adults
Yamamoto et al.	2003	Case study (conference proceedings)	Musico-kinetic therapy	TBI	Adults
Wheeler, Shiflett and Nayak	2003	Quantitative study, re-analysis of data collected by Nayak et al. 2000	Group/individual music therapy	TBI, stroke	Adults

Reports of music therapy with people who have experienced traumatic brain injury are characterized by the incompleteness of relevant case information. The cases cannot be conclusively compared where information regarding gender and age is missing. Grades of severity vary widely in the diagnosis of TBI, and if this information is not provided we cannot judge the significance of reported change by therapy. Significantly, we cannot genuinely evaluate the effect of music therapy if concurrent therapies are not reported. Most authors have access to the two main sources of this information, the patient's medical records and the therapist's own clinical notes. Case material in the future *must* contain this information if we are to provide a serious base for comparative studies and from which clinical trials can be developed.

Music therapy techniques

Nineteen music therapy techniques were identified in the reports. These techniques are not unique to the field of neurorehabilitation but are found in many areas of clinical application. The techniques identified are auditive music therapy, auditory stimulation, composition, improvisation, instructional song, instrumental playing, intonation exercises, melodic intonation therapy, modified melodic intonation therapy, music reception, rhythmic auditory stimulation, rhythmic speech exercises, singing instruction, song creation, song listening, song reminiscing, song story, song text writing, traditional oriental music therapy, vocalization exercises. Refer back to Table 5.3 for more detail.

Three tables present the reports in groups of empirical studies (Table 5.4), reports of the use of music improvisation (Table 5.5) and reports of techniques other than improvisation (Table 5.6).

Central topics and issues in the identified literature

Initial therapeutic approach and early signs of change

For many patients, the initial weeks following severe traumatic brain injury are characterized by a loss of usual interaction with the environment. When closely observed, the individuals may seem completely absent of movement or vocalizations. In some instances, families and carers may occasionally observe minimal and undirected physical movements or vocal utterances.

Music therapists initially approach these individuals from a 'listening perspective' and concentrate on any sounds or movements the patients make. This observational perspective provides a sensitive basis to assess any actions made by the patient within the context of the presented music therapy intervention and, it is argued, a unique form of diagnostic potential (Bischof 2001; Gadomski and Jochims 1986; Gilbertson 1999; Herkenrath 2002; Jones 1990; Noda *et al.* 2003; Tamplin 2000; Tucek, Auer-Pekarsky and Stepansky 2001).

Table 5.4 Empirical studies into the use of music in therapy with people who have experienced TBI

Author(s)	Cohen	Wit *et al.*
Year	1992	1994
Case/participants	6 treatment, 2 control	4 treatment, 1 control
Age	Adults	Age range 13–17 yrs
Gender	–	3 female, 2 male
Traumatic event	–	–
Primary diagnosis	Stroke (7), 1 without diagnosis, possibly TBI	3 with closed head injuries, 1 with ruptured aneurysm, 1 with arteriovenous malformation
Neuro-diagnostic information	–	
Clinical symptoms	Expressive speech disorders	Attention deficits, various severities
Timescale	9 sessions, each 30 minutes	Brain injury within 1 year
Assessment	–	Rancho Los Amigos scale level 6, PASAT, Seashore Rhythm Test
Music technique	Singing instruction, vocal excercises, breathing exercise, and song singing	Electro-acoustic music for training attention
Concurrent therapies	–	–
Musical biography	–	–
Results	Statistically significant positive changes in fundamental frequency, speech rate and verbal intelligibility	Diverse levels of improvement in attention measured with Paced Auditory Serial Addition Task and Seashore Rhythm Test Differences in change measured between sustained and alternating/divided attention; inconclusive findings

Continued on next page

Table 5.4 continued

Author(s)	Hurt *et al.*	Carlisle
Year	1998	2000
Case/participants	8 subjects	13 in treatment and control groups
Age	Mean age 30 ± 5 years	19–64
Gender	3 female, 5 male	–
Traumatic event	–	–
Primary diagnosis	TBI	TBI
Neuro-diagnostic information	Multi-site lesions	–
Clinical symptoms	Persisting and significant gait disorder	High level of anxiety, stress and tension possibly preventing development of pyshological, physical, emotional function
Timescale	4–24 months post-trauma	–
Assessment	Pre/post test: velocity, cadence, stride length, symmetry of gait	Mann–Whitney test for the Personal Anxiety Report and for the Relax Mood Survey
Music technique	Rhythmic auditory stimulation	6 sessions: music and relaxation therapy versus verbal relaxation therapy
Concurrent therapies	–	–
Musical biography	–	–
Results	Statistically significant improvement in velocity, cadence, stride length. No statistically significant change in stride symmetry perhaps because of localization of damage	No significant differences in reduction of anxiety levels for either the experimental or control group

Table 5.4 continued

Author(s)	Nayak *et al.*	Baker
Year	2000	2001
Case/participants	Mixed treatment group, mixed control group	22 participants
Age	Adults: age range 31–84 yrs, mean 59.89 yrs	Mean 34 yrs ±15.34 yrs
Gender	Treatment: 4 male, 6 female Control: 2 male, 6 female	5 female, 17 male
Traumatic event	–	–
Primary diagnosis	TBI or stroke	TBI
Neuro-diagnostic information	–	–
Clinical symptoms	–	Post-traumatic amnesia (PTA)
Timescale	–	–
Assessment	FIM score of 4.5 or lower; Faces Scale of Depression score 4 or more	Score of less than 9 on Westmead PTA scale
Music technique	Welcome activity, improvisation, singing, composition, playing instruments, performing or listening	Live or taped music and no music as control 10–12 minutes in crossover design
Concurrent therapies	–	Occupational therapy
Musical biography	–	–
Results	Increased involvement and motivation in treatment group Positive trends in mood; self-report ($p < 0.10$), family rating on previous day ($p < 0.10$) and previous week ($p < 0.06$) Improvement also in social interaction Treatment group was more motivated to participate ($p < 0.06$) and actively involved ($p < 0.01$) in therapy	Statistically significant decrease in agitation and increase in orientation Study identified recall of music intervention after remission of PTA

Continued on next page

Table 5.4 continued

Author(s)	Magee and Davidson	Noda *et al.*
Year	2002	2003
Case/participants	3 groups	6
Age	–	–
Gender	–	–
Traumatic event	–	–
Primary diagnosis	TBI (5Ss), MS (5Ss), stroke or anoxia (4Ss)	TBI
Neuro-diagnostic information	–	–
Clinical symptoms	'Variety of physical, cognitive, communication, sensory, and behavioural impairments' (p.22)	Acute subdural haematoma, cerebral contusion, intracerebral haematoma (not linked to cases)
Timescale	–	–
Assessment	Profile of Mood States (bipolar form)	Initial Glasgow Coma Scores: 1 patient GCS=4, 2 patients GCS=5, 2 patients GCS=6 and 1 patient GCS=7) Reaction scale (Society for Treatment of Coma) used in study
Music technique	Pre-composed song versus improvisation; 1 session of each treatment	Two 1-hour sessions of musico-kinetic therapy, 3 times weekly, for 1 month
Concurrent therapies	–	Intensive care nursing
Musical biography	Interested in music, as listener, no formal training	–
Results	Statistically positive trends on continuum of composed–anxious, agreeable–hostile, and energetic–tired mood states	Positive tendency towards change in eye opening, movement, emotional, visual and phonation reactions measured using Japanese 'Reaction Scale'

Table 5.4 continued

Author(s)	Oyama *et al.*	Wheeler *et al.*
Year	2003	2003
Case/participants	2 participants	10
Age	30 yrs, 24 yrs	Range 34–74 yrs, mean 60.5 yrs
Gender	Male, female	6 females, 4 males
Traumatic event	MVA, MVA	–
Primary diagnosis	TBI	TBI or stroke
Neuro-diagnostic information	Acute subdural haematoma, brain atrophy and hydrocephalus	–
Clinical symptoms	Kohnan's score = 67, Kohnan's score =66 Both patients unresponsive	FIM score = 4.5 or lower, moderate depression
Timescale	8 months post-injury, 1 month after therapy began	During in-patient rehabilitation
Assessment	Kohnan's Score and SPECT (blood flow)	Pre–post assessment: 7-point Faces depression scale, Sickness Impact Profile, Self, family, and therapist rating
Music technique	Musico-kinetic therapy	4–10 music therapy sessions: welcome activity, song singing, improvisation, playing instruments
Concurrent therapies	–	'Standard rehabilitation' (p.143)
Musical biography	–	–
Results	Patient 1: Improvement in mouth and hand movement, eye contact, increased blood flow during treatment, returning to 'baseline original state after relaxation sessions' Patient 2: Increase in appropriate expression (laughing and crying); no change in cerebral blood flow observed	Group music therapy increased social interaction more than individual treatment Individual treatment seemed to influence motivation Family ratings correlated to improvement in mood and number of group sessions Unclear results concerning correlation between individual/group intervention and clinical change

Gadomski and Jochims (1986) suggest that through observation and interpretation of the patient's musical actions and non-musical behaviour during interactive music improvisation it is possible to gain unique information about the condition of the patient in terms of awareness, perception of the environment and communicative ability. This source of information provides additional insight into the condition of patients who show minimal or no observable responses in other diagnostic situations.

Bischof (2001) describes the use of music improvisation in the development of vocalizations of an eleven-year-old girl who suffered severe brainstem damage related to a road traffic accident. Early vocalizations, initially perceived as moans, were placed in a tonal context through instrumental accompaniment by the therapist. It is suggested the musical context of the child's vocalizations facilitates a transformation of the meaning of the vocalizations from expressions of physical effort into interactive communicative music actions.

Tamplin (2000) describes observing positive changes in breathing, eye movement and eye contact of four adults whilst improvising vocally. The synchronization of breathing tempo and music tempo and changes in eye activity are interpreted as signs of the patient's awareness of the music and of the music therapist. Changes in tension and relaxation are regarded as indicators of the patient's music perception and listening.

Improvised music offers a strategy for evaluating the perception and orientation of patients with severe brain injury who present either minimal or no observable actions, or reactions (Herkenrath 2002). Herkenrath, as we see in the following chapter, suggests that a range of observable qualities – including breathing, mimicking, body movement and vocalizations – can provide a basis and content for music improvisation. This form of intervention aims at assisting the patient in regaining orientation to his or her body, space, time, place and intentionality of action.

Jones (1990) published a report of a young male patient for whom prerecorded music was played via headphones following the initiative of his primary nurse. The patient had experienced traumatic head injury and was considered unable to respond. A cassette recording of music heard by the patient and his wife before the accident started a chain of events that demanded the primary nurse to re-evaluate the diagnosis of persisting vegetative state. The nurse reports how the patient suddenly began to cry. As the nurse turned the music off the patient's eyes 'became dark and he shook his head vigorously, dislodging the headphones' (p.196). When the nurse asked whether he wanted to continue listening to the music, the patient responded with slow and deliberate nodding. After recognizing the patient's ability to respond, the nurse encouraged and supported the patient in developing a wider range of communication. The patient increased shaking his head and added shrugging his shoulders to answer questions with gestures.

Table 5.5 Reports of improvisation in therapy with people who have experienced TBI

Author(s)	Gadomski and Jochims	Claeys *et al.*	Jochims
Year	1986	1989	1990
Case	Roland H	–	NN
Age	–	–	15
Gender	Male	–	Female
Traumatic event	–	–	–
Primary diagnosis	–	–	TBI
Neuro-diagnostic information	–	–	–
Clinical symptoms	Post-coma, severe ataxia	Problems of reality orientation	Transitional psychosis, initial aggression
Timescale	Remission from coma before admission to clinic	–	–
Assessment	–	–	–
Music technique	Instrumental improvisation	Improvised song, with texts relating to the weather, date and time of day	Receptive music therapy: German lullaby melodies, well-known songs, improvisation
Concurrent therapies	–	Reality orientation therapy	–
Musical biography	–	–	–
Results	Following about 2 months of isolated single actions, the patient played at musically fitting moments within a greeting song Development of expressive ability (piano playing) helped the patient to 'express his complete range of emotions' (p.109)	Increase in environmental awareness and orientation	Songs and lullabies were tolerated, improvisation led to increase in anxiety Patient entered a session announcing, 'I have woken up' and could not recall anything from the earlier phase except the greeting song This is interpreted as a sign of internal activity 'despite disorientation and disturbance of consciousness' (p.128)

Continued on next page

Table 5.5 continued

Author(s)	Jochims	Barker and Brunk	Jochims
Year	1990	1991	1992
Case	G	Creative arts therapy group	NN
Age	–	Adults	47
Gender	Male	Female and male	Male
Traumatic event	–	–	MVA
Primary diagnosis	TBI	TBI, spinal cord injury, stroke	TBI
Neuro-diagnostic information	–	–	–
Clinical symptoms	Transitional psychosis	No specific detail given	Post-coma
Timescale	–	–	–
Assessment	–	5-point scale used in the institution	–
Music technique	Receptive improvised song for patient	Combined arts activities: song, improvisation, drawing, craft activities	Co-improvisation and music reception
Concurrent therapies	–	Physiotherapy, occupational therapy, speech therapy, recreation therapies, neuropsychology	–
Musical biography	–	–	–
Results	Patient scratched skin severely as a result of transitional psychosis; the therapists reflected this in improvised song The patient spoke one single time asking, 'It won't turn out that bad will it?' in response to the therapist singing 'Hr G wants to scratch himself kaput' The patient returned to his previous state	Patients reached higher scores in the categories 'addressing personal issues' and 'identification with work' Increase in active participation and 'helpful leadership' Increased 'commitment to group attendance' and an increase in the relatives' ability to allow the patient to be independent	Over six sessions 2–3 deep sighs observed in each session Session 7: Patient played drum within musical structure of the greeting song and other traditional songs This new ability led to a change in the perception of the patient by the staff and resulted in an extension of the rehabilitation treatment duration

Table 5.5 continued

Author(s)	Jochims	Jochims	Kennelly and Edwards
Year	1994	1994	1997
Case	N	RK	Sally (sister of Chris)
Age	40	19	10
Gender	Male	Male	Female
Traumatic event	Motorcycle accident	Road traffic accident	MVA, as car passenger
Primary diagnosis	TBI	TBI	Closed head injury
Neuro-diagnostic information	–	–	Cerebral oedema
Clinical symptoms	Buccofacial apraxia, left-sided spastic paresis, neglect syndrome, mutism, ideomotor apraxia	No clear diagnosis given: change in consciousness	Left hemiplegia, fractured right femur, ruptured bladder, multiple pelvic fractures, facial lacerations
Timescale	–	–	Therapy began 2 weeks post-injury
Assessment	–	–	GCS = 7 at accident
Music technique	Improvisation	Receptive music therapy with passive movement of patient's arms	Improvised and pre-composed song
Concurrent therapies	–	–	Nursing, physiotherapy
Musical biography	Organ player in amateur rock group	–	Enjoyed music pre-injury
Results	Patient able to develop structured music playing after initially having no recognisable structures Discrepancy between activity in music therapy setting and apathetic behaviour in all other situations The author relates this to resignation based on negative future perspectives: 'The inner drive was missing to confront the uncomfortable elements of daily life' (p.1323)	Initial rhythmic gestures to music led to joint swinging of the patient's arms Only observed in connection with Beethoven's 5th Symphony	Responses included crying, movement of all limbs, attempts to speak, eye opening and looking at the therapist and the guitar: 'behaviours indicative of improvements in orientation and awareness' (p.23–4)

Continued on next page

Table 5.5 continued

Author(s)	Kennelly and Edwards	Bright and Signorelli	Gilbertson
Year	1997	1999	1999
Case	Chris (brother of Sally)	Mixed group	Michael
Age	7	–	9
Gender	Male	3 female, 4 male	Male
Traumatic event	MVA, as car passenger	Suicide attempt, train accident, domestic violence, other brain disease	MVA
Primary diagnosis	Closed head injury	Brain injury, anoxia, Lennox–Gasteaux Syndrome, subdural haematoma	TBI
Neuro-diagnostic information	Intracerebral haemorrhage, left frontal lobe haematoma, left occipital haemorrhage	–	Brain atrophy
Clinical symptoms	Bilateral lung contusions, ruptured left hemi-diaphragm, ruptured spleen, pelvic fractures, left leg below-knee amputation	'No purposeful movement', patients were without 'communication by word or gesture' (p.256)	Vegetative syndrome, tetraparesis, hydrocephalus
Timescale	Therapy 3 weeks post-injury	–	Admission one month post-injury
Assessment	Initial GCS = 8	QoL questionnaire	–
Music technique	Receptive songs, song creation	Improvised vocal and instrumental music	Vocal improvisation
Concurrent therapies	Nursing	–	–
Musical biography	Enjoyed music pre-injury	–	–
Results	'elicited a range of responses from Chris during his period of unconsciousness, including vocalizations, body movements, changes in breathing, orientation to the therapist and guitar, and eye opening' (p.27)	'Some level of communication with most clients and improved the quality of life for all/most clients' (p.262) TBI participants: 'notable changes in areas of enjoyment, sense of individuality and the ability to express emotion' (p.260)	Development of interactive communication

Table 5.5 continued

Author(s)	Gilbertson	Gilbertson	Magee
Year	1999	1999	1999
Case	G	K	NN
Age	Adult	Adult	30 yrs
Gender	Male	Male	Male
Traumatic event	Motorcycle accident	–	Road traffic accident
Primary diagnosis	TBI	Brain damage	TBI
Neuro-diagnostic information	Cerebral contusion, skull and other skeletal fractures	Pre-motor cortex damage	Left-hemisphere damage
Clinical symptoms	Spasticity	Aphasia, paresis, disturbed motor planning and coordination	Aphonic at admission, expressive and receptive aphasia, right-sided hemiparesis
Timescale	10 days post-admission individual therapy, group therapy 1 month later	–	Admission 7 months post-injury, music therapy began 8 months post-injury
Assessment	–	–	–
Music technique	Improvisation	Improvisation	Initially group music therapy; 12 months post-injury individual music therapy Instrumental improvisation denied; then adapted melodic intonation therapy
Concurrent therapies	–	–	Speech therapy
Musical biography	–	Proficient musician, conductor of children's choir	Active musician; guitar, composition
Results	Development of motor skills, increase in physical and psychological ability and self-assessment, self-dependency, enjoyment and development of relationships	Improvement in temporal organization of movement, physical coordination and emotional expression	'Inconsistently able to produce verbal phrases using this method, and he was continuing to show considerable change and improvement in his general functional abilities' (p.23)

Continued on next page

Table 5.5 continued

Author(s)	Tamplin	Tamplin	Tamplin
Year	2000	2000	2000
Case	John	Akim	Simon
Age	23	34	19
Gender	Male	Male	Male
Traumatic event	–	–	–
Primary diagnosis	–	–	Brain injury
Neuro-diagnostic information	–	–	–
Clinical symptoms	Coma	Coma	Coma, high tonus in neck, reduced head movement
Timescale	3 months post-injury	3 months post-injury	5 months post-injury
Assessment	–	–	–
Music technique	Improvised singing	Improvised singing	Improvised singing
Concurrent therapies	–	–	–
Musical biography	–	Listener of Hindi music	–
Results	Changes in quality of breathing, slow and deeper, turned to therapist Actions interpreted as 'changes indicative of John's awareness of myself and the music, and his orientation to my presence during music therapy sessions' (p.47)	Reduction in breathing tempo, entrained to therapist's singing, eye-opening pattern, breathing-in phrasing; the patient's wife became more involved in the clinical setting	Orientation towards the music source and turned to therapist, patient would 'visually track the movement of my head when I moved position, indicating an orientation to the music, and myself and its source' (p.48) Eye opening interpreted as sign of awareness of therapist

Table 5.5 continued

Author(s)	Tamplin	Bischof	Bischof
Year	2000	2001	2001
Case	Matthew	René	Nina
Age	25	8	11
Gender	Male	Male	Female
Traumatic event	–	Motor vehicle accident (MVA)	MVA as pedestrian
Primary diagnosis	–	Severe TBI	TBI
Neuro-diagnostic information	–	–	Brainstem damage, brain contusions, brain swelling
Clinical symptoms	Coma	Apallic syndrome, tetraparesis, instable vegetative function	Apallic syndrome, high-grade spastic muscle tone
Timescale	5 months post-injury	6 weeks post-injury clinic admission, no exact information about start of MTh	–
Assessment	–	–	–
Music technique	Improvised singing	Vocal improvisation	Vocal improvisation
Concurrent therapies	–	–	–
Musical biography	–	–	–
Results	No observable signs of change; therapy ended after 4 weekly sessions 18 months followed 'no observable progress in orientation or awareness' (p.48)	Development of simple communicative exchanges with eye closing patterns	Regaining use of the voice

Continued on next page

Table 5.5 continued

Author(s)	Bischof	Kennelly, Hamilton and Cross	Kennelly, Hamilton and Cross
Year	2001	2001	2001
Case	Emanuel	Tracey	Cathy
Age	10	12	3
Gender	Male	Female	Female
Traumatic event	MVA as car passenger	MVA as pedestrian	MVA as pedestrian
Primary diagnosis	TBI	TBI	TBI
Neuro-diagnostic information	Bilateral contusions, haemorrhage	Diffuse axonal injury, multiple cerebral contusions, intraventricular haemorrhage	Extensive cerebral contusions, haemorrhages, and multiple infarcts
Clinical symptoms	Coma	Coma, followed by post-traumatic amnesia, dysarthria	Initial coma, later vision impairment, severe aphasia, right-sided hemiplegia
Timescale	–	–	–
Assessment	–	GCS = 3	GCS = 5
Music technique	Vocal improvisation	Joint music and speech therapy, vocal exercise, singing songs of patient's song preference	Joint session with speech therapist: singing of song, instrumental improvisation
Concurrent therapies	Physiotherapy and others (not specified)	Speech pathology	Speech therapy
Musical biography	–	Piano and clarinet lessons, pop music fan including 'Spice Girls'	–
Results	Regaining use of voice, arm movements Later: early vocal and verbal ability	Increase in speech intelligibility, participation, motivation and enjoyment Rate of speech, pitch range and intonation improved	Improvement in word retrieval, indicating choice of song, song recognition, and could following verbal instructions during instrumental play

Table 5.5 continued

Author(s)	Herkenrath	Gilbertson
Year	2002	2002
Case	1	Markus
Age	Adult	34
Gender	Female	Male
Traumatic event	Accident	MVA
Primary diagnosis	TBI	TBI
Neuro-diagnostic information	–	–
Clinical symptoms	Tetra-spasticity, disorder of body perception, loss of speech ability	Tetra-paresis, dysarthria
Timescale	–	Therapy described 8 months post-injury
Assessment	–	–
Music technique	Improvised singing	Improvisation
Concurrent therapies	–	–
Musical biography	–	No musical experience
Results	Patient began to vocalize tonally with the therapist During this vocal improvisation the patient relaxed and developed trust in the situation	Positive change in mood state, opportunity to monitor changes in physical ability, opportunity to demonstrate ability at a time of severely reduced physical ability, creation of a aesthetically pleasing musical work

Though this report does not represent the work of a music therapist, it does show the potential music may hold for some patients with traumatic brain injury to enter into a dialogue with their environment. More recently, Noda and colleagues (2003) also emphasized the significance of careful visual and aural observation of patients following severe TBI.

Observable changes in the awareness of the environment are clinically highly significant in the early phases of rehabilitation following TBI. These signs may include changes in breathing, vocalizations, or minute body movements. Two children (aged 7 and 10 years) received music therapy as a part of their rehabilitation following severe injuries as passengers in a motor vehicle accident (Kennelly and Edwards 1997). At the time of the incident the children were assessed with Glasgow Coma Scores of 7 and 8. Improvised singing was used to encourage potential communicative actions during coma and coma emergence. In improvisation, the therapist mirrored musically the non-musical actions of the children, such as minimal body movement, and 'elicited a range of responses from one child during his period of unconsciousness including vocalizations, body movements, changes in breathing, orientation to the therapist and guitar, and eye opening' (p.27). During the therapy process, both children presented patterns of eye opening and attempts to speak which were understood as 'behaviours indicative of improvements in orientation and awareness' (p.23–4). Rosenfeld and Dun (1999) too have described the clinical significance of initial eye and oral movement that is temporally coordinated to songs sung by the therapist and consider these events as positive changes in environmental awareness.

Oyama *et al.* (2003) measured the positive effects on the level of consciousness in a 30-year-old man who had suffered TBI as a result of a motorcycle accident, using musico-kinetic therapy beginning 8 months post injury. A behavioural assessment scale – Kohnan Scoring Scale, reported in Fujiwara *et al.* (1993) – assessed positive increases in fine motor movement, communicative gesture and eye contact over seven months of therapy. Single photon emission computerized tomography (SPECT) showed an increase in cerebral blood flow during the intervention that returned to baseline state after relaxation sessions. The increase in cerebral blood flow suggests an increase in activation of the brain and represents an important parameter of neural recovery.

Awareness, orientation and memory

Improvised songs have been used in therapy with people who have experienced traumatic brain injuries. This technique has been used to increase patients' environmental awareness by relating the song text to the actual activities (Claeys *et al.* 1989). Improvised singing has been used also as a part of reality orientation therapy in which text related to the weather, the date and time of day has been incorporated (Claeys *et al.* 1989). Baker (2001) also highlights the importance of music therapy techniques that lead to statistically significant positive changes in the orientation of patients who have suffered post-traumatic amnesia. In this crossover study, Baker demonstrates that by playing live or recorded music there is an increase in orientation and memory measured using the Westmead PTA scale, a scale consisting of questions about age, date, place, person and recall of printed pictures. In the same study, Baker (2001) also identifies that people experiencing post-traumatic amnesia do recall events occurring in the music therapy

Table 5.6 Reports of music therapy techniques other than improvisation with people who have experienced TBI

Author(s)	Emich	Hohmann	Lucia
Year	1980	1987	1987
Case	No specific cases mentioned	Practice description, no vignettes, but cases mentioned	Practice review
Age	Children and adolescents	Adults	–
Gender	–	Both	–
Traumatic event	–	–	–
Primary diagnosis	Cerebrotraumatic lesions	Various: TBI, stroke, hypoxic brain damage, Guillain Barré syndrome	Head trauma
Neuro-diagnostic information	–	–	–
Clinical symptoms	Aphasia	Post-coma, chronic pain, disturbance of tonus regulation, transverse paralysis, headaches	Aphasia
Timescale	–	–	–
Assessment	–	–	–
Music technique	No formalized technique: music intonation of verbalizations	Auditive music therapy	Vocalization, song singing, rhythmic speech exercises
Concurrent therapies	–	–	–
Musical biography	–	–	–
Results	Author suggests increase in use of verbal communication can be expected	Technique aims at: 1. initiation of contact and communication; 2. development of awareness and concentration ability; 3. psychic harmonization; 4. supportive accompaniment in the working through of illness and healing crisis; 5. general stimulation, an increase in vigilance, 6. relaxation/harmonization of body tonus	Music therapy techniques used may lead to improvement in speech/language ability and motor function

Continued on next page

Table 5.6 continued

Author(s)	Hiller	Jones	Gervin
Year	1989	1990	1991
Case	AB	Bill	F
Age	16	32	29
Gender	Male	Male	Male
Traumatic event	TBI	MVA	MVA
Primary diagnosis	Severe brainstem and frontal lobe injury	Head injury	TBI
Neuro-diagnostic information	Brainstem and frontal lobe injury	Intracranial pressure	–
Clinical symptoms	Receptive and expressive language disorders, cognitive and affective disorders	Persisting vegetative state	Left-side hemiparesis, cognitive and memory deficits
Timescale	2 years post-injury	Describes changes during 2 years post-injury	Trauma treatment: no information Treatment described over first 3.5 weeks
Assessment	–	–	–
Music technique	Song story	No formal method: reception of biographical relevant music	Instructional song for dressing
Concurrent therapies	–	Nursing	Nursing
Musical biography	–	Music listener	–
Results	Extension of vocabulary and speech ability, development of trust, experiencing wider range of affective responses, increase in reading and writing skills and concentration	Patient began responding to caregivers through gesture, leading to a change in interaction on the part of the caregivers	Significant reduction in dressing time: 25–28 minutes reduced to *c.* 8 minutes and reduced level of required assistance

Table 5.6 continued

Author(s)	Gervin	Glassman	Livingston
Year	1991	1991	1996
Case	S	Lori	Red
Age	14	–	28
Gender	Female	Female	Male
Traumatic event	MVA	–	MVA
Primary diagnosis	TBI	Severe cerebral damage, brainstem damage	TBI
Neuro-diagnostic information	–	–	Left temporal lobe damage
Clinical symptoms	Left-side hemiparesis, problems with initiation, motor planning and attention	Initially in coma Later: extreme motor dysfunction, absence of functional speech, moderate organic brain syndrome	Loss of vocal/verbal ability
Timescale	Trauma treatment: no information given Treatment over first 3.5 weeks described	2 years post-injury	8 years post-injury, therapy over 6 months
Assessment	Initially: Ranchos Los Amigos Scale 4–5	–	Observation
Music technique	Instructional song for dressing	Song reminiscing and song text writing	Singing, breathing techniques, vocal exercises
Concurrent therapies	Nursing	Bibliotherapy	Multi-disciplinary treatment setting
Musical biography	–	–	–
Results	Significant reduction in dressing time: 15 minutes reduced to c. 8 minutes and reduced level of assistance	Provided patient with creative mode of expression following loss of verbal ability	Increase of vocal ability, rate of speech, and breath control

Continued on next page

Table 5.6 continued

Author(s)	Livingston	Livingston	Livingston
Year	1996	1996	1996
Case	Ralph	Jane	Anna
Age	–	32	29
Gender	Male	Female	Female
Traumatic event	–	–	MVA
Primary diagnosis	TBI	TBI	TBI
Neuro-diagnostic information	–	–	Right hemisphere damage
Clinical symptoms	Reduced rate of speech	Loss of verbal ability	Monotone voice
Timescale	Injury treatment: no information Therapy over 6 months	–	8 years post-injury, treatment 18 months
Assessment	Rate of speech in words per minute	–	–
Music technique	Rhythmic entrainment to pre-composed song	Instructional composed song	Breathing exercises, melodic exercises, song singing
Concurrent therapies	Multi-disciplinary treatment setting	Multi-disciplinary treatment setting	Multi-disciplinary treatment setting
Musical biography	–	–	–
Results	Initial 88 syllables per minutes increased to 130 words per minute	After treatment patient was able to select and locate pictorial communication signs	Vocal range extended from monotone to 18 melodic pitches, increase in voice volume with carry-over to speech voice

Table 5.6 continued

Authors	Livingston	Livingston	Livingston
Year	1996	1996	1996
Case	Matthew	Chantelle	Terry
Age	–	23	30
Gender	Male	Female	Male
Traumatic event	–	MVA	–
Primary diagnosis	TBI	TBI	TBI
Neuro-diagnostic information	–	–	–
Clinical symptoms	Disturbed arm and finger movement, reduced muscle strength	Depression and frustration	Memory deficits, word finding problems
Timescale	Treatment duration 6 months	5 years post-injury	Treatment duration 6 months
Assessment	–	–	–
Music technique	Instrument playing	Song composition	Instructional song
Concurrent therapies	Multi-disciplinary treatment setting	Multi-disciplinary treatment setting	Multi-disciplinary treatment setting
Musical biography	–	–	–
Results	Strengthened neck muscles, increased range and coordination of arm and finger movement	Developing coping strategy for depression, release of negative emotions	Learnt names of staff and increased recall; some cueing remained necessary

Continued on next page

Table 5.6 continued

Author(s)	Price-Lackey and Cashman	Robb	Robb
Year	1996	1996	1996
Case	Jenny	D	B
Age	38	16	16
Gender	Female	Female	Male
Traumatic event	MVA as car driver	–	–
Primary diagnosis	TBI	Closed head injury	Closed head injury
Neuro-diagnostic information	Left-sided fronto-parietal contusion, cerebral oedema	–	–
Clinical symptoms	Memory disorder, loss of fine motor ability, speech/ language disorders	Cognitive skills (word retrieval, abstract thought, verbalization)	Discharge situation
Timescale	–	–	Last 2 months in paediatric rehabilitation clinic
Assessment	–	–	–
Music technique	Playing music, not in therapy setting	'Fill in the blank' song writing, group song writing, improvisational song writing, songs used for discharge from hospital	Discharge song composed by therapist, sung by rehab team staff for patient and his family
Concurrent therapies	Occupational therapy, bibliotherapy, residential rehabilitation	Neuropsychology	Rehabilitation team
Musical biography	–	–	–
Results	None of the documented changes are related to music playing	Mode of expression to overcome frustration. D was able to develop lingo-cognitive skills	Provides emotional support and expression for closure of in-patient rehabilitation process

Table 5.6 continued

Author(s)	Kennelly and Edwards	Kennelly and Edwards	Lee and Baker
Year	1997	1997	1997
Case	Sally (sister of Chris)	Chris (brother of Sally)	Jane
Age	10	7	–
Gender	Female	Male	Female
Traumatic event	MVA, as car passenger	MVA, as car passenger	MVA
Primary diagnosis	Closed head injury	Closed head injury	Closed head injury
Neuro-diagnostic information	Cerebral oedema	Intracerebral haemorrhage, left frontal lobe haematoma, left occipital haemorrhage	–
Clinical symptoms	Left hemiplegia, fractured right femur, ruptured bladder, multiple pelvic fractures, facial lacerations	Bilateral lung contusions, ruptured left hemidiaphragm, ruptured spleen, pelvic fractures, left leg below-knee amputation	Cognitive and physical disorders, unsafe behaviour
Timescale	Therapy began 2 weeks post-injury	Therapy began 3 weeks post-injury	–
Assessment	GCS = 7 at accident	Initial GCS = 8	–
Music technique	Improvised and pre-composed song	Receptive songs, song creation	Instructional song
Concurrent therapies	Nursing, physiotherapy	Nursing	Multi-disciplinary therapy
Musical biography	Enjoyed music pre-injury	Enjoyed music pre-injury	–
Results	Responses included crying, movement of all limbs, attempts to speak, eye opening and looking at the therapist and the guitar; 'behaviours indicative of improvements in orientation and awareness' (pp.23–4)	'elicited a range of responses from Chris during his period of unconsciousness including: vocalizations, body movements, changes in breathing, orientation to the therapist and guitar, and eye opening' (p.27)	Increase in safe behaviour, risk evaluation, and better wheelchair use

Continued on next page

Table 5.6 continued

Author(s)	Lee and Baker	Magee	Rosenfeld and Dun
Year	1997	1999b	1999
Case	Liz	A	David
Age	–	30	7
Gender	Female	Male	Male
Traumatic event	TBI	Road traffic accident	MVA as pedestrian
Primary diagnosis	Closed head injury	TBI	TBI
Neuro-diagnostic information	–	–	Diffuse axonal injury, bilateral frontal contusion
Clinical symptoms	Physical, communicative and cognitive disorder	Expressive and receptive aphasia, aphonic at admission	Coma
Timescale	–	Therapy began 8 months post-injury	Therapy began 18 days post-injury; 3 months of music therapy
Assessment	–	Problem Orientated Medical Records system (Weed 1968)	–
Music technique	Song creation	Modified melodic intonation therapy	Song listening, song singing alongside instrumental improvisation, physical stimulation, family music therapy
Concurrent therapies	Multi-disciplinary	Multi-disciplinary	Multi-disciplinary
Musical biography	–	Active musician, guitar/composition, actor in musicals	–
Results	Combined therapy approach led to increase in logical argumentation, coping strategies in potential conflict situations, and tolerance of others	The patient became able to sing known songs and became inconsistently able to produce short phrases, and showed improved verbal function Patient used singing as 'an emotionally expressive outlet' (p.24)	Initial eye and oral movement, turning to music source Later improvement in physical coordination and became more independent in playing instruments

Table 5.6 continued

Author(s)	Rosenfeld and Dun	Burke et al.	Kennelly, Hamilton and Cross
Year	1999	2000	2001
Case	Matthew	AT	Tracey
Age	9	15	12
Gender	Male	Feale	Female
Traumatic event	Fall from tree	MVA as pedestrian	MVA as pedestrian
Primary diagnosis	TBI	TBI	TBI
Neuro-diagnostic information	Diffuse axonal injury, bilateral frontal contusion	Diffuse axonal injury	Diffuse axonal injury, multiple cerebral contusions, intraventricular haemorrhage
Clinical symptoms	Coma	Coma	Coma, followed by post-traumatic amnesia, dysarthria
Timescale	Therapy beginning unclear; continued over first 9 months post-injury	4 weeks post-injury	–
Assessment	–	Initial GCS = 9	GCS = 3
Music technique	Song listening, song singing, instrumental improvisation, physical stimulation	Song writing, song listening, song quizzes, instrument playing	Joint music and speech therapy, vocal exercise, singing songs of patient's song preference
Concurrent therapies	Physiotherapy	Neuropsychology, nursing, physiotherapy, speech pathology, hydro-therapy, schooling	Speech pathology
Musical biography	–	–	Piano and clarinet lessons, pop music fan including Spice Girls
Results	Initial eye and oral movement, increase in vocalizations, leading to singing elements of song texts Six months post-injury was able to create songs	Early stages: 'increased vocal intensity and more constant vocalization' (p.467) Later: self-expression and 'validation of feeling' and processing and recall of verbal information, upper-limb coordination	Increase in speech intelligibility, participation, motivation and enjoyment Rate of speech, pitch range and intonation improved

Continued on next page

Table 5.6 continued

Author(s)	Kennelly, Hamilton and Cross	Tucek, Auer-Pekarsky and Stepansky	Yamamoto *et al.*
Year	2001	2001	2003
Case	Cathy	Theoretical paper with case vignette: G	1
Age	3	–	–59
Gender	Female	Female	Female
Traumatic event	MVA as pedestrian	MVA	MVA
Primary diagnosis	TBI	TBI	TBI
Neuro-diagnostic information	Extensive cerebral contusions, haemorrhages and multiple infarcts	Brain contusions	Subarachnoid haemorrhage, acute epidural haematoma, brainstem contusion
Clinical symptoms	Initial coma, later vision impairment, severe aphasia, right-sided hemiplegia	Severe disturbance of consciousness, apallic syndrome, right-sided spastic tetraparesis	Continuous consciousness disturbance
Timescale	–	–	4 months post-injury
Assessment	GCS = 5	Coma Remission Scale (CRS)	–
Music technique	Joint session with speech therapist: singing of song, instrumental improvisation	Traditional oriental music therapy	Musico-kinetic therapy
Concurrent therapies	Speech therapy	Nursing	–
Musical biography	–	–	Enjoyed folk-songs
Results	Improvement in word retrieval, indicating choice of song, song recognition, and could follow verbal instructions during instrumental play	Increasingly gave eye contact, stereotypical movement of the left arm CRS score increase from 9 to 12 points	Describes process of regaining expressive and communicative ability. Increase in expressing preferences and later became more independent in eating and drinking. At the end of therapy, patient was able to learn new songs and participate in 'walking practice' (p.115)

intervention better than events occurring in other situations. This provides strong support for the provision of music therapy at early stages of rehabilitation of people with post-traumatic amnesia.

Jochims (1990) reports a patient with transitional psychosis who was able to remember a greeting song used in the music therapy setting from the phase of treatment otherwise forgotten.

Knox and Jutai (1996) suggest that music listening activities are effective in music-based attention rehabilitation. The authors review the literature on music, attention and rehabilitation theories, and suggest that music-based attention rehabilitation may lead to better outcome in rehabilitation because of the activation of specific neural pathways: 'The partial localization of attention and musical processing in the right temporo-parietal lobe areas suggests that music seems to engage the most important and complex neural system for human attention and memory' (p.174). Wit et al. (1994) carried out an investigation into the effects of electro-acoustic music-based attention training with adolescents who had suffered closed head injuries. Though inconclusive, the results suggest further inquiry is warranted into the potential of this method in facilitating positive improvement in sustained and alternating/divided attention.

Speech and language

Many authors refer to the benefits of music therapy strategies in the rehabilitation of speech and language disorders resulting from traumatic brain injury (Aldridge 1993a; Bischof 2001; Cohen 1992; Emich 1980; Jungblut 2003; Kennelly, Hamilton and Cross 2001; Livingston 1996; Lucia 1987; Magee 1999b; Robb 1996).

Alongside vocal exercise, pre-composed song and song creation, improvised singing has been used in joint music and speech therapy interventions with children who had experienced TBI (Kennelly et al. 2001). Combinations of music therapy techniques, reported earlier in Kennelly and Edwards (1997), are used with children emerging from coma and post-coma. In this report, the authors discuss the importance of a therapy approach that combines elements of music and speech therapy interventions to adequately meet the specific needs of children with speech/language dysfunction following TBI.

Robb (1996) describes the use of song writing in music therapy with traumatically injured adolescents. To build a therapeutic relationship with the patients, Robb suggests the use of songs to introduce the participants to each other. The song-writing techniques described in this article include 'fill in the blank', in which patients place their own words in spaces left in the original text. Other song writing techniques included group song writing, improvisational song writing and songs used for discharge from hospital. A 16-year-old, who had sustained a atic closed head injury, took part in music therapy and used song writing to ont issues of self-expression and cognitive retraining. The 'fill in the blank' mode was chosen due to challenges in the areas of word retrieval, abstract thought, vocabulary and association (pairing words to ideas).

Emich (1980) suggests that singing provides for children and adolescents with a variety of traumatic and non-traumatic neurological diseases an opportunity to become vocally active. The singing of common verbal communications is suggested as a possible step in the regaining of speech function that must be explored in cases of severe verbal disorders. The author does not provide any further detail to support this suggestion.

Intonation activities, singing instruction and singing of pre-existing songs have been incorporated in a structured model of intervention for people following traumatic brain injury or cerebrovascular accident (Cohen 1992). In this study the independent variable was singing instruction, and there were five dependent variables: speaking fundamental frequency, speaking fundamental frequency variability, vocal intensity, rate of speech and verbal intelligibility. Clinically significant change was seen in the areas of speaking fundamental frequency variability, speech rate and verbal intelligibility.

Livingston (1996) describes the use of singing and breathing techniques, alongside vocal exercises and song singing in the treatment of adults following traumatic brain injury. Therapy led to an increase in the rate of speech, breath control, vocal range and loudness of the voice. The author highlights the carry-over of these significant changes to the patient's speech voice and emphasizes the relevance of the effects of the therapy in the lives of the patients outside of the music therapy setting.

Lucia (1987) too reports the use of vocalization, song singing and rhythmic speech exercises in the rehabilitation of patients with aphasia, a speech/language disorder commonly related to traumatic brain injury. In her review of practice, Lucia identifies suggestions that these music therapy techniques may lead to improvements in vocal ability, breath control, pronunciation and articulation. Bischof (2001) describes the use of vocal improvisation in the rehabilitation of two children following severe TBI. After initial mutism, both children developed the use of their voices in vocal improvisations with the music therapist.

In a report of music therapy with a patient with expressive and receptive aphasia, Magee (1999b) describes the use of modified melodic intonation therapy in speech/language rehabilitation. This technique relies on the mapping of words or short phrases to distinctive melodic phrases. The patient portrayed in the report became able to sing known songs and was later able to produce short spoken phrases in everyday life situations, albeit inconsistently.

Emotional expression

Music therapy has been suggested as a relevant therapeutic strategy in providing patients with traumatic brain injury with an adequate form of emotional expression (Bright and Signorelli 1999; Burke *et al.* 2000; Gadomski and Jochims 1986; Gilbertson 1999; Glassman 1991; Hiller 1989; Jochims 1990, 1992; Robb 1996).

Bright and Signorelli (1999) carried out a study into changes in the quality of life as a result of music therapy with a group of individuals who had experienced severe brain injury. At the start of the study, the participants showed 'no purposeful movement' and were 'without communication by word or gesture' (p.256). The authors report the music therapists to have 'achieved some level of communication with most clients and improved the quality of life for all/most clients' (p.262). Of the participants with TBI, notable changes were observed in the areas of enjoyment, sense of individuality and the ability to express emotion measured in the authors' own quality-of-life assessments during the individual music therapy sessions.

Glassman (1991) describes the use of song reminiscing and song writing in the treatment of a young woman who had experienced severe cerebral trauma as a result of a motor vehicle accident. The young woman suffered brainstem damage that led to motor dysfunction including the loss of speech function. Songs were chosen which topically related to feelings and thoughts originating from the patient, and the therapeutic activities included adapting the texts to express her thoughts and feelings.

Robb (1996) describes the use of song writing to confront issues of self-expression and cognitive retraining. The 'fill in the blank' mode was chosen by the therapist because of challenges the patient experienced in the areas of 'word retrieval, abstract thought, vocabulary, and association (pairing words to ideas)' (p.33). Through song writing, it was possible for the young girl to work simultaneously on her cognitive and language abilities. An example is given of 'fill in the blank' mode song writing through which it was possible for the singer to express her awareness of the effects of her injuries and her frustration about the reduction of her writing ability caused by the injury.

Burke *et al.* (2000) describe the use of song writing, song listening, song quizzes and instrument playing in music therapy with a 15-year-old girl who had suffered diffuse axonal injury as a result of traumatic brain injury. In the description of the therapeutic process the patient increases her repertoire of self-expression through music and attains a 'validation of feeling' (p.467).

Oyama *et al.* (2003) discuss the development of 'facial expression appropriate to conversational context' (p.125) of a 24-year-old female with severe traumatic brain injury. They remark that changes in crying and laughter are observable only when specific music is played. No further detail or explanation is provided.

Change in mood

Nayak *et al.* (2000) identified changes in their study of the effects of group music therapy with 18 hospitalized patients following stroke or traumatic brain injury. The music therapy interventions used were 'typical of music therapy practice' (p.278) and included a welcome song or activity, followed by instrumental improvisation, singing, composition, playing instruments, performing, or listening to music. Positive trends were seen in mood state in a week-to-week comparison made by family members ($p < 0.6$). Weak positive trends were observed in the measurement of mood in self-report ($p < 0.10$) and family rating in a day-to-day comparison ($p < 0.10$).

Baker (2001) too identified statistically significant positive change in the reduction of agitation in a group of patients suffering from post-traumatic amnesia ($p < 0.0001$). No statistical difference was observed between the effects of the live or recorded presentation of the music intervention.

Three groups of patients with multiple sclerosis (5), traumatic brain injury (5), or stroke- or anoxia-related brain damage (4) participated in two music therapy sessions in a pilot study carried out by Magee and Davidson (2002). These sessions involved the use of either pre-composed song or clinical improvisation. Both of these main activities were contained within a greeting and farewell musical activity. Mood state was measured pre- and post-session using the Profile of Mood States, Bipolar form (POMS-BI). Results showed significant positive changes on the continuum of composed–anxious, agreeable–hostile, and energetic–tired mood states. There were no significant changes in the elated–depressed continuum. No correlations were observed between patient group or treatment modality. The authors suggest that 'the type of therapy may not be the critical determinant in mood change' (p.26). However, the interventions used in this study, consisting of one single session of song singing or improvisation, do not represent usual practice and do not represent the planned use of song or improvisation as a technique embedded in a therapeutic process evolving over time. Though there is a wide diversity in the duration of therapy epochs, single sessions of music therapy are highly unusual in neurorehabilitation.

Carlisle (2000) investigated whether the application of receptive music and relaxation therapy is more effective than only verbal relaxation therapy in reducing anxiety of patients following brain injury. The study is based on the hypothesis that anxiety may block potential positive change in psychological, physical and emotional functioning. No statistically significant differences in the reduction of anxiety levels were observed in either the experimental or control group.

Level of involvement in rehabilitation

Barker and Brunk (1991) describe the role of music improvisation in the context of a creative arts therapy group. Group members were involved in five activities including painting, the singing of songs, and music-making. In 'partner projects', two members of the therapy group 'create compositions through imitation and/or improvisation' in response to the art works they have created (p.28). There is no specific description of the form or role of music improvisation. There are four key findings in this study. Members of the creative arts therapy group attained higher scores on the institution's assessment scales in the areas of 'addressing personal issues' and 'identification with work' (p.30). Increases in active participation and commitment to group attendance were noted on behalf of the participants and an increase in the relative's ability to allow the patient to be more independent was also seen.

Jochims (1994) describes how a musically experienced patient with disturbed musical ability as a result of traumatic brain injury, regained the ability to play music in a structured and rhythmically organized manner through music improvisation techniques. She describes the patient as being more active and involved in music therapy than in all other situations in the rehabilitation clinic. This contrast, she explains, is related to the fact that his 'inner drive was missing to confront the uncomfortable elements of daily life' (p.1323) (my translation). The implication here is that music therapy can offer patients the opportunity to behave differently in music therapy sessions compared to other situations and settings.

Exploring physical abilities in non-directed instrumental improvisation was important in the therapy of a 10-year-old boy who suffered traumatic brain injury as a passenger in a car accident (Bischof 2001). Bilateral brain contusions caused initial tetraspastic muscle tone and ataxia and a temporary loss of spontaneous speech. Instrumental improvisation was seen as clinically significant in the young boy's rehabilitation as he reacted to physical contact and aversive stimuli with uncontrolled defence reactions. Any attempts to influence the boy's movement in physiotherapy were unsuccessful. In later music improvisations, the young boy was able to use his foot to play on a wind-chime, and his arm to play a cymbal without physical support from another person. Initial vocal sounds develop into pre-verbal communications, and these are imbedded in musical form providing a basis for improvised songs.

Nayak *et al.* (2000) too describe clinically significant changes in the level of involvement of patients with traumatic brain injury in rehabilitation after participation in group music therapy. Though clinically significant, these changes do not reach statistical significance.

Interpersonal aspects of human experience

Jochims (1992) suggests that basic functional ability is a prerequisite for self-dependency, a reduction in required assistance in self-care, and increased participation in everyday life. However, Jochims also argues that intra- and interpersonal aspects of human experience are commonly neglected in neurorehabilitation. By attending to the emotional and psychological state of these patients, she suggests that music improvisation in therapy can provide a balance to the dominating aspect of functional retraining of physical ability. In this sense, music therapy provides a balance to the overall rehabilitative treatment strategy.

Magee (1999b) asserts:

> The social and emotional needs of the client are often seen as being less important than the more visible functional needs and certainly appear more difficult to measure objectively... It is often immensely difficult to illustrate the value of this type of contact in a neuro-rehabilitation setting in any quantifiable way, other than incorporating more physical and functional goals within a music therapy program. In doing so, however, we risk neglecting the enormous potential for emotional rehabilitation which music therapy offers. (p.20)

Magee points here to an important issue for researchers in the field of neuro-rehabilitation. Researchers are aware of the difficulties when challenged to demonstrate effectiveness of music therapy as a significant therapeutic strategy in emotional rehabilitation. However, focusing on functional ability may direct our attention away from other facets of music therapy in clinical practice that are more relevant. We need to relate research and practice that investigate effectiveness in everyday practice, but the assessment of effectiveness must include parameters other than functionality alone.

Some research methods may simply not be capable of measuring change in the non-standardized qualities of human life. We need research methods that actually fit clinically relevant questions (Aldridge 2001a, 2004). How can researchers be expected to provide evidence of effectiveness if their own work is hindered by methodological inappropriateness and irrelevant parameters? Case study methods (Aldridge 2004) stay close to practice (Edwards 2004) and so tackle clinically relevant questions.

Arm and hand coordination

Burke *et al.* (2000) described the use of instrument playing in music therapy to positively affect the hand-to-hand coordination of a 15-year-old girl who had suffered diffuse axonal injury as a result of a motor vehicle accident. Livingston

(1996) also describes the successful use of instrument playing in the rehabilitation of arm and finger movement of a young man who had suffered traumatic brain injury.

Gait

Hurt *et al.* (1998) studied the effects of rhythmic auditory stimulation (RAS) on gait in five males and three females between 25 and 35 years of age diagnosed with traumatic brain injury. The patients were between 4 and 24 months post-injury and received physiotherapy before the start of the study. The inclusion criteria included the diagnosis of a static state of gait disorder. All participants were able to walk without assistance but might have required a supportive device. Velocity, cadence, stride length and symmetry parameters were recorded pre- and post-intervention. All participants showed deficits in all the measured parameters before the intervention. An increase in average velocity was observed over the baseline with RAS (+18%). With RAS, the participants showed an increase in the swing symmetry (28%). After five weeks of RAS training there were significant increases in velocity (50%), cadence (15%), stride length (29%) and symmetry (12%). In fast walking exercises there were increases in average percentage of cadence (2%), stride length (18%) and symmetry (13%) (Hurt *et al.* 1998, p.238).

Independence

Following traumatic brain injury, many individuals experience changes in their functional independence.

Gervin (1991) describes the use of a pre-composed song with instructions for dressing. All participants had experienced TBI and were assessed using the Ranchos Los Amigos Scale 4–5. The participants presented 'minimum to moderate physical deficits, and exhibited difficulties initiating the sequential steps to dress' (p.88), and required a high level of verbal instruction or cues and a minimum of physical assistance.

Two case reports of individuals receiving music therapy intervention in addition to occupational therapy whilst dressing are discussed by Gervin. A 'dressing song' commented on the individual steps involved in changing from pyjamas into daytime clothing. Both cases achieved a reduction in the time required to dress. A 29-year-old man, who initially required 25 to 28 minutes to dress, required only 8 minutes after the intervention. A 14-year-old girl managed to dress in approximately 8 minutes after initially requiring 15 minutes. Alongside the reduction in time needed, both patients required less supervision by nursing staff – a highly prized resource in rehabilitation centres.

Lee and Baker (1997) report the use of an instructional song to increase safe behaviour and risk evaluation in wheelchair use by a young woman challenged by a cognitive disorder as a result of a closed head injury. The change in safe behaviour led to an increase in the patient's independent movement, so therapeutic supervision became unnecessary.

What constitutes an independent life is variable from person to person. For people who have experienced traumatic brain injury, basic abilities such as eating and drinking may be primary issues in regaining initial independence. Yamamoto *et al.* (2003) describe the use of musico-kinetic therapy as a part of rehabilitation with a 59-year-old woman who suffered a continuous disturbance of consciousness. The authors argue that this type of therapy directly affects brain activity and helps 'to recover the disorder region or activate the residual region for producing a new neural circuit, that allows perception and motion' (p.109). After regaining expressive and communicative ability, the patient increasingly expressed her preferences and later became more physically independent in eating and drinking. A direct link between the intervention and the reported results is not provided in this report.

Identity

Music improvisation has been used successfully in therapy to assist the redevelopment of self-identity following emotional trauma (Jochims 1992), but the author does not make explicit the actual processes involved in this redevelopment, nor are references to conceptual models provided. Bright and Signorelli (1999) too suggest that improvisation in individual music therapy can lead to an increase in the patient's sense of individuality, but they do not provide detail as to how this may be achieved nor what it means specifically.

Price-Lackey and Cashman (1996) present the results of qualitative research based on life-history interviews of a woman who had experienced moderate head injury. The young woman is reported to have become involved in playing music alongside writing, studying, graphic design for computers, and theatre production, 'to create a new identity' (p.306).

A young man who had suffered traumatic brain injury as a result of a motorcycle accident expressed the importance of creating music improvisation recordings to demonstrate his abilities and skills at a time characterized by a focus on possible residual physical disability (Gilbertson 2002). The patient used a music CD of the recordings of improvisations taken from music therapy sessions as Christmas gifts for his family, his therapists and doctors, and his friends at home. He explained the importance of these recordings for his sense of identity by stating: 'That is, more than everything, something which I can present later – then I can say "Here people – I have managed this in spite of everything".'

The families

Family members of people who have experienced traumatic brain injury have been involved in studies into the effectiveness of music therapy to help determine changes in mood and levels of involvement. Nayak *et al.* (2000) asked family members to rate changes in involvement, motivation, mood and social interaction of their relatives who had experienced TBI or stroke. The report by Wheeler *et al.* (2003) also mentions the involvement of family members in music therapy assessment; this study is, however, a re-analysis of the same data published by Nayak *et al.* (2000)

Though it is known that TBI significantly influences not only the lives of those injured but also their families and relatives (NIH Consensus Development Panel 1999), there is no mention, in the identified literature, of the provision of therapy for the families of those injured. The dramatic nature and severity of TBI generates specific forms of trauma for family members and relatives. I suggest that music therapy may offer a relevant and appropriate form of therapy for these people too. This is matter for future investigation.

Choice of music therapy method

There has been limited discussion of strategies in choosing appropriate music therapy methods at the beginning of therapy. My review identifies 19 music therapy techniques in the rehabilitation of people who have experienced TBI, which leads to the question: 'How do music therapists choose which methods are appropriate for their clients?'

In one study, the author mentions an 'ongoing music therapy debate about the appropriateness of live and taped music in treatment protocols' (Baker 2001, p.188). Baker's research demonstrates that patients show a preference to listening to live music and attain better recall of the live presentation of music than recorded music. In response to this she states:

> With respect to music therapy practice, both live and taped music may have their advantages and a place in practice. Taped music is the easier mode to administer and hospital staff could be trained to implement the programs at appropriate times when the music therapist may be unavailable. (Baker 2001, p.188)

Thus, the use of recorded music in the treatment of people with post-traumatic amnesia may be a therapeutic strategy that is available to many professionals and not restricted to trained music therapists – although patients prefer, and improve better, with live music.

Uncertainties about the effectiveness of different music therapy methods have been expressed in the study by Magee and Davidson (2002). Though the study does not reflect usual practice in the use of song or improvisation, the authors came to the conclusion that 'the type of therapy may not be the critical determinant in mood change' (p.26). No correlations are observed between patient group or treatment modality. The question remains: 'How it is possible to determine differences between treatment strategies when we do not yet know the specific effects of each of the treatments?' Basic research on existing treatment strategies is needed before we begin to carry out comparative studies.

Multi-disciplinary approaches to rehabilitation

Some authors have suggested that a multi-disciplinary approach is necessary in rehabilitation with people who have experienced traumatic brain injury (Kennelly *et al.* 2001; Lee and Baker 1997; Paul and Ramsey 2000). All of these authors emphasize that this approach is not simply a multiprofessional provision of a variety of therapies, but a unified strategy that fuses therapy-specific methods in attaining shared rehabilitation issues.

Box 5.1 Checklist for reporting cases

Checklist item	Information required in case reports
1	Age
2	Gender
3	Traumatic event
4	Primary diagnosis
5	Neuro-diagnostic information
6	Clinical symptoms
7	Time between injury and therapy beginning
8	A description of the therapy or therapies
9	Documentation of concurrent therapies
10	Results of the therapy
11	Assessment tools and ratings (e.g. Glasgow Coma Scale or Coma Remission Scale)
12	Musical biography

Lee and Baker (1997) discuss the use of a combined therapy approach in the rehabilitation of a young woman who had suffered closed head injury. The shared aims of the rehabilitation included the development of coping strategies in potential conflict situations and the tolerance of others. Song creation was used as a technique to approach and formulate the targeted issues in the music therapy setting. The songs created in music therapy were then taken up in the social work setting and were used as a basis for the development of coping strategies.

Kennelly *et al.* (2001) describe joint music and speech therapy with children who had experienced severe TBI. A selection of therapy-specific techniques, including song singing and vocal exercises, were combined to focus on improving vocal, speech and language ability with the children. The joint therapy approach is described as being successful in assisting the children in reaching improvements in word retrieval, speech intelligibility, rate of speech, pitch range and intonation.

The reception of music has been used to increase the participation of patients in physical rehabilitation, to ease discomfort, and to lead to an increase in functional independence (Paul and Ramsey 2000). The authors suggest that patients involved in challenging physical or occupational therapy tasks can be provided with a means to focus away from pain and movement limitation through music reception. Patients taking part in these combined therapy interventions may be able to reach a higher level of their potential physical ability.

Checklist for reporting cases

We have seen in this chapter the consequences of missing case report information. To establish a common base from which to compare case study material we need an underlying structure of the data. Case study reports should include information as noted in Box 5.1. In addition to these elements, it is important to mention any assessment tools used, such as the Glasgow Coma Scale or the Coma Remission Scale, as well as information about the musical biography of the patient. Given this information we will be able to share the authors' understanding of the cases they present and improve the overall quality of research. We can then develop a database of studies in traumatic brain injury as a platform for further clinical trials.

In conclusion

This review set out to identify, collect and analyse literature related to the use of music therapy in the rehabilitation of people who have experienced traumatic brain injury. As we have seen, mention of music therapy first appeared in one single publication related to rehabilitation of people who had experienced TBI (Emich 1980). During the 1990s there was an increase in reports of the application of music therapy in neurosurgical and neurological rehabilitation settings. The relevant studies provide varying levels of evidence and information about the positive benefits of music therapy in neurorehabilitation in a wider range of therapeutic issues than has been previously identified. A review of this literature provides an overview of the efforts music therapists have made in adapting and developing therapeutic strategies for, and with, people who have experienced TBI. As a result, core aspects of music therapy with these people are clearly discernible and are summarized in Box 5.2.

As stated in the introduction to this review, the World Health Organization defines the term 'rehabilitation' as the combined and coordinated use of medical, social, educational and vocational measures for training or retraining the individual to the highest possible level of functional ability. The NIH Development Panel also emphasizes the importance of focusing on improvement in functional ability and declared:

> The goals of cognitive and behavioral rehabilitation are to enhance the person's capacity to process and interpret information and to improve the person's ability to function in all aspects of family and community life. (NIH Consensus Development Panel 1999, p.978)

Though changes are required in the collection and measurement of evidence of change, this review has identified a variety of areas in which music therapy plays a valuable role towards reaching these rehabilitation goals.

Although many therapy strategies in neurorehabilitation focus on regaining functional ability, this review has shown that music therapy is not simply an additional therapy that can be added to the list. The application of music therapy in neurorehabilitation can facilitate improvements in both functional and psychological aspects of life of people who have experienced TBI.

Traumatic brain injury presents extreme challenges to health care systems and to society. Music therapy has been shown to be valuable in responding to these challenges and broadens the scope of treatment possibilities.

Box 5.2 Core aspects of music therapy
with people who have experienced traumatic brain injury

Music therapy provides a unique non-verbal assessment strategy in initial phases of rehabilitation following traumatic brain injury

Music therapy offers musical dialogue-based interaction for patients emerging from coma or who are initially diagnosed as 'minimally responsive'

Music, in a therapeutic setting, is an integrative medium that provides a logical context for initial attempts towards orientation and cognition following trauma

Music therapy provides a strategy to enhance memory of events and information during phases of post-traumatic amnesia and neuropsychological disorder

Music therapy leads to improvements in vocal ability, and some aspects of speech ability including voice control, intonation, rate of speech and verbal intelligibility

In therapy, music provides an adequate field of interaction for emotional expression, communication of feelings and validation of emotionality

Music therapy offers a strategy to positively influence mood state often affected by traumatic brain injury

Music therapy can lead to an increase in the level of involvement in therapy and rehabilitation in general

By focusing on social and psychological areas, music therapy enhances rehabilitation success and, in turn, provides a balance to therapies focused on physical function

Music has been used in therapy to influence gait positively, particularly with patients presenting a static level of disability

Music therapy is appropriate for patients of many ages, and has been applied with patients between 3 and 84 years of age

Music therapy provides a unique therapeutic possibility with patients with severe traumatic brain injury (Glasgow Coma Score 3–8)

Music therapy can lead to an increase in independence in activities of daily life

People who have experienced traumatic brain injury have used music therapy to redevelop some aspects of their personal identity

Music therapy may offer a relevant and appropriate therapeutic resource in the future for family members of people with traumatic brain injury

CHAPTER 6

Encounter with the Conscious Being of People in Persistent Vegetative State

Ansgar Herkenrath

Sono ergo sum – *I sound, therefore I am*

This chapter is based on qualitative research of music therapy with patients suffering from traumatic, ischaemic or hypoxic brain damage whose condition is described by the medical terms *apallic syndrome, coma vigile* or *(persistent) vegetative state* (in German: *Wachkoma*). These patients are seen as unable to perceive, and communicate with, their environment. Participants in this study were between 20 and 50 years of age and had been in the described state for between 18 months and seven years. All therapy possibilities were considered as exhausted. The patients were living in a long-term nursing institution for adult residents with severe neurological handicaps in Haus Königsborn, Lebenszentrum Königsborn, Unna, Germany, where I have been working as a music therapist since 1997.

From the beginning of my music therapy activities, my work with these patients confronted me with their condition, its definition, diagnosis, progress and prognosis. My personal impressions in music therapy sessions, where I experienced changes in patients not only as reflexes but as re-actions, and thereby expressions of their awareness, were in direct contrast to the opinion common among physicians that patients of this type are unable to perceive and react. I found them to be resounding personalities who met me with their entire being. This impression finally led me to the motto of *sono ergo sum.*

This motto comprises more than considerations on the sounding of a human being in the musical sense. I *sound* – man also *sounds* in his innermost body, in his state of being, in his inner harmony or his dissonance. Man *sounds* in his mood and his self in relation to himself and others. The words I *sound* are therefore an image of our inner self in our relation to ourselves and others.

The words *I am* raise the questions *Who am I?*, *Where am I?* – and most of all *What am I?* Observing myself in a mirror, I can see my body in its various forms of expression. But I would vehemently reject a description of me, my being, my self or my soul based exclusively on my body. My personality comprises more than a mere organic structure. Observing patients with apallic syndrome in my work, and perceiving not only their body but also an expression of their personality, their self, and seeing how many different brain regions can be affected without a loss of the self, the personality, then I must wonder where this self of a human being is located in the body. Is it an element of the brain? Where does this part come from that is conscious of itself and says *I am*; what is it and where does it go when this body dies?

The word *ergo* (therefore) implies a conclusion in the sense of 'because'. I am because I sound, and as long as I am able to sound, I will be. But what about those people who are impaired, ailing, seriously ill, and what about patients in persistent vegetative state who are considered unable to show intentional reactions? Are they able to sound at all, if they cannot show any directed reactions? Or would it be true to say in their case *I do not sound therefore I am no longer (myself)*?

Persistent vegetative state and awareness are mutually exclusive according to the medical tradition. The general term *Wachkoma* in German is an attempt to describe summarily the acute state and also the rehabilitation phases of the condition specified by the medical terms 'apallic syndrome', 'vegetative state' and '(persistent) vegetative state' that are often used synonymously; the inherent dilemma is that the above medical diagnoses exclude the existence of a conscious-ness in itself in the afflicted patients. The title '*Encounter with the conscious being of people in persistent vegetative state*' therefore appears contradictory at first and will have to be further verified.

Consciousness generally implies a consciousness of the self that perceives the self and others, defining the self in contrast to the environment and inducing a communicative behaviour in dialogue with this environment; it is a core element of existence and human life. Persons who have no consciousness and are therefore considered unconscious are without this element of their human existence. But the defined loss of consciousness means not only loss of this core element of human life; according to the generally accepted prognosis of this illness it is impossible to recover it. This diagnosis and prognosis push a patient aside, to the verge of human existence.

The irreversible loss of consciousness is a sign of transition from life to death (Valarino 1995). A patient in the long-term phase of the vegetative state is therefore in danger of not being recognized as a 'living person' any longer. This conclusion leads to discussions on the basic rights of such patients, on the economics of their long-term care, and on euthanasia. The objective of this study is to demonstrate that patients with apallic syndrome are by no means unable to perceive, or in the process of dying, but human beings who live in their own specific form of life and animation.

A necessary precondition for the music therapy approach described here with patients with apallic syndrome is the existence of an elementary form of consciousness in these patients and a potential that allows them to react intentionally to what they perceive in this consciousness; the approach is based on 'creative music therapy' as initiated by Paul Nordoff and Clive Robbins and involves joint improvisation and joint interpretation in the therapeutic encounter. The medical definition and prognosis for the condition apallic syndrome/persistent vegetative state either nullifies this therapeutic approach, which is based on the potential of every person to enter into mutual communication, or is a contradiction within itself. A consequence was that I saw the need to raise my personal observations and assumptions from the area of subjective experience and feelings, to objectify them and to explore a scientific basis for my interpretation and therapeutic approach.

This essay presents a basic introduction to the neurological condition and the terms 'brain' and 'mind', 'perception' and 'consciousness' from the perspectives of medicine, neurophysiology and neuropsychology, philosophy, theology and ethics, and describes a concept of a human being on this basis. I shall then relate the observed changes in patients with apallic syndrome to generic terms like 'reaction' and 'reflex', significance of respiration, speech and music, distance and nearness. This combination produces various findings that will be presented in a conclusion. Necessary preconditions will be described for an encounter with the consciousness of such patients, and I shall formulate detailed questions on medical and social consequences involved.

Apallic syndrome: a form of life in search of a name

'Wachkoma' is no term to be found in the general medical terminology. In medicine, the terms (persistent or permanent) vegetative state, coma vigile and apallic syndrome are used synonymously to define this condition. In Germany, Kretschmer (1940) was the first to describe case studies of a disease with failure of all cerebral functions and a lowered level of cerebral functions to the midbrain level with disinhibition symptoms, in Zeitschrift für die gesamte Neurologie und Psychiatrie. Kretschmer called it a transitional syndrome that may disappear either completely or almost completely. He differentiates between a supposed state of alertness and the inability to enter into meaningful contact with the environment or to react to it. Later Gerstenbrand (1967) described the condition in more detail in a monograph, from its onset, progress, fully developed state up to the remission phases. Jennett and Plum (1972) described an analogous condition and called it 'persistent vegetative state', and they added to the title 'a syndrome in search of a name'. Observations made by nursing staff, relatives, therapists and physicians led to the term *Wachkoma* (literally: 'awake-coma') in German, since this term summarizes the discrepancy of such observations between recognizable sleep–alert phases and seeming inability to enter into contact.

Coma vigile is mostly caused by brain damage due to severe craniocerebral injury trauma, cerebral haemorrhage, or hypoxia. Advances in rehabilitative medicine and emergency care facilitate successful reanimation and treatment in a growing number of patients. They survive such acute events, and are even fully rehabilitated in most cases. Some, however, remain in a permanent state of coma vigile. All descriptions of the state assume a functional failure of the cerebral cortex and complete loss of cognitive potentials while brainstem functions are maintained. There are various descriptions of a possible remission, and all assume that recovery cannot be expected after a period of more than 18 months in this condition (Andrews 1996; Mummenthaler and Mattle 2002; Poeck and Hacke 1998).

The title of this chapter may be held as provocative. It is based on an assumption about a phenomenon that is generally deemed to be non-existent – the consciousness of a patient in persistent vegetative state and the possibility of an encounter with this consciousness.

On brain and mind, perception and consciousness

Consciousness – this term is used as a matter of course in medicine, but the question remains, 'What is consciousness?' Is it reducible to neurological processes, or does it go further? May we locate it within the brain or does it exist as a mental phenomenon only, and as such, can it be explained at all in neuro-scientific terms? Is it of decisive significance for us, is it the essence of human individuality? Consciousness, and questions about its existence, significance, generation, localization and demonstrability, and a differentiation between brain and mind, provide such a wide range of issues that it is impossible to cover them exhaustively in this essay. But further deliberations on consciousness require a short survey of its various definitions and interpretations in medicine, philosophy and theology.

Brain and consciousness in medicine

Medical theory relates consciousness directly to brain functions as a biological phenomenon generated by the cerebral cortex. Part of consciousness is the ability to perceive the self and the environment, and a disorder of this ability is defined as pathological, with a differentiation between qualitative disorders (content-related consciousness, awareness) and quantitative disorders (alert awareness, response). Examples of qualities of consciousness are alertness, orientation (time, space, personality), attention, thought processes and memory.

The medical literature provides no definition of consciousness in itself but defines it in the negative form as the absence of pathological disorders; that is, consciousness is defined through a description of its deficit, not in its existence, but as a lack of pathological disorder. A recognizable, expected and therefore adequate response to defined stimuli is seen as proof of its existence. This means that everybody who is neither somnolent, nor soporific, nor comatose, and responds adequately to all levels of stimulation is 'conscious', and those who do not correspond to the expected stimulus–response correlation are 'unconscious'.

Despite intensive discussions of the term 'consciousness', the general and uncontroversial view in medicine appears to be that brain function determines consciousness. Attempts at a medical definition of consciousness inevitably lead to questions of brain functions and their significance for the human mind. Neurophysiology as a field that covers among other functions those of the brain should therefore provide more information on consciousness.

For centuries, generations of brain researchers have tried to define consciousness and always been faced with the much-discussed problem of body and mind. The main problem today is not to demonstrate which neurobiological processes produce certain states of consciousness and perceptions in the brain. According to Searle (1997):

> the second and more difficult problem consists in explaining how consciousness actually works in the brain. I believe indeed that a solution to this second problem would be the most important scientific discovery of our time. (p. 10)

Numerous brain researchers have explored brain physiology and the concept of consciousness and have chosen many different methods, from an analysis of various imaging and electrophysiological procedures to discussions on a 'stream of consciousness', the self-healing potential in the brain, the functions of the prefrontal cortex, and even quantum mechanics (Bayne 2001; Blackmore 2001; Calvin 1998; Goldberg 2002; Kotchoubey *et al.* 2002; Müllges and Stoll 2002; Pickenhain 1998; Rudolf 2000; Stein, Brailowsky and Will 2000; Sutherland 2001; Wilber 1997). They all can contribute significantly to an explanation of the physiological preconditions for something to function that may be called consciousness. But all of them are unable to explain or localize this specific thing, consciousness in itself. Kotchoubey *et al.* (2002) conclude their study by saying that consciousness is a heterogeneous concept both philosophically and physiologically.

A cooperation between neurologists and psychologists has been demanded repeatedly. Neuropsychologists have started to explore correlations between psychic functions and anatomical, physiological and biochemical states. A literature research, however, revealed a significant deficit in that only a few articles by neuropsychologists or neuroscientists address the concept of consciousness with the intention to clarify the meaning of consciousness itself. Attempts to explain consciousness are often connected with hypotheses. This interplay between existing knowledge and assumptions, demonstrability and subjective interpretation, findings and questionable premises, characterizes the discussion and appears to be an effort to find a way out of this controversial situation (Edelman and Tononi 1997).

Today, neuroscientists are aware of the existence of a consciousness that permits us to perceive us as individuals and self; and many of them believe that consciousness cannot be associated with any definite brain region (Beckermann 1996; Deikman 1996; Dennett 1996; Eimer 1996; Ross 2003; Smythies 2003). We often find a mixture of neurological, neurophysiological and neuropsychological concepts. But no area of neuroscience is able to give a satisfying explanation of consciousness. Attempts are made to reinterpret consciousness phenomena as results of culturally conveyed interpretations or results of cognitive processes (Prinz 1996), or to discuss self-perception in a differentiation between 'I' and 'self' (Deikman 1996); but such efforts seem mere tricks to bridge the gap between neuroscientific findings and the fact that every person perceives something he calls his consciousness, the perception of his ego or his innermost self.

> The phenomenon of human consciousness is almost our last big secret. A secret is something that men are – still – unable to explain … And as is the case with all previous secrets, there any many who hope it will never be de-mystified, who insist that this last taboo remain untouched. (Dennett 1994, pp.37ff)

If the question of consciousness is to be answered at all, it has to be extended to comprise philosophical, theological and ethical aspects as well.

Aspects of philosophy, theology and ethics

In the discussion of human consciousness we come across terms like 'ego', 'self', 'human existence', or 'soul'. We cannot avoid such terms. We have to take them up and try to express what goes beyond the activities of neurons in the brain and permits us to experience our individuality. 'What is man?' is a question asked not only in consciousness research but also philosophy, theology and ethics.

From times of antiquity, consciousness has been seen as an integral part of mind and soul. Plato saw the body as a prison of the soul that is controlled by the mind. The middle ages differentiated between a body-soul and a mind-soul (*anima rationalis*) that was seen to comprise conscience as well. The mind-soul was superior, was associated with immortality, and remained free from physical illness. Against this background, the Cartesian theory of a separation between body and soul appears an almost logical consequence, a release of the biological body from the soul. 'Thought' for Descartes is 'consciousness'. Soul for him is an immaterial thinking substance.

Such considerations formed the basis of the body/spirit problem that was addressed by a wide range of philosophers, including Spinoza, Locke, Leibnitz and Berkeley. Kant saw the soul as transcendental, as an idea without substance, as something beyond the reach of human experience. According to his scientific empirism, any knowledge presumes sensory information. Sensory information requires interpretation and order. He believed thought to be the only source of cognition, on the basis of reason. In his opinion, reason can neither prove nor disprove the immortality of the soul. Kant accepted self-recognition as the objective of human efforts and advocated soul research on an empirical basis. Schopenhauer in his theory of the 'primacy of volition' sees the human mind as determined by urge, instinct and volition. In his phenomenological approach, the body is subject, an embodiment of the will. For him, the human mind is more unconscious will and less conscious reason (Hannich 2003; Hinterhuber 2001; Spering 2000).

Again and again, philosophers underlined the directedness of activities as a characteristic of the mind. Brentano called this intentionality a characteristic of the mind, Heidegger found an explanation of a person's being in that person's activity, and Sartre saw the intentional directedness of actions towards a world of objects as an expression of consciousness (Feinberg 2002). According to Searle, intentionality is not the same as consciousness; rather, the former is a phenomenon that depends on the latter (Searl 1997). Humanistic psychology according to Assagioli, Fromm, Jung, Maslow and others comments on human consciousness among other things: 'The human being is more than a sum of his parts...there is something in us, a power, a tendency...that wishes to grow and unfold, that wants to live and strive towards something' (Reiter 2003, pp.4f). Feinberg concludes:

> The personal uniqueness of mind and existence of each individual organism is what we call 'soul'. The soul of each brain is indeed something unique and unrivalled. We can donate an organ or blood for transfusion, but the sense of

myself has a reality for me that only one person may experience: myself.
(Feinberg 2002, p.223)

The term 'soul' is deeply rooted in the theological history of the Christian churches. The bible contains differentiations between 'soul' and 'spirit'. For the Christian religions, the significance of the soul transcends human existence on earth and from the very beginning is enhanced by the idea of a life after death. The soul is considered immortal and goes on living in the hereafter. These are the concepts on which church doctrines are based. Mind or reason (*anima rationalis*) are located on the highest level of the mortal world according to St Augustine. The human mind forms a direct connection with the invisible, elusive world. The mind allows the soul to reach that world. It is located between the material world and God. The orthodox churches take up these concepts and state that man is an indivisible entity of mind, soul and body. Luther and Calvin retain the concept of the soul as an integral part of human beings. 'Consequently, man does not *possess* a soul, man *is* soul' (Hinterhuber 2001, p.103).

In contrast to this historical tradition, terms like 'soul', 'human existence' and 'consciousness' are almost insignificant in current theological concepts. Current discussions among neuroscientists on such ideas do not find any expression in current theology, although the latter should feel challenged to address these questions, as some neuroscientists have pointed out (Roth and Prinz 1996). The obvious conclusion is that, as God does no longer figure in modern psychology, philosophy or neurosciences, soul and human existence seem to be no issue in current theology.

Schweitzer maintained that true philosophy has to be based on the most immediate and comprehensive fact of consciousness. This means that I am life that wants to live, surrounded by life that wants life. It is good to maintain life and promote life and it is evil to destroy and suppress life (Quester, Schmitt and Lippert-Grüner 1999). Albert Schweitzer's words address the ethical issues involved in brain research, philosophy and theology that concern man's consciousness, brain and existence, self and soul. Philosophy and theology play an important part in the ethics of any society.

Ethical principles in medicine are demanded and postulated even today. The draft proposal of an ethics charter that was set up on the occasion of the European Council's 'Human Rights Agreement in Biomedicine' says, among other things, that the right of life has to be protected in any phase of its existence, that decisions on the value of human life by third parties are excluded, and that the unique nature of human life forbids deliberate termination. Nobody may decide on the value of the life of another (Bavastro *et al.* 1998).

There is a highly controversial ethical debate worldwide on people in persistent vegetative state. The consciousness of patients concerned and its definition is addressed again and again with a view to ethical consequences of divergent opinions and even a discussion on their right to live.

Some countries provide the option to allow patients in coma vigile to die by food deprivation. Cases like those of Helga Wanglie, Karen Ann Quinlan, Nancy Cruzan and Tony Bland are under continuous discussion (Wade and Johnston 1999). There is a clash of diverging attitudes. On the one hand, coma vigile patients are prevented from dying through forced alimentation on intensive wards, and thereby forced to lead an inhuman existence; on the other hand, such patients are neither brain-dead nor dying but human beings with a right to live and be supported by society.

These discussions reveal the essential problem; that is, a right to live for patients in coma vigile may be postulated only by those who assume the possibility of an existing consciousness in these patients. However, the medical standpoint is that they have no consciousness and no cognitive potentials, which inevitably leads to a discussion of an 'end of life'. The concept of human existence that everybody involved in the care of these patients has is, therefore, of decisive importance.

Coma vigile and the concept of human existence

There is no satisfactory answer to the question 'What is man?', and certainly not to 'What is man in coma vigile?' The basic statements of my study on the condition of persistent vegetative state and on human existence presented above in abbreviated form lead to the following general assumptions that form the basis of my concept of human existence.

The term 'coma vigile' describes a complex pathological condition concerning the human body. The nature of man, however, is more than the mere sum of his deficits or his pathologies. Neurophysiologists may be able to demonstrate a relation between consciousness and neuronal processes in the brain but cannot give a comprehensive explanation for consciousness. Similarly, neuropsychologists consider consciousness as one of the secrets of mankind. The inevitable conclusion is that each human being constitutes a physical, emotional and social entity that is basically preserved even in case of illness. Even persons in permanent vegetative state are therefore unique human beings with individual needs and potentials. The depth of consciousness is inviolable and must not be narrowed down.

The most essential characteristic in each person is consciousness. I discover a person's consciousness only in his or her reactions. The persistent vegetative state is a form of life that in the first instance offers no access. A lack of access, however, does not imply its non-existence. It is still impossible to find medical proof of consciousness in such patients. The challenge is to find and offer new ways of access.

Everybody is directed towards development and lives and acts intentionally and purposefully. There are no validated medical data on whether, when and to which degree changes occur, or may occur, in the brain of patients in the long-term phase of coma vigile, even years after the traumatic event.

I start from the assumption that a patient in coma vigile is a living person in possession of his most essential characteristic, consciousness, and who lives a form of life that for him is normal although I am unable to perceive or understand it. He has not lost the basic potential for development and is able to choose and decide whether to accept or refuse offers of an encounter and accompaniment in his life.

> Man needs a you to become an I. The you comes and goes, relational events take shape and dissolve again, and it is during this change that the consciousness of the unchanging partner grows, the consciousness of self. (Buber 1962, p.32[1]

This quotation from Buber expresses the essential concept of access that Hannich and Ziegler have demanded repeatedly as interpersonal dialogue (Hannich 1999; Zieger 1999). This approach describes a path I embark upon as a therapist, the objective of which is dialogue with the self of the other person.

I go in search of this self. I see the path as a continuous togetherness, and not as a one-way road with myself as the starting point. When Buber postulates that real life is always about encounter, then this encounter cannot be reduced to a therapist's directed activities (Buber 1962, p.15). What is required according to the hermeneutic theory is '*Zwischenleiblichkeit*' or 'intercorporality', the relatedness to each other (Hannich 2003).

This demand is a challenge, not only for my professional knowledge, but my whole self: 'The basic word I-you can only be expressed with the entire being' (Buber 1962, p.7).[2] This approach implies a tremendous challenge for me. It involves a willingness to be open that I cannot and will not accept without reservations, and that requires that I set personal limits. I cannot evade the offered encounter in the sense of a duality in the therapeutic relationship. I get involved – according to my abilities – with the patient in coma vigile, with what we do

---

1   'Der Mensch wird am Du zum Ich. Gegenüber kommt und entschwindet, Beziehungsereignisse verdichten sich und zerstieben, und im Wechsel klärt sich, von Mal zu Mal wachsend, das Bewusstsein des gleichbleibenden Partners, das Ichbewusstsein.'

2   'Das Grundwort Ich-Du kann nur mit dem ganzen Wesen gesprochen werden.'

together, with myself. The issues addressed in this chapter obviously include a reflection of my own consciousness, my way of thinking, my emotions.

Basic aspects of work with patients in coma vigile and their significance as parameters for consciousness

Reaction and significance

In my music therapy practice, I experience situations where patients in persistent vegetative state mainly show changes in parameters of respiration, shifts in head and eyes towards the source of sounds and/or a variety of movements. I perceive most of these changes as *reactions*.

In this context I use the term 'reaction' in a sense derived from its Latin origin, as an activity that is performed as an answer (re) to another action. It may be a reflex, or may be performed intentionally and therefore have a rational origin. Situative and temporal references determine the difference between reflex and reaction. If a reaction has a rational origin, then it is intended and is an expression of a cognitive potential. In medicine, neurophysiology and neuropsychology, cognitive potential is seen as the basic requirement for consciousness.

Recognizable reactions should therefore not turn out to be mere reflexes but examples of an intentional activity in response to a stimulus situation. If this is the case then they have a rational origin and as such are an expression of a basically existing cognitive potential in coma vigile patients. The existence of basal potentials of perception and recognition – therefore of consciousness – could be observed in such reactions. In order to distinguish between reactions and reflexes, the observed types of reaction must contain an at least basic element of intention.

Respiration is among the activities we perform unconsciously and as a rule without interruption from birth to death. Respiration is controlled centrally in the medulla oblongata. Only rarely are we acutely aware of, or deliberately influence, our respiration. Sudden changes occur as a sign of a reaction, in the form of a startle response or acute anoxaemia, and may therefore be described as reflex-like. Regular interruptions in breathing or changes in intensity may also be part of a pathological respiratory pattern.

Apart from its physiological significance, respiration is highly individual and specific to each person. It is part of each human being's personality and intimate in nature. Respiration may express the mental condition, may be used intentionally (e.g. in the form of sighs) and thus become an element of non-verbal communication. Respiration has therefore not only physiological but also qualitative significance (Aldridge 2002).

Many movements may be either reflex-like, unconscious or intentional. The same applies to movements that basically belong to reflexes. Eyeblink as a protective reflex is a reflexive and unconscious process. Nevertheless we can stimulate and employ it deliberately.

Examples of pathological movements in coma vigile are primitive reflexes, mastication and mass reflexes, or extensor reflexes. Basically, such movement patterns may be the only movements a patient can use as intentional movement as well. The external appearance of such movements alone is therefore no indication of their quality. Any assessment requires the situative and temporal context in which such movements occur.

An orientation of head and eyes towards the source of a sound implies a situative connection. It must not be confused with the source of sound that is placed in the line of vision. Different and changing orientation as well as turning towards and away from such a source are examples of situative body movements.

An orientation towards the location of the stimulus that calls for attention is innate behaviour. It not only permits visual contact and control but also facilitates optimum auditory directedness. This means that not only eye contact is decisive. The same movement that at first seems an unsatisfactory attempt at establishing eye contact may also be intended to align one's hearing. In cases where visual potentials of a patient cannot be reliably defined, such movements may have a quality comparable to the orientation of a blind person. An orientation without eye contact must not necessarily signify avoidance behaviour or imperfection.

The definition of the term 'reaction' already implied its temporal reference as a response to an action. A reaction therefore presupposes a previous perception, and this is why perceptiveness may be derived from a reaction. It suggests a quality beyond mere reflex – a deliberate performance. Reactions must reveal a situative and a temporal reference in order to be distinguishable from reflexes. A situative reference means that a reaction occurs only in the specific situation, or in an intensive form only in this situation.

Music may help to discover a temporal reference. Music itself has a temporal structure. Time in this context is significant for the basic beat but also as a temporal frame for the beginning and end of a melody. The internal logical structure of music influences the time factor, a structure that is determined by the logos of music. This involves the periodic generation of melodies and specific elements of accentuation that have developed in the musical history of the Occident and influence our musical perception even today.

Every human being has an innate musicality. This is why we perceive a departure from such musical structures, irrespective of the specific quality or further education of our musicality, as unsatisfactory or wrong. This innate musicality also corresponds to our ability to convert music into movements. We have the natural skills to accompany a basic beat with a clapping of hands or otherwise joining in, and to follow musical accentuations.

Another element that is common to respiration and movement is rhythm. Rhythm provides a temporal structure for both. Improvisation on respiration or movement may direct the attention of patients in coma vigile to these elements and in addition to their temporal structure. Reactions to be observed in a temporal connection with the abovementioned musical structures may therefore indicate a basic ability for temporal orientation. Reactions occurring after a stimulus in the sense of a reflex-oriented stimulus–response pattern can be excluded here.

A movement occurring with a certain accentuation – perhaps the end accentuation of a melody in the final cadence, or a main accentuation within a melody phrase – comprises not only a simple temporal reference. If it occurs only in this instance, it indicates an expectant attitude, a temporal orientation towards the future, a knowledge of something that will happen immediately, and an awareness of the imminent start or end of a melody, of the importance of an accent. It also reflects an ability to remember: to remember something that has already been heard or experienced.

It is not the exactness, the simultaneous movement, as a chronology of events that is important; what is crucial is the *obvious decision* to move at this moment, in the sense of a distinction between chronos and kairos postulated by Aldridge (1997, 2001a, 2002) – that chronos is the time we measure, and kairos is the right moment for an appropriate and intentional action in response.

Repeatedly, we have situations in music therapy when a certain element of physical expression, such as respiratory movement, eyewink or another movement, is taken up in an improvisation by the therapist and we see an alteration in this original element. Although reference to the physical event is obvious, there must also be a perception that this is not recorded music but a live improvisation specifically for this situation; a situative orientation is required.

In addition, an awareness is necessary as to which body part or physical expression the music refers to. This also reveals the basic potential of a physical orientation. The patient in coma vigile must be able to perceive that the music directly relates to his breathing, his eyewink, or this movement he makes. This perception goes beyond the mere recognition of any physical element. This reaction implies not only the recognition of one element, but a recognition of *my* individual breathing, *my* individual eyewink, *my* individual movement. Re-action thus becomes a response to the other person. It reveals a recognition of the self, and therefore self-consciousness!

Distance and nearness

My personal way of working with coma vigile patients as a music therapist is based on the Nordoff/Robbins approach. It presupposes an active participation of clients in joint musical improvisation. Persons in coma vigile are therefore included in the music and, just like the therapist, become part of this music. A distance in the sense of musical neutrality, music randomly available from previous recordings without any reference to the client, is therefore a contradiction to this therapy approach.

Involving patients in persistent vegetative state into joint activities may have a variety of qualities for distance and nearness. The sound produced by the therapist in improvisation is related directly to one physical element in the patient that is reflected in that sound. The sound becomes a signal; an offer for nearness, an offer of an intimate, personal encounter.

Despite this general offer, the music may imply different degrees of distance and nearness. The improvisation of a melody may be oriented to the client only in very general terms. The temporal distance from one event to the next (the distance from one eyewink to the next) would be filled with several notes of one beat or even with several beats. Improvisation may, however, also involve a very close physical reference, where each event itself (e.g. each eyewink) would correspond exactly to one musical event, one single note of the melody.

Although most music therapy sessions are characterized by physical distance and auditive means, where therapist and coma vigile patient do not touch each other, the translation of one body element in a 1:1 ratio to elements in the music may create a very intensive nearness. This intensity is not a consequence of the simultaneity of sound and movement but emerges through the experience of the situation. The emotional experience of this special nearness may convey an intimate character to the therapy session. Nearness in music therapy therefore does not depend on physical nearness, body contact or touch. Where physical nearness is used in exceptional cases, it is used more to provide technical support to movement and is not an expression or stimulus of this emerging nearness.

My study revealed that nearness did not depend on the choice of instrument nor music. In almost all significant examples, I was involved with my own voice and thereby immediately and personally. The sound of the voice is an intimate expression of personality. With the offer of nearness I offer myself through my voice – and not in my professional capacity – as a person with whom a client may enter into contact.

In music therapy with coma vigile patients, the terms 'distance' and 'nearness' describe not only a musical–technical method as part of an improvisation. Distance and nearness show themselves as qualitative elements. They add the relational aspect to the approach of a music therapy offer.

Therapy and relationship

Perception is not an isolated capacity but leads to emotional experience and corresponding reactions in the sense that a situation takes shape. Listening to music means not only to perceive it, but also to experience it. Active music-making permits one to take an active part in this music and to give expression to one's own emotional experience.

Reaction is a response to action that has been perceived. Distance and nearness are qualitative elements of music therapy with coma vigile patients. If they perceive music and react to it in some way, then we may assume that they also experience the music emotionally for the above reasons. Such an emotional experience of music and nearness in improvisation creates a relationship between the coma vigile patient and his or her therapist. There are several requirements for such a relational situation that lead to further conclusions. Both may be described as follows.

A person in permanent vegetative state should be able to perceive and be aware of the physical reference of improvised music, and differentiate between a perception of his environment and himself. Only then would he be able to react with the corresponding body element. Such a reaction would express his willingness to open himself to the situation and turn towards his perceived environment. A reaction in a coma vigile patient would therefore imply that he recognizes that there is someone else who acts, that the music is actively produced by someone. This reaction to another person would illustrate the ability to differentiate between the self and the other and therefore to recognize the own self, an awareness of the self, a self-consciousness.

Healthy persons do not continuously reflect upon their self-awareness, although it is always there, and others have no way to assess it. Similarly, the depth of self-awareness in coma vigile patients in such situation cannot be described, but it exists without doubt.

The therapist must be willing to enter into a relationship with the coma vigile client. This means that his or her music cannot remain an isolated, technically skilful activity, and what he or she does in therapy cannot be reduced to professional activity alone. The focus must be directed to more than the client's pathology.

In addition, a therapist must see himself or herself as part of a social relationship, according to the definition of a relationship as a degree of connectedness or distance between individuals united by a social entity. The therapist must focus on the person, the personality of the coma vigile patient, and accept the patient as a partner with equal rights in this relationship. This implies that the therapist enters into the relationship not only as a professional but as an individual, with his or her own personality.

Both therapist and coma vigile patient must therefore be aware of their individual self in the therapy situation, as a necessary requirement for an encounter between the consciousness of the coma vigile patient and that of the therapist.

The parameters described here are confirmed in the single case studies of my thesis (Herkenrath 2004). They illustrate an encounter between the consciousness of coma vigile patients and that of their therapists. An encounter between two human beings depends on many factors and cannot be repeated in an identical fashion; despite various similarities and parallelisms, each encounter is a singular event and to be assessed as such. The sessions cannot be duplicated nor quantitatively evaluated. Each individual situation of an encounter is significant, and to be judged according to the described principles.

In general, it is problematic to examine each situation with a view to its significance. A therapy situation receives significance only from a comprehensive perspective. Basically, there is no situation without significance. With the idea in mind that normality should be an objective for the life for coma vigile patients, the everyday encounter with them without any exceptional events is already important for the emergence of a relationship.

Coma vigile: an art of living

There are widely differing views on the situation and form of consciousness of persons in coma vigile. Assessments of this situation range from a state without consciousness and without perceptions to an interpretation as an active withdrawal from the outside world. Such differences are mainly due to the problem that it is difficult to recognize and interpret movements observable in coma vigile patients as reactions to the environment. The recognition of such movements is, however, essential for an assessment of a patient's state of consciousness. The dilemma for coma vigile patients is therefore that, if their form of life is an active withdrawal or reduction of previously performed activities, they must themselves demonstrate the existence of their consciousness, although their perceptive and communicative potentials are massively impaired.

Persons with serious neurological impairments lose their orientation with regard not only to their environment but also to their body and therefore to themselves (Sacks 1990; Zieger 1998). A frequently voiced opinion in this context is that these impairments may prevent such patients from an encounter with the environment and also with themselves, so that the impairment also prevents contacts that the outside world may want to establish with the patient. This might serve to isolate and exclude coma vigile patients.

In music therapy with coma vigile patients, we have situations where changes or movements may be observed and may even be identified as reactions and therefore define orientation potentials. The occurrence of such reactions suggests that the described isolation and exclusion are broken down and a form of relationship has been established between the coma vigile patient and his or her surroundings. We must ask ourselves what makes this possible and which conclusions may be drawn for persons in coma vigile.

Respiration, eyewink or other movements are taken up in the musical improvisation and reflected as elements of physical expression. Reactions demonstrate that patients perceive and reflect this coupling with an auditive level, and thereby the physical element itself. We may conclude that persons in coma vigile are able to direct their attention to their own body, at least upon a corresponding stimulus.

All described elements of physical expression, including respiration, are movements. Movement comprises rhythm, requires time and space and receives structure through these elements. Music, too, is movement with a temporal structure. When movement is taken up and reflected in improvisation, the structures of music and movement melt into each other. Movement becomes music, and music becomes resounding movement. Reactions show that persons in vegetative state are able to recognize such temporal structures and the rhythm of their own movements and thus actively relate. Reaction in response to action is an essential part of any encounter. An individual reacts to a perceived offer in order to influence the offer and his or her own situation. Communication and dialogue result from a sequence of reactions and counter-reactions. Communication is not limited to one person but constitutes a relational phenomenon.

As a rule communication is understood as verbal communication. Persons in coma vigile have no way to express themselves verbally or through a yes/no code. In their non-verbal reaction to the therapist's action, who on his or her part shows a counter-reaction and thus produces a change in the reaction of the patient, persons in coma vigile are a link in the chain of action, reaction and counter-reaction and in this way become partners in a non-verbal communication.

In music therapy sessions, coma vigile patients frequently exhibit reactions in the form of changes in the intensity of respiration, eyewinks or movements. Intensity of physical expression not only has physiological causes but is also connected to emotions. Changes in intensity also lead to changes in the experienced emotions or are caused by them. Such patients are therefore able to have emotional perceptions in encounters with another person and are able to give expression to their emotion.

The above suggests that a person in persistent vegetative state is not only affected by a serious impairment of his perception and has lost his orientation towards the environment and himself, but also that he possesses the potential for a re-orientation in time, body and self, in space and situation. The results of this study on the form of life of coma vigile patients may therefore be summarized as follows.

Despite his withdrawal and reduction to the physical self, a coma vigile patient also lives in a correlation with his environment that allows him to respond to offers in the sense of a re-action. Like any healthy individual, he is able to live this correlation and also to participate actively in this environment. The life form of coma vigile is his normality.

Consequently, coma vigile patients are living individuals with consciousness, with emotional perceptions despite massive physical impairment, and the ability to enter into social contact. As a physical, mental and social entity, they have individual needs and potentials like any other human being.

Persons in coma vigile are able to perceive and experience themselves as part of an encounter. The degree and way of entering into contact is something they decide according to their personal competence and individual potential.

Personal competence in a coma vigile patient means that he can either accept or refuse offers of contact. Developments or changes in his situation are not to be expected in a chronological sense (chronos) and do not occur as a consequence of the offer alone. They rather depend – in the sense of kairos – on a patient's decision to tolerate them.

The above considerations lead to the conclusion that coma vigile patients live in a process where they are in need of support in order to cope with their situation and to develop new perspectives, and where as living individuals they have a right to be protected. The specific life form of a coma vigile patient is his or her way of life and art of life at the same time.

The therapist: professionalism and humanity

The encounter with coma vigile patients challenges a therapist's professionalism, but also his or her humanity. The therapeutic focus from the very beginning is on those elements that need to be treated; but in each encounter the therapist will first perceive a patient's physical appearance in its expression and recognizable impairments. Subsequent activities will inevitably be determined by the therapist's perceptions and pertinent emotions. On the basis of these combined perceptions and emotions the therapist enters into a relationship with the patient that has to be filled with life.

The way this relationship develops depends on the therapist's attitude. If he or she believes coma vigile patients are unable to perceive and therefore unable to react immediately to perceptions, activities will be directed to the patients' physical phenomena alone, denying a patient's existence as a person. This would prevent an encounter with the personality of the patient. But the basic precondition for encounter and relation is a mutual level of I and you. 'The other person encounters me. But I enter into the immediate relation with him. The relation therefore comprises being chosen and choosing, passivity and action' (Buber 1962, p.15).[3]

We see that a therapeutic relationship depends not only on the personality of the coma vigile patient but also on that of the therapist. A therapist's objective observations are connected with his or her personal experience of the situation. The therapist's subjectivity, his or her subjective experience, is therefore part of the therapeutic activity. Objectivity and subjectivity cannot exclude each other; but the acceptance of their existence and the willingness to admit them is a basic precondition for an encounter.

Among the most profound experiences in my work with coma vigile patients are situations where my personal attitude towards the patient prevented an encounter in music therapy. Only my willingness to open myself for a patient, to accept him despite his possible resistance against me, to offer him my nearness and not to see the responsibility for the situation on his side but to assume it myself – only this helps to create a background for encounters.

How to initiate a dialogue with coma vigile patients has been described in various ways in this chapter. Hannich and Ziegler repeatedly point out in their publications that this dialogue requires, apart from professional competence, also interpersonal contact on the basis of a sympathetic, emphatic and supportive attitude towards the patient (e.g. Hannich 1994, 1999; Hannich and Dierkes 1996; Zieger 1996, 1999, 2003). The obvious requirement of appropriate professional competence on the part of the therapist is expanded here by an essential aspect that goes beyond the concept of relational medicine – the need for a therapist's personal competence in the sense of an involvement of his or her personality in the encounter with the coma vigile patient. The situation is influenced by the therapist's attitude, and his or her attitude towards the patient has a decisive influence on success or failure of the intervention; but the essential aspect – apart from rational and professional action – is a willingness to enter into contact with the patient. In this encounter, the therapist must offer his or her own self – the therapist as a self that meets the patient in his or her personal being and with his or her individual identity.

This willingness to open oneself is more than a mere technicality and must be demanded not only from the therapist but also from everybody who in involved

---

3   'Das Du begegnet mir. Aber ich trete in die unmittelbare Beziehung zu ihm.
     So ist die Beziehung Erwähltwerden und Erwählen, Passion und Aktion in
     einem.'

with patients. Everybody involved in such a relationship should become a partner who not only observes the patient and tries to recognize him or her, but who also permits himself or herself to be observed and recognized. 'But in the perfect relationship, my you comprises my self without being it; my impaired recognition melts in a boundless feeling of being recognized' (Buber 1962, p.101).[4]

Human existence as a counterpoint to human brain

As mentioned before, medical specialists are not in a position to localize nor define human consciousness, despite the general opinion that brain functionality is essential for consciousness. Many brain researchers call the phenomenon of consciousness the last big secret.

The abilities of perception of self and the environment and an adequate reaction to these on the basis of existing orientation potentials are seen as part of consciousness. If the term 'adequate reaction' may be understood as a directed reaction to outside stimuli, then patients in coma vigile have consciousness because of their re-actions described above.

But are statements on orientation potentials, cortical processing of perceptions and adequate reactions enough for a comprehensive description of human existence? The spirit, the self, the ego of man is more than a mere neuronal activity, and human consciousness is so manifold that it cannot be reduced to the functionality of brain nerves.

Coma vigile is not caused by damage to one particular, isolated brain area; coma vigile patients may be affected by a variety of different impairments to the brain. But despite the different degrees of brain damage, each single one of them has an individual personality and lives his or her individual existence, as described before. This realization, however, implies the question of what human existence really is if it cannot be reduced to brain activity. First of all, we may assume that each human existence is individual, unique and not transferable to another human being. It may not be duplicated in the sense of cloning. This uniqueness of being and of human spirit is often called 'the soul' (Feinberg 2002). It is not material in any way known to us. It cannot be reduced to brain nor body and therefore cannot be explored scientifically. This may be the reason why after years of studies many brain researchers realize that they are unable to solve this last secret and have to admit: *Ignorabimus!*

---

4   'Aber in der vollkommenen Beziehung umfasst mein Du mein Selbst, ohne es zu sein; mein eingeschränktes Erkennen geht in einem schrankenlosen Erkanntwerden auf.'

The personal experience of being an individual living in his own body does not help anybody to find out when and how he became who he is and started to live in his self, his soul. The soul, the consciousness of man, constitutes a counterpoint to the brain in the musical sense, as an independent existence of equal importance. It is there, like the brain, but cannot be localized. It may be experienced but not be proved with scientific means. *Ich bin Leben, inmitten von Leben, das Leben will* – I am life, surrounded by life that wants life.

Medical and social implications

Medical knowledge on long-term phases of coma vigile turns out to be full of gaps, and many prognoses are wrong. Prior to a discussion on definition and terminology of coma vigile, the phenomenon itself urgently requires new scientific research. Such research must focus not only on the acute situation of patients or the first months after the event, but foremost on the long-term phase in order to close the tremendous gaps in knowledge.

A first objective would be to update knowledge on the illness and its progress, diagnosis and treatment in order to gain new scientific findings. The perspective must then be expanded beyond the acute stage and the first few months, and data must be collected on long-term development and the condition of coma vigile patients. The subject of this study is not the abstract illness of a patient but the entire human being himself or herself. This is why in such a research project the search for biomedical findings and concepts of relational medicine must not be mutually exclusive, but must complement each other. Only a combination of both allows us to collect comprehensive data on the illness and the patients affected, and in addition on consciousness as the core of human existence.

Accordingly, an evaluation must focus equally on the search for high efficiency in therapy and care, and on the quality of life for coma vigile patients. Such an evaluation must be free from the pressure of expectations from medicine and society on cost reduction in treatment and care, and also free from economic interests. We may assume that the ideas presented in this chapter will be confirmed by such scientific research. Medicine would thus provide new descriptions of coma vigile patients, and thereby encourage society to recognize these patients as living persons with a consciousness the depth of which is hard to evaluate.

Opinions on coma vigile patients are divided. There are open discussions on the value of life in such patients, their right to live and be taken care of by society. This study tried to demonstrate that coma vigile patients are people with serious brain damage, but also with a consciousness who in their specific form of life have the capacity to meet others or be met in an encounter, and who have the same basic rights as everybody else.

Our society must address the legal and ethical implications. Society is challenged to ensure the rights of coma vigile patients to a protected life and physical integrity. The right to physical integrity implies the right to medical and nursing care. The aspects involved here are more ethical than legal in nature. Patients in coma vigile are not in confrontation with society, but one of its parts. As a consequence of their impairments, they are among the weakest elements and in need of support. Any discrimination, any debate on the value of their lives as a cost–benefit calculation, or possible euthanasia, are in sharp contrast to the findings of this study, ethically unjustifiable and thoroughly reprehensible.

In my workplace we follow the concept that every form of life in its specific way is valuable (Haus Königsborn 2002, p.6) and this applies to coma vigile patients as well.

CHAPTER 7

'Swing in My Brain': Active Music Therapy for People with Multiple Sclerosis

Wolfgang Schmid

I liked that! As if the parts have come together again. There is this children's book about a little penguin and his mother yells at him so terribly that he is blown apart. And then his head lands on the moon, his feet in the desert, and his wings at the North Pole; really torn apart. And then the feet set out to look for the other parts. Somehow, all the parts are gathered together and he is put together again. And somehow this here is similar, you can feel so torn apart, but everything belongs together really. And if it is put together again then it is all right. And this here is like that, this here does something like that; it gives an inner balance, I am taken seriously as a person; not a superficial, external 'doing something for oneself' but doing something that reaches my inner self.

This is the story told by a woman after a musical improvisation she played on the metallophone while I accompanied her on the piano. She gives a verbal expression to her impressions received in music therapy. As a participant in the pilot study 'Active music therapy for people living with multiple sclerosis', she discovers how to make active use of music and musical improvisations. In this chapter the qualitative results of the study will be presented and discussed. Starting with a literature review and the presentation of the qualitative findings, I then establish a model for the evaluation of contact in music therapy for people living with multiple sclerosis (MS).

Identity and body experience

Multiple sclerosis is the most frequent inflammatory disease of the central nervous system in young adults aged between 20 and 40 in Western industrialized nations

(Brück 2002). A critical dimension, for both patients and carers, is the fact that this diagnosis is the start of a lifelong, unpredictable process of increasing physical, mental and emotional impairments, for which ultimately there is no cure (Littig, Schmidt and Hoffmann 2002). This process may occur either in phases or progressively. Consequently, with MS we cannot speak of 'ill' and 'healthy' with the aim of recovering a former state of physical, mental and emotional health. This is a chronic disease with drastic implications for future life.

An insecure staggering gait due to imbalance or movement disorders, indistinct speech and marked tiredness or forgetfulness contribute to the stigmatization of people with multiple sclerosis. A vicious circle begins where sufferers try to be inconspicuous, to appear 'normal', and on the other hand withdraw from social relations. The consequence of withdrawal is that the psychological and social elements of life deteriorate too.

World Health Organization descriptions of the consequences of illness differentiate between 'primary impairment as biological functional disorders, secondary disability as the resulting reduction in ability, and tertiary handicap as the resulting disadvantage' (Haupts and Smala 2002, p.321). This extended perspective also covers the implications of an illness for the individual and his or her environment, the restrictions that are imposed by disability, and the consequences that a change in the psychosocial milieu has for an optimization of care. People with MS have to cope with lifelong insecurity and restrictions; they are confronted daily with their deficits, and are well aware of the restrictions the disease imposes on their identities and bodies. Their original plans for life, roles in family and personal relationships at work are massively endangered (Poser and Schäfer 2002; Wiesmann, Machtems and Hannich 2000). Various theories on coping agree on describing a chronic illness like multiple sclerosis as a permanent stressor that makes continuous demands on a person, and this stress in itself may influence progression (Griesehop 2002; Klauer and Filipp 1987; Lazarus 1995; Muthny 1992; Schüßler 1993).

The way in which an individual copes may have an impact on his or her physiological reactions and mental state, and may also change the patient's health care behaviour (Filipp and Aymanns 1996; Schifferdecker 2002; Welter and Schönle 1997). Basically, coping is seen as mainly dependent on a person's social and individual resources. A series of different factors has an impact on how patients cope with the disease and its psychosocial consequences (Görres et al. 1988).

Physical impairments accompanying MS are less significant, whereas the 'continuous, latent or manifest fear of deterioration threatens long-term plans [and] under these conditions a coping of multiple sclerosis [means] far more than an arrangement with physical losses and impairments, since all sick persons are faced with a permanent danger to their self-image and social identity' (Görres et al.

1988, p.275). Symptoms like visual impairment, paraesthesia or imbalance that frequently accompany an episode that can be quickly relieved with medication may lead to fear of loss of control, since the body seems to resist and patients perceive this as a threat to identity and continuity. The sense of personal continuity, being 'the same' as oneself and like significant others, is interrupted. A personal perception of self and body has to be modified continuously due to changes caused by the disease (Diebel 1981). If our bodies are experienced as the centres of perception and communicative expression, then they become direct sources and means of satisfaction for a variety of needs. Physical sensitivity plays an important part in how we experience ourselves. Our body image is based on how we experience activity and interactivity with our environment (Bielefeld 1986). We may assume that the changes in physical sensitivity of multiple sclerosis influences self-image.

A healthy body is replaced repeatedly by a new and more adequate one adapted to changing physical conditions without having to balance a restricted activity with restricted self-esteem (Rohde and Burges 1993). However, if our potential for individual action is restricted due to functional impairment, then this may pose an existential threat to a person's self-acceptance (Paulus 1986).

Assessment and organization of abilities play an important role in the coping process. If I perceive myself as competent, I will be self-assured in coping with the situation, whereas a sense of failed competence leads to insecurity and tension. For people with multiple sclerosis in particular, control over one's life is an important predicator of mental wellbeing and an optimistic outlook (Filipp and Aymanns 1996; Wiesmann, Machtems and Hannich 2001). An individual sense of competence is influenced by the potential for personal action and also by deliberately chosen strategies to cope with multiple sclerosis and its consequences (Sullivan, Mikail and Weinshenker 1997). This explains different coping results:

> The different degrees of success in coping shown by patients with the same level of impairment indicate self-organization principles of the organism that have to be understood in relation with its environment. The more a patient tries to 'organize himself', to 'update' himself in dependence on changed potentials, i.e. to create a correspondence between the current state and the previous self and body image, the better are his chances to heal. (Ludwig-Körner 1992, p.14)

For renewal the individual must attend more to himself and his feelings than to the environment. Resource-oriented interventions are well suited to promote processes of self-organization and renewal. Resources are those factors that help a person to develop better resistance to adverse events and thus contribute to health and wellbeing. Individual resources used for coping are personal commitment and a belief in one's own importance and value, the conviction to be able to control events sufficiently, and the recognition that not stability but continuous change is a characteristic of life (Filipp and Aymanns 1996). In addition, a resource-oriented treatment concept allows the definition of positive features such as individual health-supporting factors and possible starting points for therapy planning at an early time in the anamnesis of a patient (Rimpau 2000).

Living with multiple sclerosis

Multiple sclerosis implies a multitude of needs and problems to be addressed in therapy. Traditional medical and therapeutic concepts for MS patients – like therapeutic exercises, occupational therapy and speech therapy – focus on symptoms and aim to maintain physical and cognitive functions (Poser and Schäfer 2002; Wötzel et al. 1997), whereas there are almost no therapy concepts available to take care of secondary psychosocial consequences. This is why it appears essential to find appropriate interventions that support patients in their coping processes and take them out of their social isolation. Patients themselves wish to be more actively involved in treatment, having a wider choice of therapies including those that address their psychosocial needs (Alcock et al. 2001; Apel, Greim and Zettl 2003; Springer et al. 2001). They declare themselves dissatisfied with traditional methods and want to play a more active part in therapy. Opting for a complementary method, they believe they assume personal responsibility for their health in a pragmatic approach to chronic disease (Thorne et al. 2002). From this perspective, the evaluation criteria for therapies must be reviewed and redefined.

Studies into criteria of quality of life also reveal that people with MS are well able to assess their own physical impairments but do not see them as the decisive factor that defines 'quality' in quality of life. Quality of life for sufferers comprises factors of vitality, general wellbeing and mental state (Altmeyer and Tietze 2003; Rothwell et al. 1997). In general, multiple sclerosis patients perceive therapists who offer alternative and complementary interventions as more helpful for the coping process than 'traditional' physicians. A possible reason is the decision in favour of alternative and complementary therapies as a consequence of dissatisfaction with the doctor–patient relationship (Apel et al. 2003; Vincent and Furnham 1996).

A patient should therefore be involved in his or her own treatment as an active partner so that his or her powers of self-preservation and resources may be discovered and mobilized as important elements in the healing process. This view is supported by findings from psycho-neuroimmunology where the inherent protective and adaptive mechanism that is responsible for stress regulation may have an impact on the degree of sclerosis through overactivity but also through insufficient activity (Heesen 2003). Against this background, we must see all forms of activity in multiple sclerosis patients as attempts to remain closely involved in social and community life to counterbalance the stigma of chronic disease. Their pronounced interest in alternative and complementary methods indicates that these areas provide chances for individual activity and exploration of potentials and limitations. From a patient's as well as from a therapist's perspective, there is a demand for therapies that go beyond those currently available, that support the emotional suffering and the growing loss of independence, that offer resource-orientated services to encourage activities, that help to fight stigmatization and isolation, and that incorporate a patient's elements of *health* (Prosser *et al.* 2003). In the lifelong progression, starting with the diagnosis of MS and requiring repeated adaptation to altered circumstances, those therapies are of specific significance that address and encourage patients' creative powers (Kriz 1994).

Music therapy for people living with multiple sclerosis

Systematic studies into music therapy for people with multiple sclerosis started about 15 years ago when the use of interferon to control episodes was authorized, which was followed by a growing demand for interventions going beyond medical needs.

Five studies and five single case studies have so far been published on music therapy interventions. The authors of these studies generated hypotheses against a specific background of clinical experience with qualitative methods (Lengdobler and Kießling 1989; Magee 1998; O'Callaghan 1994; Schmidt and Hennings 1998) and quantitative methods (Wiens *et al.* 1999). The question of specific criteria for group therapy versus single therapy or for patient selection has remained unanswered in all these studies and seems to depend on practical and infrastructural factors. Only the quantitative study described a control group and a therapy group for which physiological improvements in breathing were demonstrated through specific voice training in music therapy.

The qualitative studies show some similarities (Table 7.1). All publications underline the role of patients' activities, since these stimulate personal competence and initiative and help to create space for emotional expression and interpersonal encounter.

The authors generally agree on the beneficial effects of singing known or self-composed songs for coping. Issues related to the disease, and also memories and hopes, may be addressed and expressed in songs. Music-making with instruments may produce feelings of insecurity in some patients because of their motor impairments. Authors offer different interpretations of this aspect. While Magee (1998) mentions such feelings of insecurity, Lengdobler and Kießling (1989) find that it is not so much physical impairment that affects motivation but rather a

Table 7.1 Literature review on issues and questions addressed in music therapy for multiple sclerosis patients

Elements in music therapy	Address areas like
Patients' individual activities	Get involved or gain control
	Experience competent activity
	Emotional experience and expression
	Body experience
	Challenging emotional and interpersonal
	Encounters
Singing pre-composed or self-composed songs	Support in coping
	Social interaction
	Emotional support
	(Re)construction of identity
	Improved breathing
Instrumental improvisation	Communicative abilities
	Expansion of expression and movement
	Motor insecurity

performance-orientated concept of music and a fear of confusing emotional and interpersonal encounters. We may therefore assume that any impairment in motor abilities depends in equal parts on the degree of a patient's disability and on the type of improvisation offered by the therapist. Playing on instruments is particularly appropriate to experience and develops communicative, expressive and motor skills.

These aspects of music therapy appear highly relevant in view of the psychosocial consequences of multiple sclerosis and the need for appropriate interventions. The role of improvisations in music therapy in particular needs to be explored in detail. For this purpose I have chosen a qualitative evaluation method in my study.

The progress of the disease is highly individual and makes comparison between patients difficult. Therefore, an individual and active type of therapy was chosen in order to address the needs of individual patients with music therapy adapted to their requirements and, on the other hand, to find general therapy-specific factors common to all cases on the basis of the comparable setting. Internal qualitative specifics of active music therapy with MS patients may thus be studied in single cases and discussed with regard to quantitative test results. In this way, the study is based on the findings of previous research but takes them a step further. For the first time, data of qualitative contents and changes in music therapy are contrasted with quantitative findings from validated questionnaires in a controlled flexible study design.

A controlled pilot study

Fourteen female and six male subjects with episodic primary and secondary chronic multiple sclerosis participated in the controlled pilot study over a period of one year. The age range was 29 to 47 years, with an average disease duration of 11 years. Ten subjects formed the therapy group, ten the control group. Groups were comparable according to a neurological disability classification scale (Kurtzke 1983) for age and progress of the disease. The therapy group received three blocks of creative music therapy (Nordoff and Robbins 1977) with 8 to 10 single sessions respectively over the study period. My main questions in the study were:

1. Are there objectifiable parameters that can be assessed using standardized instruments currently in use?

2. Which qualitative aspects characterize active music therapy with MS patients, and are they reflected in clinical change?

3. What is the role of music therapy in an integrative treatment concept for MS?

Qualitative data from music therapy and quantitative data using questionnaires on anxiety and depression, self-acceptance and quality of life were collected and assessed prior to the study, every three months and in follow-up. Data on motor and cognitive performance were also collected. There was no significant difference between the music therapy treatment group and the control group. However, the effect size statistics comparing both groups show a medium effect size on the scales measuring self-esteem, depression and anxiety. Significant improvements were found for the therapy group over time in the scale values of self-esteem (Cohen's $d = 0.5423$), depression ($d = 0.63$) and anxiety ($d = 0.63$).

Over a one-year period, the therapy group showed significant improvements regarding anxiety ($p = 0.013$) and depression ($p = 0.036$) as well as a significant improvement in self-acceptance ($p = 0.012$), whereas no changes were found for quality of life and motor and cognitive parameters. Follow-up half a year after music therapy sessions revealed that improvements were not sustained and the levels for anxiety, depression and self-acceptance in the therapy group had again fallen to the original levels prior to the study (Schmid and Aldridge 2004).

Qualitative evaluation

An immediate reference to original events helps to understand and interpret processes in therapy. The basis for such an analysis is the empirical material from therapy – audible and observable phenomena such as audio or video tape recordings. The subsequent interpretation of the material is an active, dynamic process in various steps of abstraction, leading away from the original therapy towards its description, discussion and assessment depending on the researcher's theoretical background.

'Therapeutic narrative analysis' (Aldridge and Aldridge 2002) is a research approach for qualitative studies that includes Kelly's *personal construct methodology* (Aldridge 1996; Kelly 1955). It is a systematic methodology for qualitative analysis of art therapy processes and remains closely connected to the artistic–therapeutic medium with the intention of establishing both therapeutic and clinical validity (Pilz 1999). This evaluation method reveals how the therapist constructs his or her own understanding of therapy from those of the persons involved. As Bruscia (1995) remarks, reflection about the research process and the knowledge gained as a result is as important as the findings themselves.

Episodes and triangulation

The qualitative evaluation presented here is based on 37 video episodes from single music therapy sessions in the course of the project. The therapist selected these episodes subjectively from a total of 226 sessions; they document characteristic situations and subsequent changes. The criterion for selection was that each episode, in the therapist's judgement, was a prime example of what he wanted to say, although he might not at the time have been able to say in words what it was. Each selected episode was then exemplary. In a way, this is a form of data reduction, as attempting to assess 226 examples would have been simply too much. It is important in qualitative research to maintain a focus on what is necessary.

The titles given to the episodes refer to what happened in the session, some being chosen by the patients themselves, like 'Swing in my brain'. It is useful to give episodes names as they help in remembering the content for the grid analysis. Episodes were assessed according to the therapeutic narrative analysis. All episodes were fed into the computer-aided repertory-grid program (Kelly 1955) and then categorized for differences and similarities, first randomly and later in relation to episodes already evaluated.

This triad comparison of episodes served to elicit constructs and, in a further step of abstraction, general categories for developments in music therapy with MS patients.

The constructs and categories show differences in how patients respond to an offer of active improvisation. Attention to motor aspects is important as a performance and exercise perspective, but there is also a playful attitude of delight that may be decisive for improvisations. Another discovery is that patients require time in music therapy to develop a perception of their own activity and their musical creative potential, despite their impairments, and time also to enter into active exchange. A flexible temporal structure and tonal-dynamic musical expression are supportive factors in this respect. Backed by a relationship of trust with the therapist, patients learn about their own abilities and limitations, contribute their musical ideas, and thus employ personal resources to conquer new realms of activity. This is the precondition to discover music as an expressive medium, and the repertoire of expression becomes audibly more flexible as a consequence.

The common element in all 37 episodes is the way in which patient and therapist make music together. Various qualities of their musical activities lead to various qualities of interaction and therefore of contact and encounter. Kelly calls this common element of an evaluation its 'core construct' (Kelly 1955, p.482) that reflects and relates all constructs involved. The specific way of music-making, the 'contact' between the persons involved, constitutes the core of qualitative assessment and is a characteristic of music therapy with MS patients. This result expands the perception of patients' requirements and indicates needs beyond basic functional and medical care. 'Contact' and 'encounter' are essential forms of social interaction and characterize the style of many therapy concepts irrespective of the medium. Nevertheless, it may come as a surprise that 'contact' is relevant for therapy in a treatment context with a focus on recovery and compensation of cognitive and motor impairments.

Encounter in active music therapy

From the seventeenth century onwards, the term 'contact' has been used for 'touch and connection'. It is derived from the Latin *contactus* for 'touch' or 'encounter' (Pfeifer 1993, p.711). Contact may therefore be understood as an event with temporal and sensory components. This 'touch' may equally be a sensitive expression and impression, a 'touching' and 'being touched' for the persons involved. In psychology, 'contact' is generally defined as a 'meeting of, or entering into connection or relationship between, two – or more – beings' (Häcker and Stapf 1998, pp.456–7). It is based on the mutuality of at least two persons and has a mainly 'emotionally based connection' (Peters 1990, p.291). The elements leading to such a relational connection may be 'physical-bodily touch, expressive variants or linguistic statements' (Häcker and Stapf 1998, p.456). A certain minimum duration of being together is a precondition of contact between people.

Twelve representative episodes as 'contact areas'

Twelve differing representative 'contact areas' were chosen from the 37 episodes as the basis for further assessment. The basis of this choice was that the episodes represented what I wanted understood, even if I could not put that understanding into words straight away. The episodes expressed what I knew as tacit knowledge (Aldridge 2005).

My intention is to describe the original events in these areas of contact for a more detailed analysis of what contact qualities occur in music therapy and to define these qualities with regard to the actions and reactions of the people involved. Constructs and categories gleaned from the repertory grid analysis were used in the description and are identified in *italics* in the text below.

CONTACT AREA 1: SINGING

The musicians are 'all there', collected and able to become active, as may be seen from their body posture. Both musicians contribute to the emotional interpretation of the music. The musical roles are clear, that of a soloist and that of an accompanist. The musical material is clear and has an inner structure. The music develops continuously out of itself, has pace and structure through phrases and intervals; the endings of improvisations result from the musical progress. *The contact in music is clear and alternating.*

CONTACT AREA 2: THINKING MUSIC

'Keeping up' an idea is the main thing in this contact area. The music is frequently continuous without intervals or endings. The pace is unclear and halting. Metric alterations in the music are due to (often minimal) motor difficulties and lead to abrupt stresses and unpredictable changes in emphasis. The patient may wish to prearrange an idea for joint music-making or make a suggestion (for example, through alternation of instruments) so that the music remains constructed but without a seeming 'inner' structure or development. The patient is rarely open to unpredictable musical events. *Reliable contact* in music is difficult and therefore happens via *visual joint play*. Both musicians may come under pressure to perform, and this may become obvious in a fast pace or hurried movements. The absence of spontaneous body movements in connection with music may be a sign of tension.

CONTACT AREA 3: BECOMING PLAYFUL

This contact area documents a transitional situation with changes in the musicians' attitude and also in the way the musical structure is handled. Complex music with motor characteristics may become simpler and clearer. The participants have well-defined musical roles and can alternate in leading and accompaniment. Both play similar instruments. Alternating play with dialogue character makes the music more spontaneous and unpredictable. A concentration on one's own activity and performance brings a new quality of *contact to the music if the offered dialogue is accepted so that alternate play can begin*. Increasingly spontaneous body movements and eye contact indicate that the players are more related to each other and that a new quality of contact is emerging.

CONTACT AREA 4: FREEDOM IN SINGING

Contact is clear and open if both participants have an impression of play. The fact that the voice is chosen as the 'instrument' seems to be relevant: in joint or alternate singing the music can develop all by itself. Free singing gives physically impaired people the chance to find new ways of activity in pace and tonal expression, independent of motor skills. Spontaneous body movements in connection with the interpretation underline the gesture in singing or music-making.

CONTACT AREA 5: 'MY VOICE IS RELEVANT!'

Contact is clear or becomes clear if the patient succeeds in taking the initiative and causing musical changes. He may be encouraged to do so by the therapist and be delighted to pursue an interpretative intention in improvisation that permits a freer use of metre and pace and stimulates various tonal qualities of expression (e.g. tremolo or dynamic qualities of volume). Now it is more important to attend to sound, so that motor problems and resulting insecurities are no longer significant and may be integrated.

CONTACT AREA 6: FACE TO FACE

The patient regulates himself in instrumental play and strives for regularity and exactness. He thus creates his own pressure to perform. He takes no initiative for changes. The therapist can encourage this tendency with simultaneous and supportive play. He may demand too much if he challenges the patient to change something, because the latter needs to find *contact with his own activities*. He needs time and space to listen to himself, to find his own music and to trust that this will emerge. The important thing therefore is to support a patient's independence; in this case, the therapist does not play together with him but rather 'at his side'.

CONTACT AREA 7: SOUND TO THE FORE

The patient sticks to one musical idea; she is almost unable to introduce changes in her music-making. *The contact to her own activity is in the foreground.* She is deeply involved in achieving a successful series of movements, and appears to be searching for, or holding on to, a recurring temporal structure. The mere repetition of one motif is her interpretative principle. Motor impairments are addressed again and again. She requires much support in order to direct her attention, to tonal variations for example. These may come to the fore by special exercises.

CONTACT AREA 8: EXPERIMENT WITH SOUND

The play with musical timbres is part of a patients' repertoire. He uses the music as a form of expression, loves to experiment and is able to change the music by himself. Musical initiatives alternate between patient and therapist, and *contact is clear and alternating.* Singing, and above all the discovery of one's own register, plays an important part.

CONTACT AREA 9: CREATE TRANSITIONS

The patient shows flexibility in improvisation; she is able to develop and vary an established idea spontaneously. She is able to change the pace and/or dynamics of the music and to create transitions. *Contact between patient and therapist is lively and spontaneous and takes place in music.* The players develop musical form when they find orientation in musical interaction and make decisions without further prearrangement.

CONTACT AREA 10: 'O DU STILLE ZEIT' (O SILENT TIME)

Within a given form, a patient gradually succeeds in becoming more flexible and free in her music. The important point is that both musicians interpret the music and that their musical roles are clear. A given rhythmic–melodic form (e.g. a song) may produce contact because the music-making is prearranged. The patient can be sure that nothing can be done wrong. Therefore, *contact within a given musical form is clear.* Important elements are short, distinct phases or songs in which the patient may experience, and also permit, an idea of rhythmic stability and flexible inter-pretation.

CONTACT AREA 11: 'GIRL FROM IPANEMA'

The patient may pursue a clear idea within the form of one song and may achieve individual musical expression. Her own voice becomes an instrument to express her emotions. *Contact is clear within a given musical form.* The temporal continuity defined by the melody of a song appears helpful to produce and maintain contact.

CONTACT AREA 12: 'JUST START AND SEE WHAT COMES...'

The patient uses the improvised music as an individual form of expression and is not irritated by discordant notes or dissonances but discovers them as part of her play and incorporates them as expressions of negative emotions. She identifies with what she does and profits from the fact that there is no pressure to perform. The emotion inherent in music becomes significant: writing songs or choosing certain instruments or songs as favourites the patient assigns unique character to her music. Physical impairments hardly count any longer, or not at all. Music develops *in clear, equal contact*, and ideas, once grasped, are pursued and taken further.

The 12 contact areas are characterized by a multitude of interactions, and a detailed description of various contact qualities in music therapy with MS patients becomes possible. Contact between the persons involved may:

- be clear, unequivocal, spontaneous, open and mutual (contact areas *Singing, Freedom in singing, Experiment with sound, Create transitions, 'O du stille Zeit', 'Girl from Ipanema', 'Just start and see what comes...'*)

- be in a transition from ambiguity to unequivocality, as in the contact areas *'My voice is relevant!', Becoming playful*

- also mean that a patient will have to find contact with his or her own activities first (contact areas *Face to face, Sound to the fore*)

- be difficult, as in the contact area *Thinking music*, because an immediate contact in joint music is almost impossible at this point.

For all 12 contact areas, clear and mutual contact in music therapy with MS patients is remarkably often achieved in sung improvisations or songs. The human voice as our most immediately available instrument permits direct expression, irrespective of physical impairments. Flexible musical–temporal structures in instrumental improvisation lead to qualities of contact that are less equivocal. Alternate and more impulsive play that breaks out of the temporal regularity makes the people involved more aware of each other; contact becomes denser, more committed. A further aspect resulting from the above evaluation is that some patients need time to relate to their own musical activities. Exercises that offer musical alternatives concerning tonal material as well as instruments seem to be helpful in this respect. I found no contact areas without any contact-related phenomena; this may be due to the selection of original episodes, but also – with more probability – to the fact that in the context of music and music therapy and everywhere else human beings are unable not to communicate (Watzlawick, Beavin and Jackson 1990). There is always some form of musical communication, and we can only define the factors that determine, stimulate and limit this communication.

Constituting parameters for contact

To get an idea of how contact constitutes itself in the episodes – which factors encourage or limit its emergence and maintenance – the defined categories were categorized as constituting parameters for contact in music therapy with MS patients. Derived from the categories of all three therapy phases (see later), nine constituting parameters were described as being relevant for contact in music therapy (see Table 7.2).

Table 7.2 Generation of parameters from categories

Categories become	Parameters
Coping with the situation	1. Coping with the situation
Physical level, several senses involved	2. Movement
Interpretative elements, actively formed expression	3. Musical-dynamic elements
Intiative for change	4. Initiative for musical change
Structural elements and temporal structure	5. Musical roles
Flexibility in temporal structure	6. Temporal structure
Choosing voice or an instrument	7. Material
Points of orientation in play	8. Idea as a point of orientation
Improvisation or form	9. Improvisation or form

These parameters allow us to explore contact in more detail – the nature of joint music-making, as well as preconditions, possibilities and limitations. Apart from musical aspects, it is also necessary to consider categories as how patients are coping with the situation and the physical challenges. Each parameter will be described below. With a view to the different qualities of contact within the contact areas, I shall also describe supportive and limiting qualities that contribute to the quality of contact in a particular situation.

COPING WITH THE SITUATION

This parameter describes the general attitude of the people involved in a therapy situation. Participants in therapy, whether they be patients or therapists, reflect their attitudes and expectations in their behaviour. Contact may be improved if those involved experience the therapy situation free from pressures to perform in a specified way and are willing to enter into a spirit of playfulness and pleasure. On the other hand, contact may be hampered if they do not wish to relinquish anything but try instead to rigidly control the musical process and direct the course of events.

MOVEMENT

This parameter describes the non-verbal factors of physical communication in music therapy. These factors include body tension, spontaneous body movements in singing and playing, mimicry and gestures, and eye contact. Their significance has to be understood in context. The parameter 'movement' alone therefore does not allow any definite statement on contact: several parameters taken together must be assessed to describe and interpret a certain contact quality. Eye contact as part of non-verbal communication can signal agreement as well as helplessness. No eye contact may mean that someone is either deeply involved with himself or herself and in musical contact with the partner, or that he or she is absolutely 'not there' and thinking of something different. Body movements may have qualities supportive of contact in combination with the music, since they indicate a connection between physical expression and musical movement, whereby a person may be seen as using his or her body as a means of expressive interpretation. It may have a dampening effect on contact if one participant does not or cannot exhibit spontaneous body movements in singing or playing, or if the movements shown appear inappropriate for this music. This may be an indication that the player has little connection to what he or she does.

MUSICAL–DYNAMIC ELEMENTS

Musical–dynamic elements are the components of musical change in music therapy. They produce variations and help to develop new musical ideas. Musical–dynamic elements refer to changes in all musical components: pace, metre, dynamics, rhythm, melody, harmony, musical expression, phrasing and sound. The dynamics of these components unfold in transitions and changes from one polarity to another – from slow to quick and vice versa, from metrical to non-metrical, from atonal to tonal. We perceive changes in musical elements only over time, in transitions or contrasts, and they may serve as a means of interpretation for contact – supporting play and its continuation. A change in musical elements, as a consequence of motor impairment or disturbed coordination, can be integrated into the music when the patient tolerates this.

INITIATIVE FOR MUSICAL CHANGE

This parameter describes the ability to take the initiative for musical change and thus to expand one's immediate intentional and expressive scope for interpretation and action. The initiative for musical change may come from the therapist to introduce alternative modes or may occur spontaneously in improvisation to realize an idea. Contact may be negatively affected if none of the participants takes the initiative for musical change over a longer period. Phases without change may be important, above all in the beginning, to create stability and confidence; but if contact is to be maintained, a potential for change seems to be required in the long run.

MUSICAL ROLES

Musical roles as a parameter stand for the musical parts assumed by the participants in their joint music-making. This comprises the question of who leads and who follows in musical interaction. Well-defined musical roles in a song are conducive to contact since all participants are able to detect and hear themselves and the other. In the form of continuously changing roles, the musical guiding and following may itself become a game and thereby promote contact. Contact may be impeded if it is not clear who follows whom, or if the musical role demanded of him or her is too much for one participant.

TEMPORAL STRUCTURE

A decisive factor for joint musical play, and therefore for contact in music therapy, is the temporal relation between the individual events. This parameter describes various different qualities of temporal structure in music that may be continuous or fragmentary, in free or bound metre. The ability of human beings to make use of a metrically continuous temporal structure is a quality that is basically supportive of contact. The temporal order inherent in music ensures predictability and thereby anticipation and repetition, and contact is stabilized. A regular and, therefore, dependable temporal structure may be found in the form of a song or an exercise. This may be a relief for the player and direct his or her attention to new modes of play. This furthers contact as much as playing with the temporal structure itself, with changes of pace or an alternating metre. If a patient tries to rely on a continuous temporal structure then this may even impair contact. Abrupt metric changes 'caused' by motor impairments expose patients to these changes and this can lead to additional insecurity. The same may happen if a temporal structure has become automatic and the music is nothing but a repetition of one and the same motif.

MATERIAL

This parameter refers to the choice of instruments and therefore basically the decision in favour of a certain instrument or the singing voice. The choice of material is significant because it suggests a person's individual musical preference where he or she can personally relate to the activity. A patient with physical handicaps may opt for his or her own voice as musical material. In this way, the person is less dependent on the function and mobility of arms and hands. Singing would be a contact-supporting quality of the parameter material as independence from physical mobility. Reliance on breathing may give this patient self-confidence and flexibility. On the other hand, sound produced on an instrument may be a positive, confidence-boosting feedback for handicapped and insecure people and therefore have a positive effect on contact. Of particular significance in this context are instruments that do not mainly underline the rhythmic–metric element of music but, like the steel drum or ocean drum, impress with their tonal qualities.

IDEA AS A POINT OF ORIENTATION

This parameter addresses the idea a person uses for orientation in music-making. It may reveal the way he or she relates to activities in music therapy and makes sense of them. An idea may be expressed explicitly or in the form of a certain musical mode. It may consist in a certain motif or song that evokes memories in a patient. The wish to listen to live music or taped music and to discuss music, or to use texts or images – all these are ideas for music therapy. Contact may be improved if both sides are clear about which idea they take as a point of orientation. Contact may be impaired if the idea is only maintained for exercise purposes. With an exercise or a given form as an idea for therapy, music therapy is mainly concentrated on the structured offer, while the relational level may be arranged or be of minor importance. Exercises and pre-composed music thus provide a structural and also interactional basis on which a freer interpretation of relationship may be built. The decisive point is that this parameter is significant as it may indicate the musical reference points of a patient, comparable to the parameter 'material'.

IMPROVISATION OR FORM

This parameter stands for the basic decision whether to choose improvisation or a song, a musical exercise or prearranged music as the focus of activity. We cannot assume that each patient is immediately able, or willing to, improvise. Improvisation as well as form may both have positive or negative effects for the contact situation, depending on a patient's demands, abilities and interests.

Combinations of parameters

The next step in evaluation illustrates how an interlocking process of modes leads to contact in music therapy using constitutive and regulative rules (Aldridge 1999b). Musical developments are first described as events in their temporal sequence with the help of constitutive rules. Each constitutive rule then became part of a regulative cycle whereby events are interpreted. This step constitutes a dynamic understanding of contact and interaction, of 'if…then', so that a more formal evaluation of contact areas becomes possible.

In practice, the musical changes and expansions in a patient's play can be documented as observable developments in his or her expressive and active powers. A correlation between the nine parameters described above and all regulative circles of the twelve contact areas is illustrated in Figure 7.1 showing the positions and combinations of parameters.

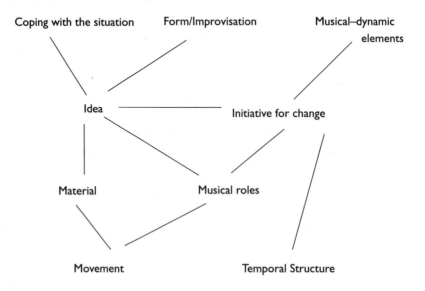

Figure 7.1 Combinations of parameters

Consider a combination of the parameters *material, the idea as a point of orientation, coping with the situation* and *form/improvisation.* The idea as a point of orientation has direct or indirect implications for the way somebody copes with the situation if, for example, he or she wants to do specific exercises, or expresses surprise or frustration after an improvisation. The choice of material again may indicate the idea and the coping mechanisms. The choice of a battery of instruments and several sticks may be an indirect indication of high expectations and performance orientation.

If a patient opts for singing, then this choice of material probably leads to the idea to sing a song. The idea of a song is connected to the concept of who takes which musical role. The therapist may accompany the singing patient, or they can sing a duet. This illustrates the combination of the parameters 'idea' and 'musical roles'. The choice of a song, as a pre-composed form with a beginning and ending, also makes a temporal structure available. A regular temporal structure provides security and is also the basis for initiative for musical change that may become evident when a song is sung in an increasingly individual interpretation.

As in singing, temporal structure may be important in instrumental improvisation in order to clarify the musical roles. If it is undecided, in musical improvisation, who leads and who follows, then it may be important for the therapist to introduce temporal structure and thus to help clarify the musical roles. On the other hand, a change in musical roles may stabilize the temporal structure in a patient's play. The parameters 'initiative for musical change' and 'musical–dynamic elements' are connected with the musical roles and the temporal structure.

A clear definition of musical roles as well as temporal structure over a long period of time may prevent any further initiatives for musical change, so that the music 'plays itself'. It will then be necessary to introduce change in order to maintain contact and liveliness. Clarity, or clarification of musical roles and/or temporal structure in instrumental play, are preconditions for initiatives for change. Therefore, the two parameters 'musical roles' and 'temporal structure' have a stabilizing function for contact in music therapy and at the same time are sources of change.

Playing with roles, either in dialogue or in alternation of leading and following, can be an initiative for change and act as a catalyst for lively contact. Comparable to the parameter 'musical roles', we discover the parameter 'movement' also in temporal structure and in initiative for change. A person's movement is closely connected with his or her musical activity.

The combination of contact parameters as described above is a central argument in favour of music therapy, since an understanding of these can serve as a basis to use individual needs and strengths of patients for future developments.

A model for the evaluation of contact

Contact, as encounter, in improvisational music therapy can be formulated as a model of three phases: exploration, interaction and development. Figure 7.2 illustrates how mutual contact in music therapy with multiple sclerosis patients may be established, stabilized and taken further over time. The circumstances and the speed with which the three phases and intermediate stages are passed, repeated or avoided depend on the people involved. Therefore, contact cannot be performed or measured in a linear way but is determined by individual, subjective factors.

The wide and diverse range of material gained from the episodes suggests the possibility of going through the three phases and intermediate stages again and again, in improvisation as well as from session to session, and that they achieve stability in the therapy process. The progress of music in time permits us to observe not isolated single events in music therapy but rather actions and reactions that blend and build upon each other. All acting persons are equally involved, change their roles and functions in the process and expand their expressive repertoires in interaction. The concept of phases provides a theoretical framework for complex developments in music therapy, which also permits an approach to a comprehensive understanding and reflection of practice; on the other hand, certain simplifications of music therapy processes have to be accepted.

Contact phase I: exploration

In the first contact phase, a patient selects an instrument, tries it out and says what kind of music he or she wants to do. The person is thus actively involved from the very beginning and accompanied and supported by the therapist at this stage of orientation. The attraction of playing a fascinating instrument or song associated with memories is a basic motivating element for the first phase in active music therapy. Structured offers in the form of exercises and songs can facilitate the introduction of music therapy as the focus is on prearranged musical forms and less on relationship.

The etymological meaning of 'contactus' (Pfeifer 1993, p.711) suggests both sensory touch and encounter with the self. In music playing, various sensory areas and impressions are organized in a specific way, and their integration and processing is supported. Singing in particular, with its immediate connection to breathing, stimulates a dialogue of the body with itself that may then be expanded to include the environment. Singing freely gives some people a sense of flexibility and spontaneity that they do not achieve with instruments. Increasingly, they use the creative sphere for an experience of the self, and the inner musical dialogue of the first phase gives way to progressively outward-directed interaction in the second contact phase.

Contact phase II: interaction

In music therapy, musicians realize their identities through musical performance. The temporal structure of music offers a coherent matrix in which participants coordinate their actions and reactions, challenge or complement each other or draw lines, and this becomes audible in the alternating character of the music. We may assume that changes in music become clearly perceivable only if they take place in the relation with another person or on the basis of a structured temporal matrix. This hypothesis is particularly relevant to the issues addressed in this chapter since it provides a theoretical basis for interaction in music therapy as the driving force for quantitatively measurable improvements in self-acceptance and mental state.

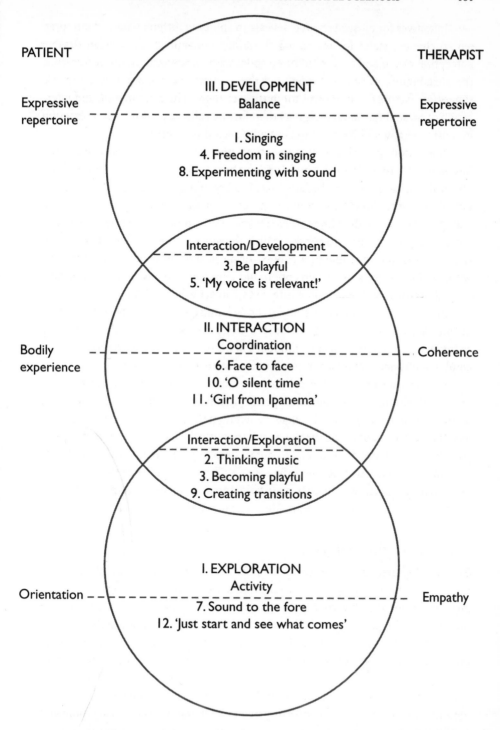

Figure 7.2 Three phases of contact (exploration–interaction–development) in active music therapy with people with Multiple sclerosis

'Initiatives for musical change' reveals an ability to differentiate and interpret: tempo changes stand for increasing flexibility, dynamic changes mean flexible perception of self and others. In the episodes with improvisations on instruments, the unambiguity of 'musical roles' and the existence of 'temporal structure' are supportive factors for 'initiatives for musical change'. The combination and interaction of these three parameters may therefore be called a platform for interaction in music therapy and its development with regard to contact.

In addition, participants integrate their physical expression more and more into musical activity in the second contact phase. This becomes obvious in those physical musical processes that are related to breathing in singing or playing the saxophone, or to direct hand contact on a conga in drumming. The inner musical dialogue of an individual finds an observable outward physical expression that is increasingly integrated into contact. Music therapy provides an active body experience that is only possible in a context of musical improvisation involving the whole being as the axis of perception and experience. Thus, physically handicapped persons, without explicit directives, can achieve flexibility and coordination that both players perceive through body language and is the basis for further action. Active music-making includes a body experience and therefore may encourage a patient to (re)gain confidence in his or her body and to mobilize and employ a physical expressive repertoire for interpersonal contact.

The relation between the parameters 'musical roles', 'material' and 'movement' constitutes a phenomenon specific to music therapy and indicates the degree to which interpersonal contact depends on the participants' body expressivity. It is a strength of music therapy that it supports the entire spectrum of expressive abilities of individuals to make contact despite physical impairments. People with multiple sclerosis thus get a chance of a physical experience that is without normative pressures and which may help them to come to terms with their physical existence, with their individual abilities and their limitations.

Contact phase III: development

The development phase relies on familiar interaction as a dependable outer framework. A clear temporal structure forms a basis for musical initiatives that introduce unpredictable changes and make interpersonal contact dynamic and interesting. The parameters of the second phase, interaction, are stabilized and changed in the third, so that the experience and expansion of expressivity produces a wide range of contact possibilities. Participants develop joint perspectives; together they explore possibilities to become active because they want to continue their interaction. Their expanded musical interaction leads to expanded identities independent of the roles of patient and therapist. They create room and confidence for the unpredictable, for developmental steps resulting from joint musical action and stimulating them to go on striving for inner and outer balance. Such an expansion of potential leads to a more competent body experience and has a positive effect on self-acceptance. Music in the third phase is highly personal and emotional, and includes negative and worrying feelings as well. In singing, this feeling of competence happens through finding and stabilizing register and playing with timbre, dynamics and expressivity. In instrumental play, there is a freer use of tempo and metre and an interpretation with tremoli, pauses or alternating sections with free and bound metre. Chronological, mechanical passages are thus increasingly replaced by kairological, situative, spontaneous impulses.

A musical metaphor

Music therapy can be an invitation for impromptu play and offers a sphere where each and every human activity may be taken up as an idea for improvisation. People who are ill or handicapped in some way get a chance to become active themselves, to mobilize their creative potential and specifically to find access to their inner self and their abilities. They are stimulated to balance their music-making with their perceptions and rely on an emphatic understanding of their skills as well as their insecurities. We synchronize ourselves in playing an instrument, in perceiving that we play and listening to what we play. Similarly, we synchronize ourselves with a partner in play who is willing to adjust, to contrast and to lead us on. Uexküll *et al.* (1997) describe these aspects as the 'subjectively perceived anatomy' (p.21) of a person whereby the physical body is not seen as a medical–biomechanical model but as a place of continuous dialogue of the body with itself and its surroundings. Proprioception, a kind of sixth sense, permits the body to recognize itself and to grasp automatically and precisely the positions and movements of all body parts, their mutual relations and their location in space. For joint improvisation in music therapy this implies that music is the audible inner dialogue of musicians with their own bodies, and also that music emerges from dialogue among musicians when they accompany and complement each other.

For people with multiple sclerosis, who suffer a loss of body perception and control because of sensory and visual disturbances as well as impaired coordination and movement, the chance to re-enter into dialogue – internally and externally – constitutes a significant relief. Aldridge (1999a) states that personal identity is formed like music – in performances. Comparable to an improvisation in music therapy, the biological form of human beings is continuously being created, that is, being brought into form. Unconscious physiological processes in the immune and nervous system, just like human communication, take place within a temporal context that follows musical rhythms. The core concept is to see individuals as 'symphonic beings', not 'mechanical beings', and to bear in mind that they 'are born as whole and creative beings' and have an inborn potential for health and wellbeing.

Aldridge (2001a) identifies a loss of emotional coherence as a core problem in neurodegenerative diseases, apart from loss of physical identity, and therefore speaks also of dialogic-degenerative diseases. He believes that multiple sclerosis patients feel a threat to their identity not so much through increasing impairment to active potential but rather because they have less and less coherence to actively counteract such limitations of action and communication. Appropriate therapies for such patients must comprise a variety of dialogue offers and must permit well-tuned responses to a wide range of human expressions because 'dialogue is an existential need in order to become healthy in the sense of becoming whole' (p.8). The temporal structure of music allows us to generate musical coherence in music therapy so that a sense of identity may be stimulated. Even if a patient is only able to produce sporadic sounds, the partner may provide continuous accompaniment and thus create a wider musical framework to which both musicians can feel they belong. Singing or playing, in whatever way, becomes part of a wider temporal context and thereby conveys a feeling of coherence.

If we combine the perspectives of Uexküll and Aldridge then we have a musical metaphor whereby the identity of an individual recreates itself continuously in dialogue with itself and others. Such a concept of a changing identity, that has to adapt to new conditions, fits the reality of the chronically ill person and lends itself to active music-making. Improvisation helps the patient to prepare for various possible changes due to the disease. A repertoire of strategies and residual abilities promote active coping with the situation as opposed to passive strategies like withdrawal and subsequent anxiety and depression or attempts to gain more control.

Patients find flexibility and new perspectives for activity, enhanced self-perception and possibilities for self-actualization, irrespective of their perceived deficits. These assumptions are validated in humanistic psychology and specifically in Rogers' personality theory. The individual actively strives to develop his or her personality and permanently tries to actualize and realize himself or herself (Rogers 1959). One of the core constructs is the 'self' (p.223) that in early childhood develops and differentiates from body perceptions on the one hand, and on the other as an organized whole in interaction with the environment; whereby the efforts of self-actualization lead us towards what may be described as growth, maturation and enhancement. If a disease threatens the self-structure, and there is a growing conflict between self-image and the image reflected from the environment, then those perceptions that threaten the structure are either denied, distorted or over-symbolized. Such 'distorted perceptions may increasingly restrict what we experience, and these restrictions again may aggravate or at least keep up the distortions' (Kriz 1994, p.208). We may safely assume that such processes of denial of the disease and its symptoms also happen to MS patients. If we add the immediate distortions of perception caused by MS in the form of misperceptions, sensory disturbances or motor impairments, and if we assume further restrictions as a consequence, then it appears appropriate to offer therapies with a marked experience character to these patients. A playful invention of music may curb the tendency to have one's perceptions distorted and restricted, since a person's individual abilities, ideas and potential become the basis for action, irrespective of any standards and scales. The patient may experiment in active music therapy without external pressures or doubts and is encouraged to set his or her own standards and to change them.

The improvement in self-acceptance reported by participants of the present study supports Rogers' assumption that the self continues to develop throughout life. Our re-creation of the self is stimulated and encouraged in all phases of life. For that reason, the perspective of the individual in music therapy plays a central role. His or her experience is less that of a static balance but rather an imbalance in musical interaction. This is due to the nature of improvisation, where participants play impromptu without knowing in advance who is going to do what, and what will be the final result. On the other hand, the temporal character of music makes music disappear as soon as it has sounded. These two aspects are possibly what gives music a decisive advantage in therapy. Music develops in unpredictable ways and knows no fixed rules; although a subsequent analysis and reflection of the sequence of musical impulses is possible, music remains dependent on the specific situation and the spontaneous acts of the people involved. Participants are permanently challenged to find an inner and outer balance that at a moment's notice may be upset again and require a new balance or complementation. Like jugglers, musicians toss their musical ideas up into the air, in the moment of impulse, and give them up immediately so that they can be passed on and changed in interaction before they come back or a new idea is thrown in. As a result, no one participant is in control of the musical development. The players pass the musical impulses around until some form of balance emerges. They move continuously between the poles of activity and rest, change and stability, renewal and consolidation, chaos and order. They are inundated by a permanent flow of mobilizing, unstable data that links up with their abilities and preferences but at the same time undermines familiar structures and stimulates combinations and self-organizing processes that produce new skills and experiences (Vieth-Fleischhauer and Petzold 1999).

Sociologists call such developmental steps 'emergences' (Fuchs-Heinritz *et al.* 1994; Martin and Drees 1999). They occur as effects of social acts when two people relate to each other and provoke an exchange of mutual responses that are not linear but unpredictable, new and incalculable, sustained by an independent will. Mutual interaction in improvisation produces spontaneous 'musical emergences' that become immediately audible as new abilities on the part of the participants. These developmental steps are integral elements of joint music-making. They introduce new qualities of experience and movement that may be felt subjectively but cannot be measured by any standards. As part of the contact development they cannot always be traced back in linear direction since they may either emerge in joint singing and playing or not. 'Musical emergences' are a positive stimulus to find an inner and outer balance. Iljine (1990) strives to provide such a stimulus for the participants of his therapeutic theatre performances through manifold sensory impressions like colours, smells, sounds and noises. He believes that therapy does not end with talking but 'enters into the co-creative play of senses and expression, offers [a] play to senses. Therapy needs intensity, needs a creative sphere, creative time, needs creative interpersonal contact, needs the aesthetic sphere of interpretation where creativity can be played out together' (p.220). Musicians do not become dependent on each other in this co-creative play in music therapy but develop a sense of uniqueness and autonomy. The transcription of an emerging improvisation into a musical score with one voice for each musician reveals their characteristics but also the way in which the individual voices complement each other, lead along or form contrasts and strengthen the role and position of each partner in the harmony of the music. People with multiple sclerosis are insecure as to self-perception; in musical improvisation they listen to themselves and their music, find orientation, position and definition, and this is a vital experience.

A synaesthetic experience

The human body is the interface for sensory perception and sensory expression. In active music therapy, the body is the instrument of perception and performance through which an individual may perceive himself or herself and become perceivable for others in joint music-making and singing. A therapy with this focus on sensory perception is based on an aesthetic understanding that human beings may 'perceive, feel or be aware through their senses' and receive an impression of themselves and the world through 'physical or sensory perception' (Pfeifer 1993, p.67). This addresses a level of experience and awareness established by the philosopher Baumgarten in 1750 as an independent 'science of sensory cognition' (Menke 1999, p.1) and a complement to the rational cognition of logical thinking prevailing in the eighteenth century. In singing or playing, we may be touched so immediately by our perceptions, feelings and memories that this physical reaction to our creative activity makes us aware, we recognize ourselves and come into sensory 'con-tact' with ourselves. An individual's entire inner wealth is externalized as a performed whole in the creative process (Aldridge 1996) and transcends the person and his or her existential needs (Scruton 1999).

It is not the created work of art that is the point in this process but the way in which an individual perceives and interprets the relation to his or her inner self in the creative moment (Ingarden 1968). Comparable to aesthetics as a 'science of sensory cognition' in the eighteenth century, music therapy complements traditional symptom-oriented interventions for people with MS. For the individuals concerned, the chance of a sensory access to their inner self appears imperative, specifically in view of their unnerving sensory impairments. The perception of self becomes tangible. What may be understood as impaired may also be satisfactory and complete.

The emotional context of active music therapy allows patients a wide range of sensory impressions and therefore a synaesthetic experience of self and of physical, mental and emotional wholeness. They can find a balance that cannot be trained in a mechanical–functional sense but organizes all their senses, guides their expressive potential to an inner stability and serenity and may be experienced and performed in the aesthetic sense as a 'being put together again'. The narrative quoted at the beginning of this chapter illustrates this well. With expressions like 'being torn apart' and 'being put together again', the woman describes her sense of identity and body perception, and changes in these caused by the improvisations. Music therapy is of essential significance in the process of coping with MS since a patient may influence developments through musical engagement and is stimulated to direct his or her attention towards current body perceptions and feelings.

It is not possible to arrest the progress of MS with active music therapy. However, strengthened individual and unique creative resources of a patient are possibly more important in coping with the disease than believed so far. The concept of phases in music therapy contact described in this chapter illustrates how people with MS may be supported in coping with the identity of chronic disease; musical dialogue provides time and space to discover and use their creative potential for life as individuals.

My results challenge the existing clinical practice where the short times in hospital make process-oriented relational therapy almost impossible. A creative therapy approach contributes to a better understanding of patients' needs and reveals that a comprehensive treatment concept cannot be based on functional considerations alone. The maintenance of social relations and networks should be encouraged at all stages and expanded by the offer of new contacts and relationships. This may counteract the vicious circle of stigmatization and social withdrawal. An offer of active musical improvisation with a focus on resources and not on symptoms that improves the psychic–emotional condition and acceptance of a permanently changing identity addresses the state of wellbeing and the remaining abilities of a patient and therefore is an essential factor of psychosocial care. Active music therapy is a meaningful complement to traditional therapeutic and medical concepts and procedures that is forward-looking and defined by a sense of purposeful activity.

CHAPTER 8

Music Therapy for People with Chronic Aphasia: A Controlled Study

Monika Jungblut

About 2400 people per one million inhabitants in Germany are estimated to survive a stroke each year. Up to 30 per cent of these suffer from aphasia, and about half of them will have an aphasia that will last for weeks, months or years, sometimes for the rest of their lives. With a total population of 80 million, about 24,000 people become impaired by aphasia as an after-effect of stroke each year (the incidence rate). The prevalence rate is about three times as high. If brain injuries, tumours and encephalitis are further added as causes of aphasia, then about 85,000 people are affected by aphasia in Germany at every given moment. The number is even higher if we also include senile diseases (Hartje and Poeck 2002).

The course of aphasias

Aphasias change over time (Leischner 1987). The most distinct and unpredictable changes occur during the first week after a stroke. Afterwards clinical syndromes become more stable. Authors agree that a chronic condition arises after 12 months at the latest. Intensive and deficit-specific speech therapy supports an improvement beyond spontaneous recovery; chronic aphasias are considered to be relatively recalcitrant to therapy (Hartje and Poeck 2002). However, this recalcitrance has been challenged (Gutzmann 1901; Leischner 1998; Taylor Sarno 1991) and an increasing number of researchers report that certain compensatory mechanisms are activated several years post-stroke (Karbe and Thiel 1998; Naeser and Palumbo 1998; Schlenck 1990).

It may be necessary then to revise the traditional view that activation patterns of the remaining speech areas in the left hemisphere (superior temporal cortex) indicate quick recovery, while activation patterns in the right hemisphere suggest incomplete compensation over longer periods. Patterns of reorganization are highly individual. Some patients use the remaining unimpaired areas of the left hemisphere but functional recovery may also include homologous speech areas of the right hemisphere to a greater extent than widely assumed (Risse and Gates 1997; Silvestrini and Troisi 1995; Thompson 2000).

The role of music therapy

Certain similarities between music and language recommend the use of musical components especially in the treatment of aphasia patients. Music and language both consist of melodic and rhythmic elements. Temporal structure, duration, rhythm, motor control and simultaneity are essential for processing in music and speech (Aldridge 1996).

Music therapy can play a valuable role in aphasia rehabilitation (Lucia 1987). Melodic intonation therapy (Naeser and Helm-Estabrooks 1985; O'Boyle and Sandford 1988) has used such musical elements to fulfil a rehabilitative role and involves embedding short propositional phrases into simple, often repeated, melody patterns accompanied by finger tapping. The inflection patterns, of pitch changes and rhythms of speech, are selected to parallel the natural speech prosody of the sentence. The singing of previously familiar songs encourages articulation, fluency and the shaping procedures of language which are akin to musical phrasing. In addition the stimulation of singing within a context of communication motivates the patient to communicate and, it is hypothesized, promotes the activation of intentional verbal behaviour. In infants the ability to reciprocate or compensate a partner's communicative response is an important element of communicative competence (Murray and Trevarthen 1986; Street and Cappella 1989) and vital in speech acquisition (Glenn and Cunningham 1984).

Music therapy strategies in adults may be used in a similar way with the expectation that they will stimulate those brain functions which support, precede and extend functional speech recovery – functions that are essentially musical and rely upon brain plasticity. Combined with the ability to enhance word retrieval, music can also be used to improve breath capacity, encourage respiration–phonation patterns, correct articulation errors caused by inappropriate rhythm or speed, and prepare the patient for articulatory movements. In this sense music offers a sense of time that is not chronological, which is fugitive to measurement and vital for the coordination of human communication (Aldridge 1991a, 1996, 2000a; Aldridge and Brandt 1991).

Jacome (1984) tells of a stroke patient who was dysfluent and had difficulty finding words. Yet:

> he frequently whistled instead of attempting to answer with phonemes...he spontaneously sang Spanish songs without prompting with excellent pitch, melody, rhythm, lyrics and emotional intonation. He could tap, hum, whistle and sing along... Emotional intonation of speech (prosody), spontaneous facial emotional expression, gesturing and pantomimia were exaggerated. (p.309)

From this case study Jacome goes on to recommend that singing and musicality in aphasics be tested by clinicians, a point also recommended by Morgan and Tillduckdharry (1982) in terms of aphasia following stroke.

Evidence of the global strategy of music processing in the brain is found in the clinical literature. In two cases of aphasia (Morgan and Tillduckdharry 1982), singing is seen as a welcome release from the helplessness of being a patient. The authors hypothesize that singing is a means to communicate thoughts externally. Although the 'newer aspect' of speech is lost, the older function of music is retained possibly because music is a function distributed over both hemispheres. Berman (1981) suggests that recovery from aphasia is not a matter of new learning by the non-dominant hemisphere but a taking over of responsibility for language by that hemisphere. The non-dominant hemisphere may be a reserve of functions in case of regional failure, indicating an overall brain plasticity (Naeser and Helm-Estabrooks 1985; Naeser and Palumbo 1998), and language functions may shift with multilinguals as compared with monolinguals (Karanth and Rangamani 1988) or as a result of learning and cultural exposure where music and language share common properties.

Those who are dealing with aphasia, whether patients, relatives or therapists, know that processes of planning, programming and motor control executed automatically become impaired. It is very difficult for a sufferer to concentrate on speech articulation, keep in mind the intended sentence, and simultaneously prepare the next utterance. Parallel processing, a characteristic feature of our entire cerebral activity, represents a tremendous task for aphasics as a problem requiring 'divided attention' (Erickson and Goldinger 1996).

Timing

When working with patients suffering with aphasia, we hear that speech rhythm and syllable stress have 'lost the beat', unstressed syllables are left out, sometimes the pause pattern is completely destroyed – there is a fundamental timing deficit. One explanation for these problems is that components involved in the processing of timing parameters are essentially controlled by the left hemisphere (Berthold 1983; Bradshaw 1989; Gates and Bradshaw 1977; Joseph 1988; Robinson and

Solomon 1974). This is why parameters referring to timing are often affected by aphasia; hence, the potential of music therapy to rehabilitate that timing.

Studies into the motor rehabilitation of patients suffering from gait disturbance as a consequence of stroke, Parkinson's disease or Huntington's disease report improved synchronization processes through rhythmic–auditive stimulation. The timing of motor coordination is facilitated, so movements become more fluent and even (Thaut and Miltner 1996; Thaut et al. 1996; Thaut et al. 1999). Rhythmic exercises are also applied in the therapy of speech apraxia in particular, for a synchronization of articulatory movements and computer-generated signals (Brendel and Ziegler 2001; Brendel, Ziegler and Deger 2000).

In the 1970s, the Bostonian school of aphasia researchers created a method called melodic intonation therapy (MIT) that uses musical elements in the treatment of aphasia patients (Albert, Sparks and Helm 1973; Sparks, Helm and Albert 1974; Sparks and Holland 1976; Sparks, Deck and Deck 1986). It is based on the phenomenon that even severely impaired aphasia patients are able to *sing* well-known songs, even if they cannot speak a single word deliberately. The singing voice becomes the focus of attention in this therapy. Melodic intonation therapy uses the dominance of the right hemisphere for melodic and emotional components of speech. Perception and control of non-verbal components are processed in the right hemisphere, which is essential for timbre, body language and facial expression, and also for expressivity, sound and melody of speech. Components like intonation and melodic contour are highly significant in this context (O'Boyle and Sandford 1988; Peretz 1990; Zatorre 1984). These melodic components of speech are mostly preserved in aphasic patients. Access to the musical structures of the right hemisphere described above in the form of songs or melodies function like a 'detour mechanism' providing the foundation for music therapy interventions in the treatment of aphasia patients.

Hemispheric processing of musical material follows the same strategies as cognitive processing in general, at least in non-musicians. The left hemisphere processes music analytically, in sequence, whereas the right processes music rather globally as sound gestalt. An active exchange takes place between the two hemispheres via the corpus callosum, so that laterality in music processing is a dynamic process, and to a great extent a 'process-specific rather than a material-specific phenomenon' (Bradshaw 1989, p.97).

An activation of these right-hemisphere language functions seems to be very important in recovery from aphasia and therefore offers a decisive starting point for music therapy intervention as well. Compared to language, music as the phylogenetically older function is processed by both hemispheres; specific music therapy interventions may reactivate remaining speech functions in the right hemisphere, and also speech-related areas of the left hemisphere, depending on the specific musical parameters chosen in each case.

As described above, temporal structure, duration, simultaneity, rhythm, motor control, intonation, melody and timbre are essential elements in both music and language. The human voice provides an 'instrument' to express these structural elements in music and language. If music and language are combined by the human voice, then we can say that singing is language set in music (Figure 8.1). Singing has a bridging function (Jossmann 1927; Ustvedt 1937): the left hemisphere controls temporal impulses and the right hemisphere intervenes subsequently and modulates the pitch. Singing, therefore, is an activity involving both hemispheres, not least because it combines words with melody (Crowder, Serafine and Repp 1990; Samson and Zatorre 1991).

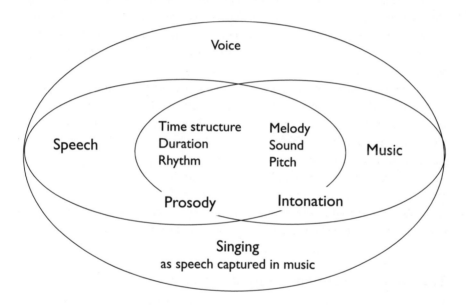

Figure 8.1 Singing as language set in music

Intonation and prosody

If we proceed from singing towards speech, then the next stage would be intonation followed by prosody, which is nearer to speech. The transition from intonation to prosody is an essential aspect of aphasia therapy, since 'prosody appears to be a multifaceted process which is not organized in the same manner as other aspects of speech and language' (Dykstra, Gandour and Stark 1995, p.474). Prosody also seems to be a bihemispheric activity since it describes temporal as well as melodic elements.

Recent studies have shown that prosodic structures facilitate recognition and availability of other linguistic structures (namely, from word to sentence level) (Lindfield, Wingfield and Goodglass 1999; Speer, Kjelgaard and Dobroth 1996). Compared to controls, aphasics show much greater comprehension for emphatically stated sentences than for those without stress. This means that due to their semantic deficit they learn to pay more attention to prosodic cues (Kimelman and McNeil 1987; cited in Langenmayr 1997).

Melodic contour in music, and intonation in language, share common cognitive and neural processing strategies, in addition to parallel processes at the levels of motor, imaginative and emotional processing. While we speak because we have content to convey to another, that content must be conveyed in a context of understanding; it is not simply what we say, but the way that we say it.

The human voice is the basis of speech. Vocalization is not an acquired skill – like speech – but constitutes an instinctive and congenital function that has to be assessed in its close relation with the older parts of the brain. Contact with and use of the singing voice are among our earliest experiences and might touch the deepest realms of our personality (Rittner 1990).

Singing together conveys a sense of community and belonging and evokes an atmosphere where inhibitions may be shed. This feeling of connectedness in singing contrasts with the experience of speaking, where aphasia sufferers very often feel separated from others because of their impairment. The lives of many patients are changed from one moment to the next. They undergo a loss of structure, order and orientation. To those patients, in particular, the possibility of returning to singing as a resource can be a tremendous support.

Aphasia in the widest sense means a 'fluency deficit'. The use of the singing voice can be a way to get back to flowing what has 'lost the beat' or has 'got stuck'.

The SIPARI treatment method: a study

The focus of this study is on music therapy with aphasia patients who suffered strokes years ago and who have to cope with the consequences, either alone or, ideally, with the support of relatives. Up to now there have been almost no concepts, nor facilities, for the long-term rehabilitation of aphasia sufferers. Health insurers and social institutions concentrate on early rehabilitation because professional integration is their main concern. But what about all those patients who have exhausted the conventional rehabilitation plans, who are too impaired, too old in many cases, and cannot stand up for themselves precisely because of their impaired expressive skills? In the late stages of rehabilitation, efforts to improve a patient's condition are tedious and often lengthy. However, the studies mentioned above about compensatory mechanisms becoming reactivated years after the event suggest treatment plans that can combine resource-oriented and training-centred music therapy interventions.

This is why a treatment method – SIPARI – was designed based on an impairment-related use of the human voice. It is applied in its various tonal qualities, ranging from Singing to Intonation to speech-adequate Prosody, and involves concentrated breathing. The focus is on an Activation of the remaining right-hemispheric speech abilities in aphasia patients. In addition there are Rhythmic exercises to encourage phonological and segmental capacities of the left hemisphere, in particular. Improvisations are used in the form of musical role plays and associative improvisations, on the basis of a holistic perspective that incorporates linguistic–cognitive as well as socio-emotional learning processes.

The purpose of the study to be described below was to assess the efficacy of the method in the treatment of patients suffering from global aphasia and Broca's aphasia in comparison with a control group with no treatment. The hypotheses presented were:

1.   there would be significant improvements in expressive linguistic skills as shown by improved score on the Aachen Aphasia Test overall profile in the treatment group

2.   the treatment method would encourage specific improvements in those subdomains responsible for linguistic expression.

THE PATIENTS

Seventeen patients were recruited over a period of six months in cooperation with the Aphasiker-Zentrum NRW e.V. (Aphasia Centre, North Rhein Westphalia) and self-help groups in Duisburg, Mülheim and Essen, Germany. Nine test persons with apoplectic insults in the left hemisphere were examined (4 female, 5 male), in addition to eight controls (4 female, 4 male). All patients were right-handed. The duration of aphasia the patients examined was between 4 and 26 years (mean 11.5 years). Criteria for inclusion in the trial were that they had suffered with a chronic aphasia with a duration of more than four years; had a non-fluent aphasia (global aphasia or Broca's aphasia); would partake in no speech therapy for the duration of the study; and would consent to participating.

THE METHOD

The instrument used for assessment in this study was the Aachen Aphasia Test. This is the best-known psychometric standardized procedure for aphasia diagnosis designed specifically for the German language. It is applied repeatedly over time to assess the efficacy of speech therapy interventions and is a recognized standard measure (Table 8.1). Three independent and experienced testers performed the test with all subjects in a comprehensive pre/post test design and detailed linguistic data were recorded for each subject.

Table 8.1 Aachen Aphasia Test subscales

AAT-Test sections	Structure	Points Per scale/ item	Total
1. Spontaneous speech	6 scales	0–5	
2. Token test	5 sections with 10 items	1/0	50–0[1]
3. Repetition	5 sections with 10 items	0–3	0–150
4. Written language	3 sections with 10 items	0–3	0–90
5. Naming	4 sections with 10 items	0–3	0–120
6. Comprehension	4 sections with 10 items	0–3	0–120

Duration: 60–90 minutes, evaluation *c.* 60 minutes
[1] The token test measures errors; therefore a lower score indicates a better result.

PROCEDURE

Participants were informed in writing of the purpose and procedures of the study. Patients with impaired comprehension of written language or suffering from alexia received a verbal explanation. The Duisburg self-help group provided a room for group therapies; single therapy sessions took place at patients' homes.

In the case of two patients (1 test person, 1 control) it was not possible to include their data in the official data collection since they were not identified unequivocally as non-fluent aphasics, despite evidence of non-fluent spontaneous speech. The data of two further controls were not included as a consequence of serious illness in the period under consideration. Table 8.2 and Figure 8.2 summarize the characteristics of the groups.

Rhythmic–melodic voice training on the basis of the music therapy SIPARI method was offered over a period of seven months. All eight test persons attended 20 group sessions of music therapy once a week. Each session lasted 60 minutes. In addition, all test persons received 10 single therapy sessions (60 minutes per week over the last three months of the therapy). All test persons had a music therapy exercise CD available with training sequences from therapy sessions; this was updated continuously. Each session was based on training exercises and the patient could then take the CD home and practise.

Table 8.2 Group comparisons at entry:
age and duration of aphasia in years

Treatment	N		Mean	Std. deviation	Std. error mean
Therapy	8	Age	63.75	7.7413546	2.7369822
		Duration	11.50	6.4142698	2.2677868
Control	5	Age	68.40	4.5055521	2.0149442
		Duration	14.00	7.8421936	3.5071356

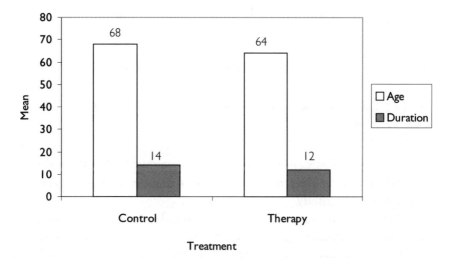

Figure 8.2 Group comparisons at entry: age and duration of aphasia in years

RESULTS

A Mann–Whitney U test was conducted to investigate the hypothesis that aphasia patients, when treated with this music therapy intervention, would improve their expressive linguistic skills as an overall profile score on the Aachen Aphasia Test. The results of the test were in the expected direction and significant ($z = -2.932$, $p < 0.005$). The music therapy group had an average rank of 9.50, while the control group had an average rank of 3.00. Figure 8.3 shows the distribution of the total scores on the test for the test profile; see also Table 8.3 for the statistics.

A secondary hypothesis was that specific expressive language abilities would be enhanced. We see this in the subdomain scores for repetition ($z = -1.984$, $p < 0.05$). The music therapy group had an average rank of 8.69, while the control group had an average rank of 4.30 (see Table 8.3).

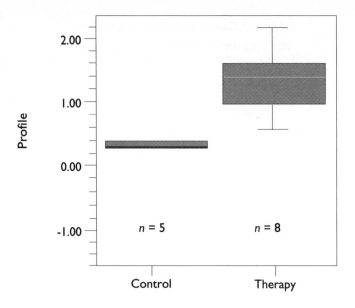

Figure 8.3 Distribution of Aachen Aphasia Test profile scores for the music therapy treatment group and the control group

Both our hypotheses were confirmed. We can see this graphically in Figure 8.4 where there are clear differences between the profile score changes, repetition, and articulation and prosody.

However, if we scrutinize a subset of the data and compare the patients suffering with Broca's aphasia, then we see another factor emerging in the argument: articulation and prosody. There were four patients in each group (Table 8.4).

A Mann–Whitney U test was conducted to investigate the hypothesis that Broca aphasia patients, when treated with this music therapy intervention, would improve their expressive linguistic skills as an overall profile score on the Aachen Aphasia Test. The results were in the expected direction and significant ($z = -2.323, p < 0.05$). The music therapy group had an average rank of 6.50, while the control group had an average rank of 2.50. When specific expressive language abilities are considered, we see an improvement for repetition ($z = -2.323, p < 0.05$) and for articulation and prosody ($z = -2.049, p < 0.05$).

For both groups there were significant changes in the Aachen Aphasia Test profile that can also be recognized in the subscales of repetition, and articulation and prosody (see Figure 8.4).

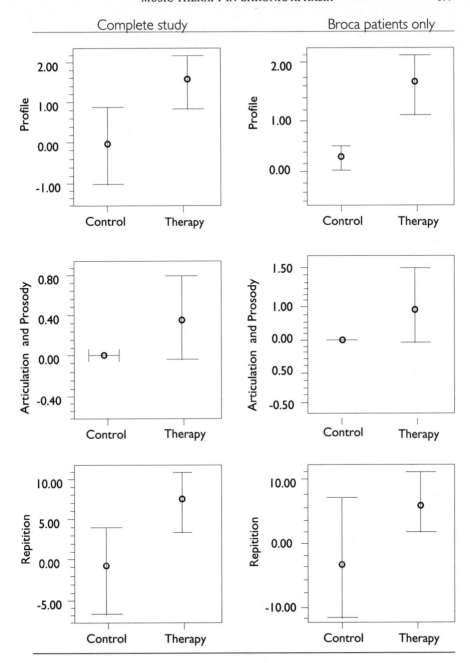

Therapy: *n* = 8 Control: *n* = 5   Therapy: *n* = 4 Control: *n* = 4
Error bars at confidence interval 95%; group means included by vertical error bars

Figure 8.4 Error bar charts and means for comparison changes in the principal variables of the complete study population and selected Broca group alone

Table 8.3. Mann–Whitney U test for the Aachen Aphasia Test profile, and subset scores, for the complete study population with the grouping variable *Treatment*

Descriptive Statistics

	N	Mean	Std. deviation	Minimum	Maximum
Spontaneous speech					
Communicative behavior	13	0.0769	0.27735	0.00	1.00
Articulation and prosody	13	0.2308	0.43853	0.00	1.00
Automated speech	13	0.0769	0.27735	0.00	1.00
Semantic structure	13	0.1538	0.55470	-1.00	1.00
Phonematic structure	13	0.2308	0.72501	-1.00	2.00
Syntax structure	13	0.0000	0.81650	-1.00	2.00
Token test	13	-1.3846	3.35506	-8.00	5.00
Repetition	13	2.3077	6.87246	-11.00	12.00
Written language	13	0.3077	4.57137	-8.00	8.00
Naming	13	5.9231	10.64943	-7.00	29.00
Comprehension	13	1.5385	3.47887	-3.00	6.00
Auditory understanding	13	3.0769	3.22649	-3.00	9.00
Reading understanding	13	-1.5385	4.11532	-12.00	3.00
Profile	13	0.7600	0.91711	-1.46	2.18

Ranks

	Treatment	N	Mean rank	Sum of ranks
Spontaneous speech				
Communicative behavior	Music therapy	8	7.31	58.50
	Control	5	6.50	32.50
Articulation and prosody	Music therapy	8	7.94	63.50
	Control	5	5.50	27.50
Automated speech	Music therapy	8	7.31	58.50
	Control	5	6.50	32.50
Semantic structure	Music therapy	8	8.25	66.00
	Control	5	5.00	25.00
Phonematic structure	Music therapy	8	8.25	66.00
	Control	5	5.00	25.00
Syntax structure	Music therapy	8	8.06	64.50
	Control	5	5.30	26.50
Token test	Music therapy	8	6.25	50.00
	Control	5	8.20	41.00
Repetition	Music therapy	8	8.69	69.50
	Control	5	4.30	21.50
Written language	Music therapy	8	8.19	65.50
	Control	5	5.10	25.50
Naming	Music therapy	8	7.81	62.50
	Control	5	5.70	28.50
Comprehension	Music therapy	8	8.44	67.50
	Control	5	4.70	23.50
Auditory understanding	Music therapy	8	8.50	68.00
	Control	5	4.60	23.00
Reading understanding	Music therapy	8	7.25	58.00
	Control	5	6.60	33.00
Profile	Music therapy	8	9.50	76.00
	Control	5	3.00	15.00

Continued on next page

Table 8.3 continued

Test Statistics Grouping Variable

	Communicative behaviour	Articulation and prosody	Automated speech	Semantic structure	Phonematic structure	Syntax structure	Token test
Mann–Whitney U	17.500	12.500	17.500	10.000	10.000	11.500	14.000
Wilcoxon W	32.500	27.500	32.500	25.000	25.000	26.500	50.000
Z	-0.791	-1.500	-0.791	-1.803	-1.792	-1.429	-0.896
Asymp. Sig. (2-tailed)	0.429	0.134	0.429	0.071	0.073	0.153	0.370
Exact Sig. [2*(1-tailed Sig.)]	0.724	0.284	0.724	0.171	0.171	0.222	0.435

	Repetition	Written language	Naming	Comprehension	Auditory understanding	Reading understanding	Aachen Aphasia Test profile
Mann–Whitney U	6.500	10.500	13.500	8.500	8.000	18.000	0.000
Wilcoxon W	21.500	25.500	28.500	23.500	23.000	33.000	15.000
Z	-1.984	-1.408	-0.955	-1.700	-1.784	-0.296	-2.932
Asymp. Sig. (2-tailed)	0.047	0.159	0.339	0.089	0.074	0.768	0.003
Exact Sig. [2*(1-tailed Sig.)]	0.045	0.171	0.354	0.093	0.093	0.833	0.002

Table 8.4 Mann–Whitney U test for the Aachen Aphasia Test profile, and subset scores, for the Broca patients with the grouping variable *Treatment*

Descriptive Statistics

	N	Mean	Std. deviation	Minimum	Maximum
Spontaneous speech					
Communicative behavior	8	0.1250	0.35355	0.00	1.00
Articulation and prosody	8	0.3750	0.51755	0.00	1.00
Automated speech	8	0.0000	0.00000	0.00	0.00
Semantic structure	8	0.0000	0.53452	-1.00	1.00
Phonematic structure	8	0.1250	0.64087	-1.00	1.00
Syntax structure	8	-0.1250	0.99103	-1.00	2.00
Token test	8	-0.5000	3.25137	-5.00	5.00
Repetition	8	2.2500	7.06602	-11.00	12.00
Written language	8	-0.3750	5.82942	-8.00	8.00
Naming	8	5.7500	9.88144	-1.00	29.00
Comprehension	8	1.8750	3.48210	-2.00	6.00
Auditory understanding	8	2.1250	2.64237	-3.00	5.00
Reading understanding	8	-0.2500	2.91548	-6.00	3.00
Profile	8	0.8537	0.73971	0.16	2.18

Continued on next page

Table 8.4 continued

Ranks

	Treatment	N	Mean rank	Sum of ranks
Spontaneous speech				
Communicative behavior	Music therapy	4	5.00	20.00
	Control	4	4.00	16.00
Articulation and prosody	Music therapy	4	6.00	24.00
	Control	4	3.00	12.00
Automated speech	Music therapy	4	4.50	18.00
	Control	4	4.50	18.00
Semantic structure	Music therapy	4	5.38	21.50
	Control	4	3.63	14.50
Phonematic structure	Music therapy	4	5.75	23.00
	Control	4	3.25	13.00
Syntax structure	Music therapy	4	5.25	21.00
	Control	4	3.75	15.00
Token test	Music therapy	4	4.50	18.00
	Control	4	4.50	18.00
Repetition	Music therapy	4	6.50	26.00
	Control	4	2.50	10.00
Written language	Music therapy	4	4.50	18.00
	Control	4	4.50	18.00
Naming	Music therapy	4	4.50	18.00
	Control	4	4.50	18.00
Comprehension	Music therapy	4	5.88	23.50
	Control	4	3.13	12.50
Auditory understanding	Music therapy	4	5.00	20.00
	Control	4	4.00	16.00
Reading understanding	Music therapy	4	5.00	20.00
	Control	4	4.00	16.00
Profile	Music therapy	4	6.50	26.00
	Control	4	2.50	10.00

Test Statistics Treatment: Grouping Variable

	Communicative behavior	Articulation and prosody	Automated speech	Semantic structure	Phonematic structure	Syntax structure	Token test
Mann–Whitney U	6.000	2.000	8.000	4.500	3.000	5.000	8.000
Wilcoxon W	16.000	12.000	18.000	14.500	13.000	15.000	18.000
Z	-1.000	-2.049	0.000	-1.323	-1.667	-0.949	0.000
Asymp. Sig. (2-tailed)	0.317	0.040	1.000	0.186	0.096	0.343	1.000
Exact Sig. [2*(1-tailed Sig.)]	0.686	0.114	1.000	0.343	0.200	0.486	1.000

	Repetition	Written language	Naming	Comprehension	Auditory understanding	Reading understanding	Aachen Aphasia Test profile
Mann–Whitney U	0.000	8.000	8.000	2.500	6.000	6.000	0.000
Wilcoxon W	10.000	18.000	18.000	12.500	16.000	16.000	10.000
Z	-2.323	0.000	0.000	-1.617	-0.584	-0.584	-2.323
Asymp. Sig. (2-tailed)	0.020	1.000	1.000	0.106	0.559	0.559	0.020
Exact Sig. [2*(1-tailed Sig.)]	0.029	1.000	1.000	0.114	0.686	0.686	0.029

Although this is a small-scale study, we see in Table 8.5 that the effect size comparison for the complete study is large (Cohen's $d = 2.04$) at acceptable confidence levels ($\alpha < 0.05$, power $1 - \beta > 0.95$) such that we can say that this is a clinically significant treatment approach. The same positive result applies to a comparison of the matched patients from the treatment and control group suffering with Broca's aphasia (Cohen's $d = 2.7627$, $r = 0.81$, $\alpha < 0.05$, power $1 - \beta > 0.95$).

Table 8.5 Effect size comparisons and descriptive statistics for the complete study group

Aachen Aphasia Test complete study	Descriptive statistics			Effect size statistics			
	N	Mean statistic	Std. deviation	Cohen's d *	Effect-size r *	Alpha **	Power (1-)beta **
Study group complete	8	1.2838	0.52882	2.04	0.71	0.05	0.96
Control group complete	5	0.0780	0.77937				
Broca treatment group	4	1.44	0.58833	2.76	0.81	0.05	0.96
Broca control group	4	0.2675	0.11871				

Effect size conventions:
d small 0.20, medium 0.50, large 0.80; r small 0.10, medium 0.30, large 0.50
* calculated from http://www.uccs.edu/~lbecker/psy590/escalc3.htm
** calculated with G*Power http://www.psycho.uni-duesseldorf.de/aap/projects/gpower/

Discussion

The test measurements, when assessed by three external testers, reveal that the SIPARI method brings about significant improvements in speech ability in 75 per cent of the chronic aphasia patients treated. More than 62 per cent of treated persons achieved an improvement of at least 12 per cent in at least one subtest. In contrast, the speech abilities of the untreated control group remained almost unchanged.

The mean profile increase among the test group is above the critical difference considered statistically significant required by the Aachen Aphasia Test to demonstrate clinical change. As four Broca's aphasia patients each formed part of both the test group and the control group, an evaluation was performed to compare this specific aphasia. A comparison of both groups also reveals a mean profile increase surpassing the expectations of statistical significance (Table 8.6; see also Figure 8.4).

The significant improvements in test persons were achieved mainly in those subtests that focused on expressive linguistic performance; that is, in *spontaneous speech* 'articulation and prosody' and in *repetition*. Consequently, the first hypothesis assuming an improvement of expressive linguistic abilities through music-related interventions is substantiated. An improvement in auditive *comprehension* for the entire group appears to be a basis for significant improvements in repetition, since *repetition* requires auditive processing. These findings confirm reports from linguistic research that mainly underline the role of prosody in linguistic comprehension (Besson and Friederici 1998; Cutler, Dahan and van Donselaar 1997; Gerken 1996; Levelt 1989; Pell 1997; Speer *et al.* 1996). If we scrutinize the test scores further, then we see this relationship reflected in the correlation scores (see Table 8.6).

A remarkable finding is the good performance in repetition, and specifically naming, in the group of global aphasics on the level of more complex stimuli. On the one hand, designation requires a more comprehensive activation of speech-systematic processes, and on the other hand more complex stimuli obviously require increased cognitive performance like working memory. Another striking improvement is for those suffering with global aphasia in the token test (mean: 6.75 point rate) and in auditory comprehension, which also suggests an improvement in cognitive skills.

These results challenge speech therapy studies where the chances for improvement in chronic global aphasia are considered as being extremely small (Basso, Capitani and Vignolo 1979; Kirshner 1995). It is possible that music therapy interventions stimulate mechanisms that influence memory performance. Cognitive performance may be improved through specific rhythmic classification exercises in combination with the use of tonal memories through a specific application of melodic elements. We need further studies to confirm this. David Aldridge has suggested that music provides a time structure that enhances memory by linking events together, and repetition would fit this hypothesis (see Table 8.5). In addition, the specific music-related interventions described above appear to influence speech impairments positively, thus confirming the second hypothesis.

The group of Broca's aphasia patients showed remarkable improvements on the description level of articulation and prosody. These findings confirm reports from other therapies, but we must keep in mind that other studies were in different settings where no standardized tests were applied (Bruijn and Hurkmans 2002; Cohen 1992; Cohen and Ford 1995; Cohen and Masse 1993; Lucia 1987).

Table 8.6 Correlation matrix for the subsection scores and their relevance for the treatment profile in both the complete study group and for the Broca patients' subgroup

Correlations Spearman's *rho* for complete study group n =13

	Phonematic structure	Auditory understanding	Articulation and prosody	Comprehension	Repetition	Profile	Treatment
Phonematic structure	1.000	0.246	0.149	0.224	0.574*	0.475	-0.517*
Auditory understanding	0.246	1.000	0.050	0.134	0.169	0.522*	-0.515*
Articulation and prosody	0.149	0.050	1.000	0.641**	0.465	0.464	-0.433
Comprehension	0.224	0.134	0.641**	1.000	0.279	0.306	-0.419*
Repetition	0.574*	0.169	0.465	0.279	1.000	0.649**	-0.573*
Profile	0.475	0.522*	0.464	0.306	0.649**	1.000	-0.846**
Treatment	-0.517*	-0.515*	-0.433	-0.419*	-0.573*	-0.846*	1.00

Correlations Spearman's *rho* for Broca subset n = 8

	Phonematic structure	Auditory understanding	Articulation and prosody	Comprehension	Repetition	Profile	Treatment
Phonematic structure	1.000	0.403	0.260	-0.007	0.484	0.678*	-0.630*
Auditory understanding	0.403	1.000	0.399	0.331	0.115	0.291	-0.221
Articulation and prosody	0.260	0.399	1.000	0.803**	0.737*	0.680*	-0.775*
Comprehension	-0.007	0.331	0.803**	1.000	0.524	0.396	-0.611
Repetition	0.484	0.115	0.737*	0.524	1.000	0.843**	-0.878**
Profile	0.678*	0.291	0.680*	0.396	0.843**	1.000	-0.878**
Treatment	-0.630*	-0.221	-0.775*	-0.611	-0.878**	-0.878**	1.000

* Correlation is significant at the 0.05 level (1-tailed)
** Correlation is significant at the 0.01 level (1-tailed)

Specific rhythmic–melodic synchronization exercises involving the singing voice appear to have a positive influence on the *phonematic structure* of spontaneous speech as well. The phonematic level is also concerned with the sequential order of sounds; this is why this musical intervention may have had an influence where articulatory motor movements are synchronized with external timers in singing. The relevant linguistic findings confirm this and we see this relationship reflected in the correlation scores (see Table 8.5). One of the external raters comments: 'Improvements may be due to the fact that the patient is more successful in mastering phonological and speech apraxia-related tasks and in producing target words with only minor phonematic errors spontaneously and without delay.' Another report records a 'tendency towards more attempts of deliberate speech production and less stereotypical speech parts'.

A similar approach to the method used here with speech apraxia patients, but without the singing voice, is described by Brendel and Ziegler (2001) but their study does not contain a comparable test evaluation.

One rater commented: 'The patient now assumes distinctly longer turns and uses complex syntax more often and with more success.' This assessment suggests that systematic exercises with complex rhythmic groupings in combination with pertinent melodic phrases have a positive effect on the level not only of sounds and words, but also of sentences. The patient referred to showed significant improvements on the description level of *syntax structure.*

In conclusion

This study comprised a very small group of test persons and controls, but as we can see from the effect size score this is a treatment worth implementing. The significant profile increase for the entire test group indicates a clinically successful application of the SIPARI method.

We can argue that a larger-scale clinical study is necessary. However, an imaging study would substantiate the assumption that the use of the human voice with its possibilities to change the significance of different acoustic components – in accordance with the method described above – supports and influences a variety of reactivation patterns. The positron emission test (PET) results reported by Belin and Van Eckhout (1996) appear to confirm this assumption. This present study may serve to ensure more attention for the late stages of long-term rehabilitation. It is my opinion that this constitutes not only an objective for social and human considerations but also a challenge for therapists and researchers alike.

CHAPTER 9

Traditional Oriental Music Therapy in Neurological Rehabilitation

Gerhard Tucek

This chapter has twin aims. One is to address historical concepts of traditional oriental music therapy. The other is to present examples from music therapy practice with patients suffering from severe traumatic brain injury (TBI) that relate to this background. Since the focus of my deliberations will be on the current clinical application of traditional oriental music therapy, any historical aspects of this music therapy will be described only insofar as they appear relevant to an understanding of the argument.[1] A central point of my reflections will be the possibility that the 'maqamat' (tonalities) of this musical source material have a 'general effect' therapeutically and are culturally independent, as postulated by some members of the traditional oriental music therapy community.

Music therapy: from its origins to current issues

Traditional oriental music therapy has Islamic roots. In a way, Islamic culture is a 'culture of listening'. Nobody reacts with more enthusiasm than Muslims to the melodious sound of the divine word. This applies particularly to the Islamic mystics (Sufis). They experienced that inner tremor described by André Breton as follows: 'beauty will either be like a "tremor" or it will not be…' (Breton; cited in Kermani 2003, p.165).

According to Kermani (p.371), this susceptibility to the transcendent beauty of recitations from the Koran is behind the specific response of orientals to any type of musical and linguistic utterances. Although a strict distinction is made

---

1   For background to historic concepts see Tucek (1995, 1997, 2000, 2003).

between musical Koran recitation and secular musical performance, the great recitors of the Koran with their talent for complex 'maqam' improvisation also inspired the development of classical art music.

The age-old ambivalent relation between Koran recitation and music that existed from the beginnings of the Islamic culture is illustrated well by an anecdote passed on by Ibn Abd Rabbih about a man who is arrested for singing aloud in a mosque and is thereby giving offence. Fortunately, a noble Kuraischit is present in the mosque to say his prayers at that time and he goes to the police insisting that the accused has done nothing but recite from the Koran. The misunderstanding is explained, the arrested man is released. Back in the street, the noble man says to the sinner: 'If you had not sung so well, I would not have protected you' (Kermani 2003).

In the middle ages the Koran, in addition to being a religious text, also provided opportunity for vocal training to secular singers of both genders, despite many reservations. Recitations unfolded their deep-reaching effect not only through content but even more through the sensual and emotional listening experience. In Sufism, this susceptibility to all sound finally reached a degree of refinement that we can hardly understand today.

This delight in 'beautiful sound' in the Islamic culture stimulated the emergence of one of the oldest types of music therapies recorded in writing. Curative effects of music were interpreted in a metaphysical sense as an echo of the original divine sound, but also attributed to a highly differentiated effect of the microtonal system that is 'maqamat' (for details see Tucek 2003; Tucek, Auer-Pekarsky and Stepansky 2001).

Even if narratives on the magical effect of music and singing may appear to have legendary exaggerations today, it is appropriate nevertheless to assess the core statement of the direct impact that sound has on living beings. The following story illustrates that this impact is not limited to humans:

> In the tent I saw a negro slave in chains, and in front of the living quarters I saw dead camels. I saw an emaciated camel that appeared to be dying. The chained slave told me: 'You are the guest of my master tonight, and you are dear to him. Intercede for me that he may remove my chains. He will not turn you down.' When food was placed before me, I refused to eat. This was very painful to my host. To his question I answered: 'I shall eat only when you have forgiven this slave for my sake, and when you have removed his shackles.' 'Oh,' he answered, 'this slave has made me poor and has ruined all my possessions and caused damage to me and my family.' I asked what he had done. He said: 'This slave has a lovely voice. I lived from these camels. But he loaded them with heavy burdens and urged them on with his singing so that they covered a distance of three days in one night, so beautiful was his singing when he drove them. When they arrived here and were unloaded, they died, with the exception of this one camel. But you are my guest. For your

sake, and in your honour, I shall forgive him.' Then he removed the shackles, and we had our meal. In the morning, however, I wished to hear his voice. So he bade him sing to a camel that was used to draw water up from a well there. The slave went and began to urge the camel on, and to sing. But as soon as he raised his voice the camel was beside itself and broke away from its ropes. I fell down on my face. I do not think I ever heard a more beautiful voice than his. His owner screamed and said: 'Man, what do you want? You have ruined my camel. Leave!' (As-Sarrag, and Abu Nasr 1990, p.393).

Canon of methods

The concept of current clinical traditional music therapy is based on an integration of various different methods: receptive tonality, as specific listening to music; musical improvisation; active music-making (patient and therapist together); imaginative techniques; movement exercises for concentration; and guided, or free, improvisation of music, movement and dance. In this chapter, patients with severest traumatic brain injuries receive only therapy interventions appropriate to their condition. It is not possible to address verbal–cognitive abilities in these patients in early stages of remission. Figure 9.1 gives a synopsis of current therapy objectives, methods and therapy attitudes.

The concept of 'maqam' music: immanent in culture or genetic?

Historical documents on music therapy from the middle ages describe the structure of 'maqamat' as a healing agent. The therapeutic effects of personal relations appear only implicitly – in the sense of the 'teaching physician'. However, the predominant approach of Islam does not permit a strict separation between scientific and religious arguments. This is so even today. That is why both aspects will be addressed in the following paragraphs.

If we look at these historical sources today, we have to keep several aspects in mind. The notion of an emotion- and organ-specific description of the effects of 'maqamat' that has remained unchanged over 900 years is not correct. In the course of musical history there have been several different codices with diverging assertions on 'maqam' effects. But the general idea of specific medical effects of music has remained consistent for centuries. When making a culture-specific reception of 'maqam' music we have to take into account that, in a country like Egypt, a Koran recitation by a renowned singer is not just a religious event. In traditional Arabic societies such a recitation is an important artistic performance and attracts Christians and Muslims, atheists and believers (Kermani 2003, p.192).

Therapy objectives
Regulative perspective:
autoregulation/equilibration/allostasis*

Relational perspective:
communication and relationship/perceptive intensification

Levels of effect:
physical, emotional, cognitive, social, mental/spiritual

Therapy techniques leading to a patient-oriented **Therapy attitude**

receptive tonality-specific listening to music	philosophical/phenomenological
active movement/dance	psychological
receptive being moved	religious/spiritual
musical improvisation (dyadic, single, supporting)	musical
therapeutic conversation	relational
guided/free imagination	creative
work with elements (water, clay)	material
educational narratives, poetry	educational
artistic performance	aesthetic

*Allostasis is the process of maintaining stability through change: a fundamental process through which organisms actively adjust to both predictable and unpredictable events

Figure 9.1 Therapy objectives

The question then arises about whether or not we expect a culturally specific appreciation of such sound from an audience in middle Europe. Is the 'maqam' system a phenomenon specific to a particular culture, or are there elements that can be applied generally in contemporary settings? If we are to argue for the application of traditional healing music then we must see what it is that is applicable today.

I believe that traditional oriental music therapy can be also employed as a modern-day approach in Europe in a very efficient way, as we see in clinical practice, but the focus of any application must be on a patient's individual needs, which might require an extended range of methods beyond the traditional. Let me illustrate this seemingly banal statement with an example:

Mr P, born in 1964, lives in a day and permanent care centre for patients with multiple handicaps. He was rated as handicapped and accepted by the day care facility when he was three years old because of his mental retardation and a prevalence of epileptic episodes. Mr P is unable to speak but able to follow conversations.

From early childhood on he has taken a prescribed antiepileptic and he shows a lively interest in his surroundings and in social relations. The director refers him to music therapy since Mr P has indicated a general interest in music. She hopes for flexibility in his rigid mental structures and that this will bring an improvement in his quality of life. According to his social worker, Mr P immediately accepts music therapy as an important element of his weekly treatment schedule. In the course of the therapy a stable and safe setting, as a non-musical factor, turns out to be just as relevant to a successful therapy session as musical factors.

From the start, Mr P insists on active participation in music-making and is not so interested in receptive listening.

One day, after about six months, we have to use a different room for therapy. Although all other elements of the setting are the same, Mr P is not in a condition to respond to the intervention. He refuses to play on the instrument he had come to prefer, and signals his discomfort with the unfamiliar room via sounds, facial expression and gestures. He needs almost the entire session to adapt to the new situation. In the following week – the familiar room was available again – his reactions were as usual, just as if nothing has happened.

This incident was the reason to expand the therapy concept for Mr P. The familiar setting of the room, welcoming song, and joint music-making on the harpsichord was made more flexible and extended to include new instruments, different seats, changes in the position of the furniture and introduction of a second person. This helped Mr P to acquire noticeably more flexibility in his social relations as well.

This example suggests that a methodical 'self-limitation' to receptive music therapy alone, as the core method of traditional oriental music therapy, would not be appropriate. A therapist is called upon to find a flexible response that is adequate to meet a patient's behaviour, situation and needs.

In addition to flexibility in the canon of methods, I also postulate a widest possible range for the choice of music. It would be absurd, in a German language setting for example, to deny a patient's wish to start the session with the song 'Froh zu sein, bedarf es wenig…' simply because this song does not conform to the concept of traditional oriental 'maqam' music. This is not a question of haphazard or random choice of methods.

However, as clinicians working with patients with severe traumatic brain injury, we have found that it makes sense to put these often highly susceptible patients into a positive or joyful mood with a musical repertoire based in traditional oriental music therapy. It is our experience that Austrian or German folk songs can stimulate quite intense reactions of emotional grief mainly in elderly patients, probably as an associative effect. Consequently associative music of this type appears to be not very appropriate in early stages of remission, since the patients' cognitive and integrative abilities are extremely impaired.

What these stages require more than anything is room for a joyful experience of wellbeing, which is induced through a combination of caring attention and traditional oriental music that is new for the patient but nevertheless perceived as pleasant. We have observed such a positive reaction many times in all spheres where traditional oriental music is employed by music therapists (neurology, cardiology, oncology, psychiatry, geriatrics, special and therapeutic pedagogy, care of disabled persons). In my opinion the essential point in successful therapy is whether or not a patient experiences emotional contact and what are the musical means to bring about this contact. How this contact is achieved is a matter of phases achieved through music, as we have seen in the earlier chapter by Wolfgang Schmid.

Excursus on connections between music therapy and brain neuroplasticity

Recent studies have suggested that neuronal connections in the brain are produced by genetic determinants as much as by interaction with the environment as by socio-cultural phenomena (Hüther 1998). Researchers use the term 'epigenetic factors' in this context. In the course of the phylogenetic development of the brain, connections are created that became established as behavioural patterns that ensure our biological and social life, and survival. According to the neurobiologist Hüther, it is fear – or rather stress expressed as fear – that stimulates such processes. Thanks to the 'neuroplastic' adaptability of the human brain, we have a lifelong ability to adapt to specific demands and stimuli. In other words, the connections produced by certain behaviours may also be cancelled or changed, which leads to relearning processes. Hüther states that all human emotions have a biological background but are also influenced by interaction with others and the environment. We may therefore say that social interactions also influence brain function.

These findings are highly significant for music therapy: there is hardly any other medium that produces such deep emotion as music. An *intense emotional agitation* stimulated by artistic means (in this case, music) permits a patient to perceive change first in his or her attitude and then (with emotional anchoring through repetition) in his or her behaviour. Deep-going processes of change are consequently linked less to cognitive analytical processes and more to a sensual experience of being.

These findings provide valuable clues for understanding basic effects of traditional oriental music therapy.

Sufi attitude

The historical roots of this therapy approach are to be found mainly in Sufism, the mystic dimension of the Islamic religion. This has, like all forms of religious expression, a specific aesthetic that is based less on a collection of rationally explained principles, standards and values but rather on a touching emotional experience through mythical images. Believers feel attracted not so much by logical argumentation but more by the poetry of its texts, or the beauty of its sounds, forms, rituals, architecture, colours and smells. Another important factor is the personal charisma of its figureheads. The same basic effects apply to a successful therapy, that involves the patient's positive sensual experience and the resulting intense emotion. In other words, knowledge gained from Sufi methods, as well as findings from art therapies, are the result of sensual–aesthetic *experience* and not of discursive–intellectual reflection alone.

Similarities between the effects of a religious–spiritual education and those of therapeutic activities have led to a certain confusion in the training of traditional oriental music therapists. There is an intense debate whether a therapist of traditional oriental music has also to be a Sufi mystic in order to learn and apply this form of therapy correctly. I do not subscribe to the opinion (quoted here as an example) that 'traditional oriental music therapy cannot be taught, nor even practised, without personal involvement in the philosophical–spiritual background of this therapy form' (Heck 2004; my translation). Although Heck's paper indicates the author's serious commitment, and expresses interesting thoughts, my objection to this position is that obviously it fails to recognize the anthropological, transcultural and transreligious effects behind the therapy methods of traditional oriental music therapy.

In my capacity as director of the training course in traditional oriental music therapy in Austria, and also as a clinical music therapist, I believe that the description of the therapy effects of traditional oriental music as an 'echo of the original Divine sound' is not purposive in the current debate on educational and academic issues. My intention is, however, not to dismiss this Sufi position as irrelevant. Experience from therapy practice has taught me that sometimes music may give rise to the manifestation of a curative and comforting dimension that eludes any attempts at measurement. Practice requires an experienced and sensitive music therapist who has experienced this musical dimension himself or herself and now – beyond mere instrumental technique – is able to 'move' a patient emotionally through sound. This 'spiritual' dimension of music has been described frequently and is not limited to oriental or Sufi music (Aldridge 2003, 2004).

Transfer of the historical concept to the present

Let us address, from a wider perspective, the question of how far it is possible to substantiate the medical effects of 'maqam' music historically. If we take a look at historical texts, against the background of contemporary concepts of man and the world in general, then we see that any medical or therapeutic interventions in the middle ages always served the additional objective of conveying predefined religious or moral attitudes.

First attempts at scientific thinking notwithstanding, Islamic physicians were the first to introduce scientific experiment in medicine, the main idea being to reinstate humans in harmony with the divine order through music. This is reflected in classical Greek ethics that form the basis for the development of traditional oriental music therapy, as they did for Islamic physicians.

Music was incorporated in science. For Avicenna, music belonged to mathematics but had an additional element of sacredness as well. There were frequent reports of the ecstatic effects of music even on sovereigns and califs. European audiences at classical concerts today may find spontaneous actions like those of calif Al-Hadi (who governed from 785 to 786) strange. He is said to have torn his robe in rapture during a musical performance (Neubauer 1990, p.227). Such reactions were not unusual; no wonder therefore that theoretical reflections about the effect of music on the person, and substantiation of those effects, are considered highly relevant from early antiquity.

These reflections were incorporated into a categorization of medicine according to Galen, his *Theorica und Practica*, that was continued by Al Farabi and Avicenna (Schipperges 1987, p.12). Islamic physicians in particular became renowned for systematic clinical observations and the ensuing theory and were the first to introduce scientific experiments in medicine.

But music was also considered to be an expression of the divine order and in this sense was claimed to have an element of sacredness cultivated, above all, by mystics. Orthodox Muslims, however, did not approve of such a loss of control as demonstrated by calif Al-Hadi. Indeed, orthodox circles in particular attached great importance to the predictability of emotions in response to music. This may have been a further reason for an early canonization of 'maqam' music.

Becker-Glauch (1997) describes the attempt, much repeated in the history of mankind, to use music and dance to evoke certain desired or hoped-for events through anticipation or imitation. This perspective suggests a connection between the repetition of already 'successful' actions, or a hopeful anticipation of desired events, in the setting of holy rituals. This model provides another interesting explanation for a culture-dependent canonization of desired, and actual, reactions.

Music and dance then gained increasing importance in oriental culture; a culture that was sacred, with a theoretical base of reflection and substantiated by clinical practice. In addition it was found that the deep-reaching emotionalizing effect of music could be intensified with corresponding texts from scripture.

In recent times, chronobiology studies have reported similar findings on the significance of the rhythmically uttered word (Bonin *et al.* 1999). In Monika Jungblut's chapter in this book, the rhythmic use of the sung voice, combined with movements, including repetition, are a central element of her music therapy approach.

Today religion and natural sciences appear almost incompatible, whereas the historical concept of traditional oriental music combines both aspects, albeit under the primacy of the religious, as two sides of the same coin.

In Avicenna's view, music was a part of mathematics and, for mystics, a proven means to experience and convey 'Divine love'. It was seen as having an objective effect on the human soul and its emotions. Mystics saw a deliberate participation in this order as the highest form of human redemption. Consequently, the main therapy objective, beyond physical recovery, was to guide a patient towards this divine 'healing' structural order. Accordingly, the canon of methods was not limited to medical or therapeutic interventions but included an additional religious, moral and social dimension. Thus, giving food to the poor and needy was not simply a material act; it had social and moral consequences based on a religious imperative – the act of charity.

Silent witnesses to this way of thinking are former hospital installations in the Arabic or Persian world and Turkish-language regions. These were not only centres of therapy and medical education but at the same time places of religious and social activity (places of prayer, libraries, soup kitchens, bath houses).

Today's public health systems have little room for such concepts. In the middle ages a therapy concept served among other things to achieve certain moral/ethical objectives, whereas today the design of therapy concepts is influenced mainly by the respective methods of objectification and secularization. In this sense, music therapy has changed from a 'means of education' in the hands of the therapist to a way in which the patient discovers his or her own means of expression and communication.

This raises a dilemma for the therapist working with traditional oriental music. He or she has to take a decision with regard to the basic therapeutic stance (attitude). Does the therapist see himself or herself as a conveyor of certain emotional and also spiritual issues, or rather as a partner in dialogue with the patient encouraging individual expression?

In recent years I underwent a process in my clinical practice that encouraged me to focus more on the patient and less on the historical–theoretical concept. I do not intend to dismiss a traditional approach as obsolete – it would obviously be pretentious and absurd to deny the benefits of a therapy concept that has been successfully practised for approximately 900 years. But we should seriously consider the extent to which the achieved effect depends on the specific cultural and situational context in which a therapy takes place. Psychological attunement through rituals, smells, setting, the charisma of the therapist, and so on, has a decisive influence on a patient's willingness to get emotionally involved. This is the basis of healing rituals using the burning of incense, chants, sermons and repletion that we find in Christian sacred settings.

The debate must be taken to a level of scientific understanding and substantiation, and the historical concept has to be assessed with up-to-date findings from therapy research, and to be expanded if necessary in order to take the clinical concept further. Rigid adherence to traditional forms passed on over a long time would be comparable to the conviction held in the middle ages that the Earth is a flat disc. This brings to mind what Gustav Mahler once said – that tradition is to pass on the fire, not to worship the ashes.

Design for an integrative paradigm

Clinical practice has pointed me towards a concept which addresses observable and describable phenomena. This position is not far from the early empiricists and modern evolutionary epistemology. The latter assumes a basic qualitative difference between perception and its object, and includes the act of cognition into what has been recognized. In this manner *it denies the existence of absolute objectivity*.

According to David Hume, scientists considered knowledge gained from experience not as verified but only 'probable'. A few centuries later Karl Popper advocated a similar position; he challenged the term 'positive proof' specifically for empirical sciences. For Popper, theories have to demonstrate their worth, whereby 'negative proof' is possible through falsification.

In everyday life we perceive ourselves, our thoughts, ideas, wishes, bodies, as well as our surroundings. Over time, we come to integrate all our perceptions into one cohesive picture that makes sense to us. This facilitates quick and efficient orientation whenever we have to choose behaviours adequate to the situation. These 'slumbering theories' are the result of mainly unconscious 'mental' processes. As a rule, the internal process of expanding and structuring our view of the world through immediate experience happens subconsciously, which allows us to react to the environment efficiently and flexibly. Applying these reflections to music therapy, we see that the concept of each theoretical school is brought to life through the personality of the 'experienced music therapist'.

In the course of clinical practice, each therapist develops his or her own well-defined ideas on progress, potential and limitation with regard to specific clinical situations. He or she learns to assess the effects of therapeutic musical intervention and to adapt them spontaneously to conditions and needs. A therapist's competence is the result of a combination of theoretical knowledge and experience won from practice. Without the latter, theoretical knowledge would ultimately remain without substance, according to the empiricists.

From this perspective I have come to base my therapeutic activities not only on historical concepts, in order to verify them, but also on events and developments emerging in therapy. The perceived reality should be in accordance with the *wholeness of developments* as far as humanly possible.

This poses a fundamental problem in music therapy research. Researchers are called upon to design research models that provide a scientifically adequate understanding and description of sensory–emotional experience. David Aldridge criticizes a reductionist concept of science as the core problem of today's health care system that in behaviour studies of the recovery process tends to neglect the creative aesthetic elements (Aldridge 1999c, p.5). He challenges a 'scientific technocracy' that elevates 'randomized controlled studies to the only basis of evidence' and 'thereby neglect the element of care and the social dimension of health care'.

Similarly, the philosopher Rudolf zur Lippe (1987) voices his criticism that man constructs scientific theories and believes more in them than in what they were designed to explain in the first place. Followers of individual trends in medicine, psychology or musicology who are unable to perceive any other categories but those of their own line of reasoning believe their own framework of thought and perception to be essential and have forgotten the real issue – the human element.

An example from clinical practice

Mrs G, a young woman, suffered from severe traumatic brain injury and a pelvic fracture with internal haemorrhage after a traffic accident in 1998. She had numerous brain contusions and cerebral oedema that were difficult to treat. Additional severe infections led to further complications. After respiration therapy, Mrs G had all indications of an apallic syndrome.

> Mrs G came to Wien-Meidling for rehabilitation in 1999. The first examination still showed all indications of apallic syndrome with massive spastic quadriparesis that was more pronounced on the right side. She was fed via a stomach tube. While in rehabilitation she had repeated febrile respiratory infections. Surgery to close the still open tracheostoma in May finally stabilized her physical condition.
>
> The patient attended traditional oriental music therapy sessions from the start of rehabilitation. Short-term eye contact became more frequent during therapy, and later on she produced circling, somewhat stereotypic movements with her less paralysed left arm.

The coma remission scale according to Schönle (KRS – discussed later) also reflected her improved condition. Compared to an initial score of 9, she achieved 12 out of 24 possible points after conclusion of traditional oriental music therapy.

In later sessions, the music therapy team (two music therapists, one psychologist) attempted to increase Mrs G's expressive repertoire in musical dialogue with the harp. At first the main idea was not to produce aesthetic sounds but to enjoy experimenting with this instrument. Any pressure to perform was to be avoided; for this purpose the second music therapist created a relaxing musical background on the lute. It was deeply touching to observe Mrs G when she succeeded step by step to guide her left arm along the instrument with increasingly coordinated movements. Transfer from circling to plucking or stroking movements clearly was a considerable effort; what helped was her confidence in the team and the joyful atmosphere of the therapy setting. Towards the end of the therapy, Mrs G was able to remember and repeat up to three consecutive notes.

In the last group session to which we invited her, Mrs G played the harp together with the therapist to an audience of relatives. I shall never forget her radiant eyes when all listeners obviously responded to the situation with wonder and gratification, and her father who was also present was moved to tears.

The scenes described above illustrate various different situations that in themselves were 'complete'. However, none of the following perspectives provide a complete picture of the situation:

- a differentiated description of the way in which contact between Mrs G and the therapist team was established

- a musicological study of the 'maqam' structure of 'rast' where musical interaction took place with the harp

- assessment of the sound spectrum of the harp

- registration of the patient's electroencephalogram during music reception

- subsequent evaluation of the patient's condition with the KRS coma remission scale.

With the exception of the KRS which gives a quantifying description of changes after intervention (see below), each of these different perspectives illuminates an excerpt from the general condition but does not cover the entire therapy process.

In the therapy scene described above, there is something that touches the core of a human being and defies any positivistic assessment. This core cannot be decoded, nor be reduced to a release of neurotransmitters, and eludes satisfactory psychological interpretation.

An evaluation of the patient's condition prior to and after therapy sessions with a coma remission scale gives some (rough) indication of changes in alertness but no suggestion of the therapeutic development that caused the changed responsiveness in the patient. The KRS (Koma-Remissions-Skala) is a scale for external evaluation, published by the Bundesarbeitsgemeinschaft medizinisch-beruflicher Rehabilitationszentren, a national association of rehabilitation institutions, and serves to quantify communicative skills in patients with severe brain damage. The maximum number of points to score is 24. The KRS describes the following six categories:

- alertness/attention
- motor response
- response to acoustic stimuli
- response to optic stimuli
- response to tactile stimuli
- response in speech motorics.

Our previous assessments showed that, after therapy, most patients achieved a higher score for alertness/attention after traditional oriental music therapy.

What is

As director of a study programme, I need to provide a context for students within which they learn to document and reflect their therapeutic activities. From my viewpoint, a programme, while acknowledging its traditional roots, must grapple not with speculations of 'what has to be' but with a precise registration of 'what is'. Pirsig (1992) finds a literary way to address the issue succinctly:

> It was an allegory for supporters of scientific objectivity. Wherever the map disagreed with what he observed he mistrusted his own observations and followed the map. In his mind he believed that he knew the truth; therefore he put in a statistical filter, an immune system that excluded all data that did not conform to the mental image. Seeing is not believing. Believing is seeing.

> If this had been a single phenomenon it would not have been so bad. But it is a considerable element of our culture and must be taken very seriously. We erect entire highly selective mental structures based on outdated 'facts'. If a new fact does not fit into this structure then we do not eliminate the structures, we eliminate the fact. Sometimes a controversial fact has to knock and knock for centuries before perhaps two or three people will become aware. And then these two or three people must start to hammer this fact into others until these notice something, too.

Just as the biological immune system destroys a living skin transplant with the same rigour with which it fights pulmonia, the cultural immune system fights any useful addition to knowledge... Phaidros realized that a culture that tries to exclude something dynamic is not immoral. A static persistence is required to protect what the culture achieved in the past. The question is not to condemn this culture as foolish but to look for factors that render the new data acceptable – to look for keys. The metaphysics of quality were such a key... (Pirsig 1992, p.378f)

Towards a polyaesthetic approach

Allostasis theory is a regulative approach explaining the effects of receptive music therapy. It assumes a tendency towards a flowing balance in the mental and biological apparatus of human beings. This balance is produced through a variety of artistic, aesthetically attractive and affective sensory pleasures (see 'Riyazed' concept in Tucek *et al.* 2001).

The same idea is also part of more modern approaches, for example, of Roscher's polyaesthetic education (in Mastnak 1994). Roscher had the idea to appeal to people in the entirety of their senses. He used music, dance, word, image, play with light and scene in an integrative concept. The core idea of polyaesthetic therapy derived from Roscher is the thesis that 'people have certain basic needs from natural disposition that in the course of an individual's history receive a specific quality and are more or less "dominant" or "capable of compromise" (Mastnak 1994). Mental illnesses develop 'if such a basic need comes to the foreground, is not met satisfactorily and in addition is not tolerant enough'. Polyaesthetic therapy is intended to promote healthy personality traits through an artistic process of individuation and expression, and thus to defuse the pathological conflict. This approach is therefore not primarily conflict-oriented but does not evade confrontation with the '*unavoidable trauma of human conflict*'.

The artistic–therapeutic process aims to reduce the significance and effect of the mentally induced cause of the disorder and make it accessible to treatment. From a polyaesthetic perspective, the following aspects determine the therapeutic effects of music:

- musicality – as anthropogenic and genetic disposition
- individual musical imprinting
- specific endogenous factors
- current mental disposition
- situative context.

The principles of traditional oriental music therapy are mainly in accordance with the polyaesthetic approach. It is my experience that, in neurological treatment after traumatic brain injury, an individual musical imprinting is not significant in the early remission phases, where a positive experience of the self through immediate musical experience is more relevant.

Another difference between the (historically interpreted) oriental and the polyaesthetic therapy approach is the importance attributed to a patient's individual expression in therapy. Current clinical practice focuses increasingly on the request to give patients ways to express themselves actively from early on. The result is an expanded repertoire of methods and instruments in traditional oriental music therapy.

Examples from clinical practice

Mr A and Mrs F are both in minimal responsive status after severe motor accidents. Both patients are referred to music therapy of the traditional oriental method. Therapists visit these patients for single bedside sessions respectively. Both patients show obvious reactions to the (harp) music. They open their eyes and turn them towards the source of sounds.

> In the first session Mrs F starts with seemingly stereotype stroking movements with her right hand, which I associate with playing the guitar. I place the harp within her reach and ask her to allow me to guide her hand to the strings. Mrs F agrees and lets me guide her hand. Both her eyes are now wide open, her breath is deeper. I guide her hand over the strings and produce soft sound combinations. She appears to be frightened and withdraws her hand. I imitate the previous sound patterns alone. Mrs F strives for contact with the strings again – this time on her own. I take her hand – and again she permits me to guide it. The husband is present and is deeply moved by her intensive interaction and reaction capability. He reports that prior to the accident Mrs F loved to play the guitar.

> The reactions of Mr A in the first music therapy sessions are smacking sounds and a clearer look in his eyes. The therapy team believe we see a hint of a smile, but we cannot be sure. We decide to watch him closely in the next session, and actually discover mimicry changes. Mr A starts to bend and stretch his feet. He is clearly more alert and turned towards the instrument. After the second session his eyes follow the therapists when they leave his room. In the third session his reactions resemble those of last time: smacking sounds, bending and stretching of legs, clear look to the therapist. Now he begins to move his right forefinger slightly. I take up this movement and start to produce sounds on the harp – similar to therapy with Mrs F described above. He appears surprised and also excited. I explain that his plucking movements on the strings produce the sound. When we enter his room the next time he recognizes us, and his right index finger makes plucking movements.

Both examples describe patients in a first tonal expression, which has less to do with improved skills but rather with an expression of self.

Another case described by a colleague may serve to illustrate the objective and nature of traditional oriental music therapy in contrast to other therapies that strive to stimulate and promote skills (like physiotherapy):

> *Mrs K is paralysed on her right side after a stroke. She is hospitalized in a neurology clinic in Berlin with an affiliated rehabilitation unit. Apart from her physical impairment, her mental state gives reason for concern. She feels less attractive as a woman and as a result suffers considerably. In this mood she refuses cooperation in regular therapies (speech therapy, physiotherapy) that are essential for successful rehabilitation. The physician on the ward asks the music therapist for help. The physiotherapist whose efforts Mrs K has refused so far accompanies him since he hopes she might be more approachable. First, the music therapist plays a rebab (similar to a gamba) for her, and a bamboo flute called a ney. He has brought a water container with two smaller bowls. The physiotherapist accompanies the music with soft splashing sounds, pouring water from the smaller bowls into the larger one. This procedure seems to fascinate Mrs K. For the first time she signals her intention to take an active part.*

> *She takes a water bowl into her good hand and skilfully pours the water into the larger container. In the course of the session she also takes a bowl with her impaired hand and again pours water, in a somewhat awkward movement but with visible pleasure. Successful motor skills emerge, although not very coordinated, and she is clearly pleased with herself.*

> *The first coordinated movements produced in the first music therapy session in a relaxed and pleasant atmosphere were a challenge for the therapy team (music therapist and physiotherapist) to continue their cooperation. Expectations were high; they hoped to stabilize and extend what they had stimulated in the first therapy session without plan but through mere curiosity and fun.*

On studying the video recording of the first session, both observers felt deeply moved by Mrs K's initial joyful spontaneous reaction, but this was not repeated the second time. Patient and therapist tried too hard to repeat or deepen the previous experience. Suddenly the idea was no longer a playful and pleasant exploration of what was possible but a performance to be achieved. Movements were to become more coordinated, more exact. While music had been in the foreground in the first session, now it was therapy. In the subsequent evaluation of the video both therapists reported how much they had felt this pressure to make the patient perform, and the resulting loss of the original ease, and this was transferred to the patient as well.

Presence of mind and spontaneous reaction to the situation appear to be among the most essential and at the same time most difficult tasks for a music therapist. Similar factors are characteristic of music therapy according to Nordoff and Robbins. The emphasis on congruency between musical form and self seems to me to be an important dimension of both our methods, as well as a way to approach patients that is not conflict-oriented.

Music as a form of art fades into the background in favour of its quality as a means of communication. In other words, a successful therapy process does not necessarily produce attractive music. It is this aspect which in my opinion frequently causes a misunderstanding about the dictates of aesthetics among traditional oriental music therapists. To put it strongly: there is a danger that the patient becomes the 'disturbing factor' in the artistic self-realization of a traditional oriental music therapist. I will illustrate this with an example.

> In my work with disabled patients, I have a client who in every single therapy session – going on for two years now – takes his favourite instrument, the harp, mistunes it deliberately and then starts to play it and to sing with great abandon. Mr M is 25 and insists on this sequence in each session, with himself as the only performer. He does not want any accompaniment from me, neither instrument nor rhythm, he only wants me to listen. After about ten minutes Mr M returns the instrument and asks me to play for him – on the correctly tuned instrument. This 'crazy' music is his specific way of musical expression, and he seems to find it important to be accepted and appreciated in this way.

> There are some sequences during sessions when we make music together. Depending on his moods, these phases may be a search for harmonious sounds, but also quite the opposite. He loves short receptive phases in therapy. The contrast between harmonious and chaotic music seems to be important to him. The sequences with a mistuned instrument are always a challenge for my own aesthetic sense, but they are significant for the therapy process.

Regulative and relational models in traditional oriental music therapy

Let us return to the original issue of an objective 'maqam' music. Previous studies have not found any conclusive evidence of the existence of genetically determined or transcultural emotion – or organ-specific effects of 'maqam'. Recent findings from neurobiology that underline the significance of cultural and social relations for concrete forms of neuronal links in the brain (the brain as a 'psychosocial organ') do not suggest such a generally perceivable effect either.

Consequently, the therapeutic efficiency of traditional oriental music therapy must be based on other factors, as an oriental musical structure with objective effects. To avoid misunderstandings, this is not evidence that traditional oriental music therapy is ineffective; rather it is a demand to search for more appropriate explanations. I cannot deny that after years of intensive contact with the oriental culture, and its music, even Western listeners and musicians might develop a feeling for such emotions. A hospitalized patient, however, cannot be expected to fulfil this precondition. According to historical texts this is not to be expected from the perspective of the tradition itself: The 'Lauteren Brüder' (Ihwan as-Safa) wrote around 900:

> You must know, my brother – and may God assist you with his spirit! – that the humours of the body have many aspects and that the nature of creatures has many species. For each humour and each nature there is a corresponding rhythm and melody; their number is known to God alone. You will find the truth of this statement and this description confirmed if you consider that each society has melodies and rhythms of its own that please its children while nobody else takes pleasure in them. This is true for the music of the Daylamites, Turks, Arabs, Armenians, Ethiopians, Byzantians and others who all have their own language, nature, character and customs. (Shiloah 2002, p.161)

In our clinical practice at the Meidling rehabilitation centre in Vienna, we found the relationship established through music to be an essential factor. Patients with a variety of different diagnoses describe the monophonic music of traditional oriental music therapy as mainly harmonious and pleasant and this appears to be an essential element of therapy. This form of music therapy obviously motivates patients to enter into a joyful relationship with their surroundings.

Even if we found no evidence in our studies for the original theory, we gained a vast number of interesting results. Clinical practice provides a stronger focus on the regulatory and relational dimension of traditional oriental music therapy.

The EEG project at the Meidling rehabilitation centre

We also have a research project that explores the effects of receptive oriental music therapy via the electoencephalogram (EEG). Our original intention was to illustrate the organ- and emotion-specific effects of 'maqam' music. EEG mapping is a computer-based procedure to measure the frequency part for single EEG leads quantitatively and thus to record the EEG frequency range for each brain section. The EEG is an ideal method to indicate changes in a patient's conscious state (Fachner 2005). However, patients show an abnormal EEG due to multiple brain injuries in most cases, and a certain motor restlessness that leads to artefacts in EEG leads, which renders our studies more difficult. This is why several EEGs are required for some patients, prior to, during and after traditional oriental music therapy, in order to quantify its effects on the EEG frequency distribution.

We have demonstrated that:

- the extramusical factor of a 'quiet, pleasant and comfortable setting' plays an important role
- it is possible to record alpha and theta increase in healthy subjects above the central region during therapy, and in patients above both temporal regions (left/right) after music therapy.

Healthy test persons in the control group show phenomena that may be summarily termed 'unusual conscious states'. In other words, receptive treatment with traditional oriental music therapy induces a trance-like state, the therapeutic importance of which in clinical practice has not been explored in depth but will probably be an important area for future studies.

Family members and attention to their needs through traditional oriental music therapy

Traditional oriental music therapy may provide an important basis for relaxation and burnout prophylaxis during the necessary restructuring phase in the lives of all persons concerned. The need to provide specific attention and care to family members has fortunately found increasing recognition and support over the past few years. It is the relatives who – in contrast to apallic or akinetic–mutistic patients – are able to voice their concern, helplessness, grief, rage and pain. Many of our joint efforts to support family members are obviously intended as a performance-oriented training for caregivers who frequently find that emotions are difficult to express or handle.

This is why relatives, like patients, often appear tense, insecure and sometimes aggressive. Occasionally they deny the reality of the fateful accident in all its consequences (at least in direct conversation). From the beginning, receptive traditional oriental music therapy has had a very positive response among family members because it provides the opportunity to relax, to turn inward with the help of the music, and to experience and handle internal images according to individual willingness and ability, without the need to discuss all this with others.

The essential point for us is that this session opens an internal psychological and external space for joint experience, mutual acceptance and caring attention. This becomes obvious when patients and their relatives take each others' hands, or caress them. Such individual experience that unites all persons present also improves contact between family members and often prepares the way for further psychological discussion.

An example from clinical practice

Mr S was 25. After a motorcycle accident he suffered from traumatic brain injury with skull injuries and cerebral oedema on both sides. When he was referred to music therapy he demonstrated a high degree of restlessness that was so pronounced that he threatened to fall out of his wheelchair.

At first he was unable to speak. We opted for receptive therapy combined with cautious contact through touch. The latter took the form of soft massaging movements in the upper back and neck, in the rhythm of the music. We hoped to achieve some change in his stereotypical and nervous individual rhythm. In the second session, we were able to stop these stereotypical movements for a short period. When they returned, albeit less pronounced, we tried to take up his uncoordinated movements and to 'transfer' them to the harp. After a few futile efforts we succeeded. The patient's parents were present and assumed a highly motivating role in the process.

From the beginning Mr S's parents demonstrated much personal interest in music therapy. We felt that their presence had a beneficial effect on their son's therapy. They motivated him without exerting pressure. Their visible joy and concern about the therapy and their son's small advances seemed to have reached him. In addition we invited them to attend group sessions for family members (once per week in the afternoon). They accepted both invitations gratefully and described the effects of music on them as relaxing and 'healing'.

In conclusion

The main idea behind this chapter was to bring traditional oriental music therapy out from its 'conceptual ivory tower' and relate it to real-life descriptions from clinical practice. Traditional oriental music therapy has been used successfully in clinical work for years, and clinical research in the field is gradually making an impact. After previously adopting an isolationist approach over the years, we now see a movement towards integrative concepts in research and practice. For the rehabilitation of patients with traumatic brain injury this means that living and feeling human beings are not only a combination of brain activities but an embodied spirit in active dialogue with an environment, an ecology of events and ideas that we call consciousness (Aldridge 2000c).

CHAPTER 10

Art Therapies in the Primary Treatment of Paraplegic Patients: A Qualitative Study

Anke Scheel-Sailer

During my internship on the ward for paraplegic patients in the Herdecke community hospital from September 1996 to September 1998, a number of questions emerged concerning an understanding of how the art therapies influence the rehabilitation process. Apart from the clinical objective of providing optimum care through medication, nursing, physical therapy and ergotherapy, I was frequently confronted with questions related to patients' self-concepts that had an impact on rehabilitation. My intuition was that a joint exploration of such self-concepts by medical personnel, therapists and patients would promote and facilitate rehabilitation, benefiting both patients and the treatment team.

Issues to confront

The rehabilitation process in recently affected patients or those with recent accidents appeared to be divided into different periods for different types of therapies. Therapy types were determined on the one hand by physical changes, and on the other were correlated with growing skills. Patients underwent various stages with a beginning, a climax and a catharsis as a transition to a subsequent stage or task. In the course of the rehabilitation, periods of attention alternated with periods of rest, or possibly of 'silent' change. So, in the rehabilitation of paraplegic patients are there really identifiable stages, crises, developments or changes and, if so, can we recognize and categorize such stages?

The question arose frequently as to why a patient, despite his given, although impaired, physical skills did not achieve the maximum possible extent of personal independence in the shortest possible time. Apart from limitations of physical strength, there seemed to be limitations of a different type that were not amenable to 'coaxing' by the staff. The motivation to grow beyond one's self in order to achieve this independence, in contrast to regressing into a depression, appeared to be absent in most cases and had to be stimulated with some effort. Sports or joint social activities, personal changes in the family situation and other individual alternative activities with different objectives proved to be helpful in this respect. Arts-based therapies could also provide a treatment option that would strengthen this motivation.

Among all medical personnel involved, the question remained open as to whether art therapies really do influence motivation, and if so, to what extent and in what way, compared to other therapies. Do art therapies actually affect medication and its effects, the frequency of complications, independence, the process of constructing identity, and motivation? We were including such therapies in our treatment programme but knew little about their specific influence.

Observation of changes through art therapies

In this study, the art therapists opened the evolving therapy processes to all other staff of the ward, so that not only patients but also staff members had an opportunity to perceive patients in their current situation from an 'artistic' perspective. Apart from frighteningly depressive paintings or musical improvisations, despite possible 'perturbed' fronts in day-to-day life, this method also allowed us to recognize the creative developments a patient actually experienced. There is not necessarily a correlation with functional development. Such extended perceptions gained through art therapies enable staff members to understand patients better. Progress made in art therapies also means encouragement and hope for seriously ill patients, even in cases of physical and functional stagnation. A tremendous loss can be mitigated through achievements gained on a different level of experience.

This led to the question whether any congruent or alternating developments can be observed in art therapies, and how to define them. Another essential issue is to find out how patients themselves perceive such therapies and describe them.

Evaluation of successful rehabilitation

At the conclusion of a rehabilitation programme, there always remains the question of whether it was successful or not. The goal of rehabilitation is mainly defined by the extent of the paralysis. This is why any rehabilitation is intended to achieve maximum physical and functional skills, complemented by comprehensive physical and occupational therapy and nursing interventions. A measure for the quality of rehabilitative therapies is the ability of the team of therapists to train a patient in the best possible use of his or her skills within the limitations imposed by paralysis. Successful rehabilitation also shows in a patient's social reintegration, renewed fitness for work, and satisfaction with the new situation. Patients' subjective self-assessment on the one hand and objective quality criteria on the other are therefore significant for an evaluation of rehabilitative measures.

We know that many factors have an influence on rehabilitation – family situation, primary personality, age at onset of illness, social situation, cause of illness, and many others. The quality of rehabilitation may therefore be determined by the extent to which an *expected* development is achieved under given conditions. We then have to ask ourselves if there are any unequivocal and repeatable correlations between therapeutic interventions and progress in rehabilitation.

Need for and affordability of complementary therapies

Today, for economic reasons alone, every task for nursing, medical or other therapeutic personnel has to be confirmed as indispensable. This study examines the required number of therapy sessions and the length of therapies, and in addition selection criteria as indicators for art therapies and therapeutic effectiveness. This study was intended to discover, and possibly define, criteria that would make direct indications possible. We needed also to ask ourselves for how long therapies were useful, and when they were necessary, and which criteria help us to recognize these factors.

Anatomical, physiological and causal aspects of paraplegia

Paraplegia is caused by an impairment of the spinal cord due to a variety of disorders, and leads to neurological deficits in the body parts below the lesion. Seventy-six per cent of all cases are due to trauma from, for example, traffic or sports accidents, or accidents at home (Znoj, Lude and Lude 1999). The rest are caused by diseases such as tumours of the spinal cord, circulation disorders, infections, abscesses or sliding vertebrae. The average age of patients when paraplegia begins in is approximately 27 years (Buck and Beckers 1993).

Paraplegia leads to a loss of motor functions in varying degrees and the degree of paralysis has a considerable influence on a patient's autonomy. We speak of complete and incomplete paralysis, whereby muscle activity is categorized in five classes. The ASIA scale (Gerner 1992) provides a differentiated grading of remaining motor and sensory functions. Full paraplegia (tetraplegia) affects motor functions of the arms and legs. Pronounced paraplegia above the third cervical vertebra may also result in impaired respiratory function (Buck and Beckers

1993). Paraplegias such as paralysis of the legs require in addition a differentiation between spastic and flaccid paralysis. Injuries above the lumbar vertebral column are accompanied by the phenomenon of spasticity that is produced by the autonomous reflex arc between muscle and spinal cord. It results in spontaneous muscle contractions and constitutes a decisive factor in assessing quality of life. Causes of and therapies for spasticity are the subject of ongoing research projects because certain phenomena occur in this disease that are still unexplained. Sixty-nine per cent of all cases are paraplegics, and 31 per cent are tetraplegics (Znoj *et al.* 1999).

Paraplegia may in addition lead to changed sensitivity in areas below the injury. In cases of complete paraplegia, all perceptions are lost including proprioception; that is, patients feel no external stimuli like pain, cold and heat, vibration or touch. The occurrence of neurogenic pain is important for such patients; comparable to amputation pain, pains are felt in those body parts that have no perception. They affect 70 per cent of patients, with a considerable impact on quality of life (Ettlin 1978).

The third important area of deficits in paraplegia comprises the vegetative nervous system, as well as peristalsis and the function of the bladder. Neurogenic bladder paralysis can be spastic or flaccid and requires specific, individually adjusted bladder management. Renal insufficiency is significant for possible late sequelae because of relapsing renal infections or kidney stones. Neurogenic paralysis of the bowel leads to constipation that may result in a fatal crisis. Only regular discharge combined with laxatives can prevent this.

Another significant aspect in paraplegia is a disorder of the vegetative nervous system reflected in blood pressure regulation. Symptoms are hypotension crises leading to collapse, on the one hand, and hypertension crises (so-called Guttmann reactions) on the other. As patients feel neither pain, nor overfull bladders or clearly constipated intestines, the body reacts to this stress with high blood pressure.

Rehabilitation for paraplegia sufferers

At the beginning of the twentieth century Sir Ludwig Guttmann laid the basis for therapeutic interventions with paraplegic patients. Since then, our knowledge related to rehabilitation has considerably expanded. I shall present a few definitions of the term 'rehabilitation' that are pertinent to an understanding of my study. Rehabilitation means to render something that has changed familiar or manageable again. It covers (Sturm 1979):

- all medical, physiotherapeutic and ergotherapeutic interventions that are required to restore physically impaired persons as much as possible

- the acquisition of aids or devices that guarantee greatest possible mobility and autonomy from others

- adequate and psychological support to overcome any personal and family-related problems

- evaluation of fitness for work and job opportunities.

Phases of the disease are described on the basis of numerous rehabilitation measures, although no differentiated research efforts have been undertaken so far. A possible categorization in phases was presented by Sturm (1979) as:

1. *acute phase*, with preservation of life in shock

2. *consolidation phase* of bone healing, combined with immobilization

3. *mobilization phase* up to release from the paraplegia clinic.

This representation is based on various other treatment concepts, some of which are no longer in use. Sturm is a psychologist and describes in detail which psychological aspects seem to be significant. She also points out that the primary personality of a patient has a decisive influence on rehabilitation outcome and that, as part of the rehabilitation procedure, therapists may expect to recognize significant mental crises in the form of disappointment and grief, or joy and hope (Klaasen 1994; Sturm 1979).

Paraplegia and changed body perception

Numerous psychological studies have described the importance of body perception for self-esteem (e.g. Bielefeld 1991; Fachner 1994). Body perception, although conveyed via proprioceptors in the body, is interpreted from an anthropological–psychological perspective since it is construed by individual and socially conveyed experiences of a specific life narrative (Aldridge 1999, Chapter 2). Schilder (1950) uses the term 'body image'. If our body image is created from continuous self-perception, then it is essential to build up a new body schema after the onset of paraplegia. Ettlin (1978) presents specific findings from interviews with paraplegics in a comprehensive study and tries to demonstrate a correlation between an accident situation and the subsequent construction of a new 'body image'. He uses the term 'paraplegic phantom' according to which a body schema may develop as either disturbed or intact. In the first case, a patient experiences 'the infralesional part in regard of its complete de-affrentation *correctly* as no longer what is *wrong* in regard of its further anatomical existence' (Ettlin 1978, p.81). In the second case, a patient continues to experience 'the infralesional body part in regard of its complete de-affrentation *wrongly*, but which is *correct* in view of its continued, physical–anatomical existence' (p.86).

An important aspect appears to be that experience of position and movement, and paraesthesia, are significant phenomena in understanding paraplegia, and that the construction of a new body schema is part of the rehabilitation. I shall discuss this in more detail in connection with art therapies and the avoidance of chronic pain.

Principles of the research method

The diversity of research questions that emerged from practice and individual patient encounters showed that careful choice of an appropriate method was necessary for my study. The study did not primarily address criteria that may be measured in laboratory settings but rather aspects of functional skills, state of being and organization of daily life; that is, subjective experience influenced by therapy. The focus was on the efficacy of individual patient/physician or patient/therapist encounters. 'While conventional clinical research strives for objective understandings by *excluding* the opinion of individual physicians...the theory of complementary methods achieves objectivity of understanding through deliberate training and *inclusion* of the individual physician's judgment.' (Kiene 2001, p.3). If, therefore, it is impossible to give 'empty' art therapy, the ability to recognize efficacy must be acquired so that it has to be done subjectively while describing content of an extra-subjective nature (Frommer 1995, 1997; Meinefeld 1997).

In his book *Komplementäre Methodenlehre der klinischen Forschung*, Kiene (2001) argues that time of intervention, dose effect and function are convincing when understood as co-varying parameters together. Petersen (2000), who practises psychotherapy, advocates research that will help us to register the effects of an individual therapy encounter. In psychotherapy, and also in art therapy, he sees a need for research in order to meet growing demands to economize.

Aldridge (1999b) underlines the above strategies and also the need for an artistic–scientific research approach, saying that in modern clinical research rigor without imagination leads to stagnation – and imagination alone leads to anarchy. A combination then of rigor and imagination is necessary to meet the challenge of health care combining science with truth and aesthetics with beauty. This approach then is empirical and based on the careful observation of clinical symptoms without theoretical preconceptions. The first step is a comprehensive collection of various data and observations to get an overall impression. At this point, art may enhance science, since as an expressive form it frees sensory activity from its usual meanings:

> A descriptive science of human behaviour based on aesthetics is therefore possible. The tension between what we have become and what we are going to be may be solved as a creative form in the aesthetic context. (Aldridge 1999b, p.148)

Through an extension of perceptions to subjective qualities, research is able to explore the generation of what is new, and is not reduced to a confirmation of hypotheses.

Consequently, my research question had to take into account that the patient as subject shows certain observable and subjectively perceived changes caused by the therapeutic activities of individuals in a team of therapists (Lichtenberger 1993). The changes observed by subjects have to be chronologically related to the intended therapeutic interventions and subjectively perceived changes by the patients themselves, as a causal relationship. The evaluation was performed by me as a person who had taken an active part in the system described.

This work does not presume to represent an objective stance. Rather, it is an attempt to bring aspects gained subjectively from the observation of complex events within a therapeutic community nearer to an objective reality through correlations beyond the individual – that is, through the social. The central principle of 'consistent validity', in qualitative research, is comparable to Kiene's thoughts. From a psychological perspective, the intention is to develop a method to understand subjective perceptions and not to dismiss them through randomization. 'Consistent validity' may help to maintain the scientific claim that the steps of analysis and synthesis performed by the evaluating subject may be repeated, and thereby examined, by every scientist (Kiene 2001).

The researcher's personality

In research where primary perception is in the foreground, the personality of the researcher is crucial. Authenticity and credibility are possible only if researchers reveal their personal understanding of the world.

Research analysis

Research is based on analysis of phenomena and symptoms, in accordance with the level of experience. The second level, developed from phenomenological descriptions, is reflected in the generation of constructs. In presentation and decoding, groups are formed within categories, and a connection with therapy is established. This analytical level forms the basis for interpretation with a view to coding and categorization (Strauss and Corbin 1996).

Correlations

Research into single therapies is useful only if a correlation with clinical findings is possible. The clinical relevance of this type of research is revealed through demonstrated correlations between descriptions that can be derived from medical textbooks and musical ways of expression (Aldridge 2005). Even if some details are lost in the generation of these constructs, a common level of clinical–scientific relevance can be achieved in this way.

> A thought expressed in words is not an image of the actual musical play; similarly, these rules as constructs are only rough representations of what actually happens. But they are a way to structure clinical thinking and may be used in cooperation with clinicians in order to see whether such expressions correspond to their views. (Aldridge 1999b, p.261)

Aldridge also points out that it is important for research to establish structures that form the background for regular meetings and discussions of art therapists: 'It is our task to correlate changes revealed in art therapies with changes observed in this patient in other contexts of his life' (Aldridge 1999b, p.333).

This study is based on the principles described above. The analytical steps correspond to the criteria designed by Aldridge.

In the planning phase I decided on an analysis of treatments already concluded, rather than analysis parallel to therapy. I was thus able to avoid possible negative effects of intervening research on the therapy itself. Moreover, there was no need to consider ethical reservations against scientific intervention into rehabilitation, the treatment concept being in accordance with ethical guidelines. I shall describe the influence of the study on everyday life in connection with the planning and realization of the study, since therapists intensified their perception of patients and thus produced a clearly positive effect.

Planning and patients

The study concept resulted from a one-year preparatory period in which I was active as a physician in the field, working on the hospital ward.

A professional team of carers observes a patient from various perspectives (Table 10.1). The study concept is intended to check whether a patient feels perceived from various perspectives, and therefore understood, and that the individual developments seen by different team members result in a new perspective of the entire development.

Table 10.1 Foci of team conferences

Conferences	Participants	Aspects	Frequency
Ward round	Patient, physician, nursing staff	Immediate medical questions, changes in medication, therapy interviews	Daily
Team	Physician, nursing staff, physiotherapist, ergotherapist, social worker	Current state of rehabilitation with various perspectives in critical situations	Once per week
Physiotherapy round	Patient, physician, nursing staff, physiotherapist, ergotherapist	Demonstration and experience of current motoricity; joint definition of subsequent therapy objectives	Weekly on demand
Art therapy conference	Physician, nursing staff, physiotherapist, art therapists	Presentation of patient's activities in art therapies; classification into current rehabilitation	Weekly on demand
Case conference	Physician, nursing staff, physiotherapist, art therapists	Presentation of bibliographical background, discussion of critical situations in rehabilitation	Weekly on demand

Planning stage

In the planning stage I had numerous discussions with representatives of all medical professions in the team and also with researchers from qualitative and art therapy research. I was able to test and expand spontaneous and subjective assumptions, interpretations and hypotheses about the research subject. A precondition for such interviews was an honest interest in patients and their 'holistic' development. Certain processes, interactions between therapeutic interventions and reactions were defined and recognized in patients' behaviour during the planning phase. This interpretation process and the emerging hypotheses, which were continuously being reviewed, seemed to have an impact on the daily activities of various staff members, to improve their motivation and understanding.

Selection criteria

Criteria for the selection of patients to be analysed were set up as a first step.

1.   All patients to be analysed were to have received at least one of the art therapies on offer. I found that all patients in early rehabilitation and almost all patients treated for complications had received art therapy.

2.   The second important selection criterion referred to the period between onset of paraplegia and actual treatment. A comparable process, the emergence of identity in new paraplegia, was observed in all patients in this early rehabilitation.

3.   No causes for paraplegia were excluded, so that accident patients and others alike were analysed. However, tumour patients were excluded in whom paraplegia had developed as a complication.

4.   There was no age limit, so that the age factor would have to be evaluated in the study as well as the cause of paraplegia.

A deadline was defined to limit the number of patients, and it was chosen randomly so that the selection of patients was not influenced by any other aspects. All the patients analysed concluded their rehabilitation programme between August 1996 and August 1998. This period made consistent evaluation conditions possible, and there was no change in the team of therapists throughout that time. This means that all patients experienced interpersonal consistency in the team of therapists.

All treatment procedures were implemented with the claim of repeatability and analysed individually as single cases. All treatments were included in the final evaluation.

Description of treatments

After definition of the patient material to be analysed, the first practical part was a description of treatments with a focus on developmental aspects. For this purpose I studied all patient records carefully (Figure 10.1). They comprised reports of diverse length on all therapies and covered the following perspectives: medical report; changes in medication; daily nursing documentation; documentation of progress by physiotherapists, ergotherapists and social worker.

All data were summarized in a table and selection followed from the aspects described below:

•   description of physical and functional potential, and the resulting progress steps

•   all specific events with possible implications for everyday life

- difficult and complicating tasks
- all descriptions of a patient's state of wellbeing.

Specific weekly themes were selected from this huge amount of information to summarize the documented data. Weekly themes were then evaluated for possible monthly themes or phases of different length. My intention was to form general categories from primary phenomena, in the sense of open coding (Strauss and Corbin 1996). In accordance with the development theories described by Strauss and Corbin, and the phases postulated by Sturm (1979), the question emerged whether a development in phases would emerge in early rehabilitation that could be analysed. Indeed, phases in rehabilitation were defined independently for each patient, so that a subsequent characterization of phases became possible.

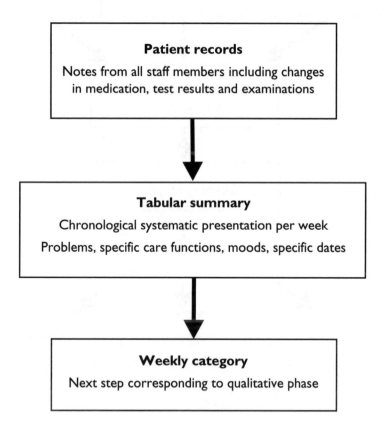

Figure 10.1 The process of rehabilitation analysis for each patient

I examined each patient and defined individual development dynamics, and then summarized all patients from a synchronized starting point in a table. This clear tabular summary helped me to define generally valid principles of development. After this abstraction there followed descriptions of specific aspects in individual patients, to be correlated with various factors. In addition, I formed subgroups with certain common factors and characteristic qualities, followed by a preliminary discussion and an evaluation of generally valid aspects and individual characteristics (Figure 10.2).

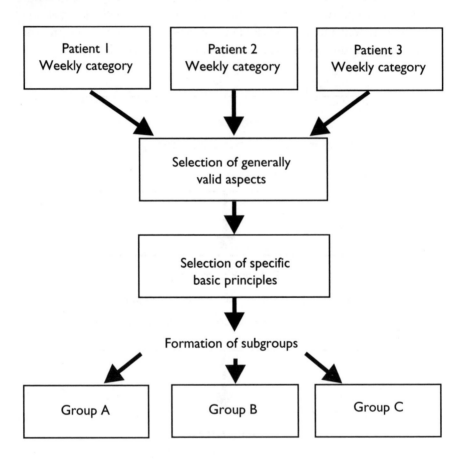

Figure 10.2 Clear tabular summary of all patients

Art therapists' descriptions of therapy sessions

The second type of input were descriptions of therapy sessions by art therapists. They were analysed for comparability and congruity using the summarized documentation by art therapists, the evaluation of paintings as part of painting therapy, and audiotape recording as part of music therapy. Paintings were evaluated with spontaneous descriptions of impressions, and also with Frieling's four-step description (Mees-Christeller, Altmeier and Frieling 2000). Assessment of music therapy was based on detailed records kept by a Nordoff/Robbins trained music therapist based upon her index of musical and therapeutic events. The assessment of eurhythmics was based on records by the eurhythmist and on my personal observations from therapy sessions.

These art therapies were also scrutinized with the intention of identifying any therapy steps as stimuli that would promote certain skills. In a second step, the timescales of the varying therapy courses were explored to find out whether there were any parallel developments and possible causalities.

Unstructured qualitative patient interviews

A third step consisted in unstructured qualitative patient interviews about their personal evaluation of rehabilitation in terms of progress achieved, the influence of the art therapy and the integration of paraplegia into their own biographies.

All the patients consented to be interviewed by me. The interviews took place in a pleasant atmosphere, in most cases at patients' homes. Each interview lasted between 45 and 90 minutes, was recorded on tape and then transcribed word for word. Interview evaluation followed the method suggested by Aldridge (1999a) and Strauss and Corbin (1996) in the form of narrative evaluation. Various theme catalogues emerged from the subjects addressed, whereby the focus was on the experience of progress and the effects of art therapies.

Fifteen patients expressed positive feedback. Nine did not feel stimulated by an art therapy intervention, but six of these described a different type of art therapy as very stimulating, so that only three patients out of 21 described either no effect at all or a negative effect.

Qualitative evaluation

A qualitative evaluation was performed on the basis of these qualitative descriptions of rehabilitation and effects documented by the art therapists. As we shall see below, it was possible to discuss differentiated indications for art therapies, and the connection between 'optimum' rehabilitation and the application of art therapies.

Presentation of results

There were 21 patients in the study group. In 11 patients, paraplegia had developed as a consequence of trauma. In 10 patients, paraplegia was caused by a disease (see Figure 10.3 for the types and levels of paraplegia). The art therapies undertaken are shown in Table 10.2.

Table 10.2 Application of art therapies

Art therapy	Total number of patients	Cervical paraplegia	Thoracic paraplegia	Lumbar paraplegia
Therapeutic eurhythmics	13 patients	6 patients	3 patients	4 patients
Music therapy	12 patients	3 patients	7 patients	2 patients
Painting therapy	10 patients	3 patients	5 patients	2 patients

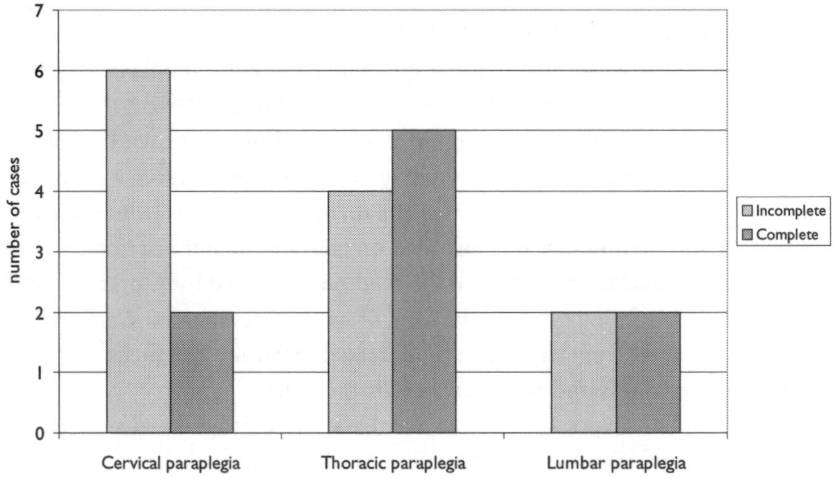

Figure 10.3 Types and levels of paraplegia

Compared to other centres for paraplegic patients (Buck and Beckers 1993; Ettlin 1978; Gerner 1992; Grüninger and Klassen 1985; Znoj *et al.* 1999), the average age of the patient group was rather high, and the group also had a large proportion of disease-induced paraplegias. Only four patients had lumbar paraplegia, so that the percentage of severe paraplegia too was rather high. Since my study is not of a statistical nature, this comparison is simply intended to provide information for possible subsequent studies at other paraplegia centres.

The qualitative analysis

In the qualitative analysis of all patient records, weekly themes and phases emerged that were characterized by typical criteria. The following is a description of phases confirmed from observations based on daily practice and the interview material.

PHASE 1: ACUTE

Life support in 'neurogenic' shock (Table 10.3)

> *From a deeply shattering and paralysing change in his or her physical, emotional and spiritual existence, the patient may be called back into life cautiously, and may raise himself or herself in a new mode of being.*

To enable a transition to the next learning phase, then:

> *The patient passes through the passivity of dependence and the abyss of grief and develops growing activities.*

PHASE 2: LEARNING

Which skills and abilities are acquired in the new situation (Table 10.4)?

> *Through a recovering mobility, the patient develops a learning and profitable attitude in the physical–functional field that is more dominant than the experience of loss.*

To enable a transition to the next consolidation phase, then:

> *The patient carries the impetus of learning and discovering over to the disillusioned acknowledgment of his or her impaired physical abilities and directs his or her view to future existence.*

PHASE 3: CONSOLIDATION

Is it actually possible to go on living with this impairment for some time? Is it possible to come to an arrangement with the impairment, to get used to being disabled (Table 10.5)?

> *Having acquired new skills, the patient must get used to the impairment, with all complications involved. This is the time to prepare the path for psychological detachment from physical boundaries.*

To enable a transition to the next acceptance phase, then:

> *The patient uses the opportunity to search for meaning in being impaired, and to find individual mental relief from physical limitations.*

Table 10.3 Phase 1: Criteria for recognition of the acute phase

Guiding principle: Life support in 'neurogenic' shock

	Necessary criteria	*Possible criteria*
Physical aspects	A pain as a result of injury or surgery	Respiratory paralysis and subsequent pneumonias
	Changed sensitivity requiring a recumbent position	Accident injuries or surgery wounds with healing by secondary intention
	Changed motoricity: rest, inhibition of movement up to onset of mobilization	Possible additional peripheral healing wounds
	Changed respiration requiring breathing exercises	Decubitus ulcers as a result of the acute situation
	Changed circulation requiring monitoring of vital signs.	Life-threatening fever or circulatory crises
	Changed digestion: constipation and laxative therapy	Therapy with medication to stabilise circulation
	Changed urinary secretion: catheter and possible subsequent urinary infections	
Functional aspects	Absolute dependence on help	
Emotional aspects	Anxiety	Misperceptions with regard to body perception
	Pain	Changed self-perception
	Disturbed sleep	Hope of recovery
	Inability to express emotions	
	Painless end of phase	
	Remembered trauma	

Duration of acute phase: 4 days to 8 weeks

Table 10.4 Phase 2: Criteria for the learning phase

Guiding principle: Which skills and abilities are acquired in the new situation?

	Necessary criteria	*Possible criteria*
Physical aspects	Vital parameters stabilized Regulated support of bladder function Wounds healing Regular rhythm of excretion Possible criteria Decubitus ulcers healing New neurological functions developed Training renders cervical collar unnecessary Functional hands ready	
Functional aspects	Reduction of regulation Regular wheelchair mobilization and prolonged mobilization periods Muscle stretching to widen repertoire of mobility Transfer training Selection of wheelchair Training to dress where possible	Weekly steps in learning and development Self-sufficiency Preparation for walking exercises Start of wheelchair sports and training Learning individual transfer Physiotherapy demonstrations to show acquired skills Training in food-intake
Emotional aspects	Discovery of acquired functions and demonstrated pleasure with achievement Experience of pain	Hope of recovery Pain-free intervals Onset of depressive behaviour Expression of aggression or auto-aggression Lack of familiarity and responsibility Visit at home Noting down questions and wishes

Duration of learning phase: 3 to 18 weeks

Table 10.5 Phase 3: Criteria for the consolidation phase

Guiding principle: Is is actually possible to go on living with this impairment for some time? Is it possible to come to an arrangement with the impairment, to get used to being disabled?

	Necessary criteria	*Possible criteria*
Physical aspects	Urinary infections Rubbings, baths, massage	'Mishaps' in excretion Involuntary enuresis Spasticity Vesicular spasticity
Functional aspects	Description of progress steps at varying speed	Maintenance of acquired degree of independence Reduction in independence as a result of complications Renewed development and progress Less frequent therapy and nursing interventions Physical therapy sessions Testing acquired skills, e.g. self-catheterization, transfer
Emotional aspects	Perception of permanent losses Growing acceptance of responsibility Signs of depressive behaviour	Dwindling hope of recovery Expression of hope 'in the face of all that' Functional relapses through depression, pain or spasticity Carelessness Suicidal ideation Participance in 'rolling out' Home visits Interviews with social worker Preparation at place of work, e.g. inspections Deafferentation pains[1] Intensive biographical interviews

The duration of this phase varied from 4 to 28 weeks, with 12 weeks on average. Patients were either released during this stage, or were hospitalized for between 3 and 23 weeks until the phase was concluded and the patient reached the acceptance phase in hospital.

1 'Deafferentation' is the freeing of a motor nerve from sensory components, as a result of severing the dorsal root central to the dorsal ganglion. Definition reproduced from the National Library of Medicine (NLM) website, Medline Plus: www.nlm.nih.gov/medlineplus.

PHASE 4. ACCEPTANCE

Why is paraplegia an integral part of my life (Table 10.6)?

Inner freedom enables patients to come to a satisfactory arrangement with their impairment and to take the initiative to determine their personal future biography.

Emerging aspects

Throughout the process a number of aspects began to emerge:

1. Emotional aspects were clearly recognizable, irrespective of the level of the paralysis. The psychosomatic aspect of the illness, emotional–physical disharmony, was apparent. Emotional crises occurred in the transition from one phase to the next, as intensive talks revealed.

2. The rehabilitation of patients with paralysis that was located lower was faster but underwent comparable phases.

3. In the tetraplegic patients, progress towards the acceptance phase turned out to be more difficult, while acceptance was more easily reached in the patients with a lower level of paralysis.

4. Art therapies were often started at times of change between phases. This 'external' initiative was the expression of an 'inner' question or need in crisis.

5. Actual changes were not immediately recognizable in the frequency of recorded comments but rather in the quality of contents.

6. Physiotherapy treatments as well as case discussions and visits at home indicated or stimulated important changes in some cases but were not significant criteria.

Length of phases in relation to level of paralysis

The length of time spent in a particular phase corresponded to the severity of the illness and the level of the paralysis (Table 10.7). This means that the respective phases had a longer impact and a more marked influence on a patient's personality and more of an effort was required to overcome difficulties due to the illness.

A further differentiation of positive or negative developments requires an analysis of the patients' development after release in order to assess the influence that the illness, the primary personality, social conditions or therapy interventions might have on the prognosis.

Table 10.6 Phase 4: Criteria for the acceptance phase

Guiding principle: Why is paraplegia an integral part of my life?

	Necessary criteria	Possible criteria
Physical aspects	Good coping strategies for possible complications Regular preventive checks	Rare complications
Functional aspects	Good coping in everyday life Specific new skills Good mobility Security in motoric processes	Maximum of independence Successful preparation for resumption of job and new start
Emotional aspects	Reassurance for troubles and anxiety Understanding of oneself and others Consistent self-maintenance Understanding of everyday necessities Personal initiative to exercise Improved sleep Expression of content and pride New discoveries of skills or activities	Good background knowledge about impairment Ability to cope with pain Attempt to integrate impairment into personal biography and family Search for new freedom despite impairment Initiatives in shaping personal future Search for meaning in this state

Table 10.7 Length of phases related to levels of paralysis

Length of acute phase	in cervical paraplegia: 6 to 10 weeks in thoracic paraplegia: 3 to 5 weeks in lumbar paraplegia: 2 to 4 weeks
Length of learning phase	in cervical paraplegia: 4 to 32 weeks in thoracic paraplegia: 6 to 18 weeks in lumbar paraplegia: 5 to 12 weeks
Length of consolidation phase	in cervical paraplegia: 14 to 27 weeks in thoracic paraplegia: 6 to 15 weeks in lumbar paraplegia: 4 to 13 weeks

In a further assessment of criteria, it is therefore important to find out which criteria indicate a serious disease, which show a close relationship between emotional and physical aspects, and which are helpful to overcome impairments so that these may be tackled subsequently.

The patient interviews were focused on specific issues. Open-ended questions permitted an individual focus, and the issues referred to were about rehabilitation, including the question of developmental steps, personal experience of art therapies, and current everyday satisfaction with the overall situation.

As mentioned earlier, all the interviews took place in a very friendly and honest atmosphere and were marked by feelings of gratitude towards the primary care clinic. This illustrates on the one hand the initial degree of dependence from which patients start out, and on the other the enormous responsibility of the primary care clinic. Despite – or even because of – this atmosphere, the style of questions was intended to stimulate criticism. All the patients experienced rehabilitation as a 'continuous' process.

The following classification of patients emerged, taking into account their development after hospitalization as they moved through the varying phases (see Figure 10.4):

- *Group 1*: Acceptance was achieved during hospitalization and maintained subsequently after release from the hospital (6 patients).

- *Group 2*: These patients appeared to be in the acceptance phase and were released but later returned to the consolidation phase with increasing difficulties (5 patients).

- *Group 3*: These patients were released from the hospital in the consolidation phase but achieved the acceptance phase later (3 patients).

- *Group 4*: Acceptance was not achieved either during hospitalization or subsequently (7 patients).

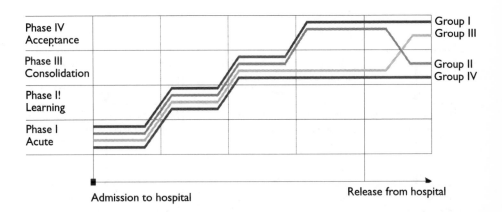

Figure 10.4 Patient development related to phases

Art therapy perspectives

Patients were first described from the art therapists' perspective. This placed the specific aspect of each art therapy into the foreground and also the question whether this type of therapy has an impact on the recovery of paraplegic patients. The qualitative analysis is based on the following sources:

- therapists' notes from therapy sessions in hospital, including the pertinent data of intervention

- classification of therapy sessions within the overall treatment to show correlation and synergy effects

- an interview with therapists on each case as a retrospective analysis, including reciprocal effects as documented in patient records

- a renewed view of painted pictures or audition of recorded tapes for a critical evaluation of development steps

- a general assessment from the physician's perspective

- a retrospective subjective assessment by patients during interviews, on the quality of interventions received and any long-term effects they experienced.

EXAMPLE 1: MR VÖGLER

Mr Vögler was 32 years old when he was hospitalized. His medical diagnosis was spinal cord contusion at level C3–C4 with consecutive incomplete transverse spinal cord syndrome sub-C3 (on ASIA impairment scale D). He had a spinal fracture. His music therapy started in the first week after admission and he had a total of 11 music therapy sessions. Figure 10.5 summarizes his progression.

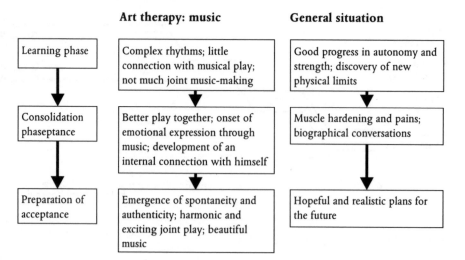

Art therapy: music		General situation
Learning phase	Complex rhythms; little connection with musical play; not much joint music-making	Good progress in autonomy and strength; discovery of new physical limits
Consolidation phaseptance	Better play together; onset of emotional expression through music; development of an internal connection with himself	Muscle hardening and pains; biographical conversations
Preparation of acceptance	Emergence of spontaneity and authenticity; harmonic and exciting joint play; beautiful music	Hopeful and realistic plans for the future

Figure 10.5 Mr Vögler's progression

Here is an excerpt from the interview:

> *Question*: In music, you just mentioned the instruments you used. Do you also remember musical scenes or melodies?

> *Mr V*: I remember that I was able to express my feelings. Well, that I went there in the morning when I did not feel so good, and I hit the instrument rather wildly, and that made me definitely feel better.

Music therapy for Mr Vögler supported his rehabilitation in various respects. In playing the saxophone, he found a way to improve his dexterity on a lasting basis. He also explored his own personality and thus gained self-confidence, which enabled him to start new professional activities in this new-found identity. The therapy had a tremendous effect in his case.

EXAMPLE 2: MR LUNG

Mr Lung was hospitalized at the age of 34 years. His medical diagnosis was a fracture of thoracic vertebrae with a complete post-traumatic transverse spinal cord syndrome. He developed an ability for playing music together with the therapist using dynamic, rhythmic and melodic alterations. Although he said that he had always enjoyed music, he was unable to admit it openly before. Sometimes he succeeded in forgetting and losing himself completely in the music. After considerable initial difficulties his personal initiatives increased, and he was able to give his music a personal touch.

Although his pains did not improve significantly, Mr Lung was able to dissociate himself from pain sometimes and to concentrate on other things, like plans for the future after release from hospital, or on music therapy. Although he received physiotherapy throughout and subsequently, he was not able to apply the learned skills to take care of himself. Given the severity of the impairment and in the light of his personality, this rehabilitation seemed to be only one element of an obviously longer process. His basic willingness to improve was also felt during subsequent periods in hospital. Figure 10.6 summarizes his progression.

Here is an excerpt from the interview:

> *Question*: How did you experience music therapy?

> *Mr Lung*: It also helped to distract me. It also helped that something moved at all.

> *Question*: Did this music...

> Mr Lung: It was also something like a motivation. This is the funny thing, this not being able to do something, and it requires courage to make this ring out. And the little one [the therapist] has often been able to make this possible. [Paraplegic patients can be as chauvinistic as any other person.]

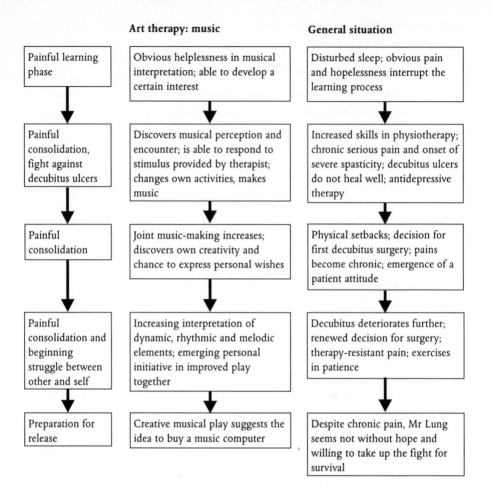

	Art therapy: music	**General situation**
Painful learning phase	Obvious helplessness in musical interpretation; able to develop a certain interest	Disturbed sleep; obvious pain and hopelessness interrupt the learning process
Painful consolidation, fight against decubitus ulcers	Discovers musical perception and encounter; is able to respond to stimulus provided by therapist; changes own activities, makes music	Increased skills in physiotherapy; chronic serious pain and onset of severe spasticity; decubitus ulcers do not heal well; antidepressive therapy
Painful consolidation	Joint music-making increases; discovers own creativity and chance to express personal wishes	Physical setbacks; decision for first decubitus surgery; pains become chronic; emergence of a patient attitude
Painful consolidation and beginning struggle between other and self	Increasing interpretation of dynamic, rhythmic and melodic elements; emerging personal initiative in improved play together	Decubitus deteriorates further; renewed decision for surgery; therapy-resistant pain; exercises in patience
Preparation for release	Creative musical play suggests the idea to buy a music computer	Despite chronic pain, Mr Lung seems not without hope and willing to take up the fight for survival

Figure 10.6 Mr Lung's progression

The traumatic paralysis that occurred under unfortunate circumstances, against the background of a disturbed personality, implied extremely adverse conditions for rehabilitation. The patient's motivation to do something about his life had been low before and was now even more reduced. He felt guilty towards others, and taking responsibility for himself as a precondition of acceptance emerged only slowly. Intensive music therapy sessions did not help this patient to achieve all objectives of early rehabilitation but, nevertheless, supported his motivation for further progress.

Indications for art therapies

I will now present indications, effects and emerging skills that may be reconstructed from the entire documentation from the perspective of therapists, physicians and patients, taking music therapy as the basis. Where patients and medical staff were able to understand the issue in question and the objective, then the art therapy process was effectively coordinated with the entire therapy process.

Apart from typical complications in patients with transverse spinal cord syndrome, such as pain, spasticity, constipation and disturbed sleep, other indications included depressive mood that led to dependency, which is counterproductive to an emerging autonomy. The most important indication for all patients was therefore an improved state of wellbeing, with positive influences on the relief of pain, depression, restlessnes and spasticity.

Consequently, art therapies relieve symptoms that are not exclusively physical. My opinion is that they encourage the emergence of a new balance and thus a new identity. The loss of various physical functions inevitably induces grief, which patients began to experience and express individually in different ways. Art therapies support a patient when he or she is unable to give expression to distress.

Effects of art therapies correlated with prognosis

The analysis revealed different groupings in the assessment of developmental progress. Criteria for assessment were the art therapist's subjective impression of therapy success and the patient's experience as described in the interview. Therapists' opinions were documented as written comments in patient notes. The four groupings can be described as follows:

- *Group A*: successful response from the perspectives of both therapist and patient

- *Group B*: successful response from the perspective of the therapist but not recognized by the patient

- *Group C*: no successful response from the perspective of the therapist, but recognition of a positive effect by the patient

- *Group D*: no successful response from the perspectives of both therapist and patient.

In the critical discussion of 'responders' and 'non-responders' to art therapies, I found that references to past experience in the wider range of art therapies had a positive influence on art therapy sessions. Personal participation in the sense of increasing motivation, like voluntariness, had positive effects. The period between the ages of 40 and 45 turned out to be the most difficult with regard to art therapies. Incomplete states of paralysis proved to be more favourable than complete quadriplegia or paraplegia. Patients with university training appeared to find complex coping processes easier. Arts therapies, however, encouraged all patients irrespective of their intellectual background. Patients who were more flexible and critical were also better able to make use of art therapies. Social or familial support had an impact on the general process but not on the effectiveness of art therapies.

All patients from group 1 (see Figure 10.4) concluded at least one art therapy session with success, in their own opinion and that of the therapist. Although we would be wrong to define the successful attendance at an art therapy session as a precondition of a successful rehabilitation, we may draw the conclusion that a successful attendance at an art therapy intervention facilitates acceptance. A differentiated analysis of patients in group 1 revealed that most of these people had a good prognosis given the degree of their impairment, so that the question about the spontaneous development without art therapies has to remain open. Indications of an unequivocally positive effect of art therapies, as beneficial for acceptance and integration into a patient's biography, are on the one hand repeated crises, which also might have resulted in a less positive development, and on the other hand the patient's subjective perceptions.

A positive effect of art therapies was noticeable in group 2, so that art therapy would certainly have to be considered positive even if it did not lead to lasting acceptance. The prognosis for rehabilitation due to illness or social conditions was less favourable for all these patients compared to those in group 1. If the effects of art therapies were considered insufficient for more lasting progress towards acceptance, then the patient's wish for art therapy sessions even after rehabilitation could be of decisive importance. This wish was not unequivocal. Art therapies had helped to achieve short-term acceptance in this particular setting, but other complications had a stronger impact.

Group 3 certainly was most heterogeneous as to patients' background and development. It is difficult to draw clear conclusions, although individual patient motivation is important.

Group 4 is open to different interpretations since it comprised seriously ill patients and those with fewer skills for self-reflection. For the seriously ill patients, art therapies certainly provided relief and thus an improvement in the quality of life. More differentiation is required in the assessment of those patients who were unable to experience positive effects of art therapies because of avoidance behaviour or their reduced introspective abilities.

Art therapies may promote the process of integration and thereby smooth the path towards acceptance if a patient is open for inner emotional coping processes. Either the therapist or the patient should decide on a continuation of an art therapy intervention after three to four sessions. It is important in this context whether a verbal or non-verbal communication was started as the basis for any new developments. The freedom to end a therapy may have a positive effect on the entire process.

It appears pertinent to have not more than three types of art therapy interventions at the same time, since a patient's attention is split between the differing forms of expression. After one type of art therapy has ended, it may be very useful to start a different kind of art therapy with a different medium of communication. A reference to previous art or music therapy experience before the impairment helps support successful treatment (Simon Gilbertson also makes this point in Chapter 5).

An important basis for successful art therapy is an integration into the entire rehabilitation process, either as interventions for short-term physical crises or longer-term interventions into the abovementioned rehabilitation phases.

Summary

The following principles have emerged:

- Early rehabilitation in paraplegic patients follows certain phases.

- The decisive criterion for rehabilitation is whether patients are able to reach the acceptance phase or remain in the consolidation phase.

- The analysis of progress in the arts therapies also reveals phases. It is possible to see direct effects derived from art therapy for everyday life, and advances in the entire rehabilitation process. Some patients profited considerably, while others gave up on art therapies after a few sessions. The subsequent analysis did not reveal any clear criteria to differentiate between these two patient groupings.

Discussion

There are clear phases in the course of early rehabilitation. The duration of these phases differs and does not necessarily correlate with the degree of impairment but is influenced by various factors (primary personality, social environment and therapy intervention).

Art therapies have a positive effect on coping abilities and promote acceptance. Patients who were motivated describe art therapies as supportive and even as a highly enhancing experience. The development in those patients who, despite an unfavourable prognosis, have experienced positive changes should be particularly pointed out in this context. Art therapies stimulate ways to develop and realize new perspectives, even though the patients may have marked inner reservations.

Thirteen out of 21 patients described the effects of art therapies as clearly positive, with potential for a long-term influence on coping. Five further patients showed positive effects of art therapies on the course of the disease but this was temporary. Only four patients did not benefit from art therapy, and therapy was stopped in these cases. All four patients had also decided against any psychological therapies while in rehabilitation.

Decisive factors for a successful response are the choice of the *right time*, the choice of the *appropriate therapy* in continuation of previous experience, or a basic *ability to get along with the therapist in question*. In cases where patients did not respond to therapy, the physician, the therapist involved and the patient decided to end the therapy after a few sessions. In some cases, however, preliminary reservations were overcome so that the patient in question experienced the therapy as a real stimulus and enhancement in rehabilitation. Decisions concerning one or another art therapy method were based on antagonistic feelings, objective reasons and a patient's potential for change.

Necessary conditions for the art therapy process were a willingness to participate and enjoyment of the therapy itself. Discussions on whether to continue or to end a therapy resulted in a 'free' choice for all patients. The paralysis itself had robbed patients of any freedom of decision in many spheres of their lives, but in the case of art therapies a freedom of choice remained. This alone supported their self-esteem and put a different perspective on their dependence on those interventions.

My perspective is that art therapies in early rehabilitation offer therapy forms that stimulate a comprehensive search for a new identity early in the process. Patients exhibit less resistance in the therapy, compared to therapeutic interviews. Personal activity experienced in art therapies encourages patients to find a unity between the physical, emotional and cognitive dimensions of their being, and thereby a new identity. A new individual experience of time, and its implications for memory, communication and mood control are promoted.

The quality of life together with a partner or family is tremendously important, and art therapies stimulate these abilities – particularly communicative abilities – in paraplegic patients.

Art therapies are generally based on the individual encounter between patient and therapist. This personal relationship gives rise to the question as to how far the assessment of a therapy can remain honest. The therapist's authenticity and introspective capability actually revealed a good correlation, which suggests honesty on the part of therapists in general.

In my study, patients' self-assessments corresponded to their therapist's assessment in 25 of 33 interventions. In three of the therapies under examination it was not possible to record patients' self-evaluation for organizational reasons. Only five therapies revealed a discrepancy between self-evaluation and external evaluation; in two of these cases, patients saw positive effects while therapists considered the 'success' as rather insignificant. This means that therapists used stricter criteria for therapy success. Where patients showed themselves satisfied, the question concerning the prognosis based on diagnosis was certainly more pertinent than a critical assessment of the effects of art therapies.

There remain only three therapies where therapists observed positive effects while the patients concerned did not register such positive effects. These results suggest that the earnestly negotiated and agreed decision either to continue or to end a therapy is probably the right one. A precondition is honesty on the part of physician, therapist and patient.

The process of individual art therapy intervention

Within the therapeutic process itself there was an initial process of learning, of familiarizing oneself with the required techniques. The second step described an emotional connection to the 'work of art'. A third step was characterized by the interpretation of a motif; art was thus individualized in preparation of an individual interpretation of life. The effects of art therapies may be seen from the acquisition or experience of new abilities like courage, trust, initiative and relaxation that subsequently make a transfer into other daily activities possible.

The people who clearly demonstrated such effects were able to advance towards acceptance, while those who experienced and developed only minor improvements remained in the consolidation phase. Even if outcome is markedly better in patients due to art therapy interventions, it must be kept in mind that these patients already have at least some of the abilities that facilitate adaptation to a new stressful situation. Art therapies have the potential to stimulate and offer a unique opportunity to make an impact on an otherwise unfavourable prognosis. These therapies promote emotional creativity and thereby support the emergence of a comprehensive new identity.

In some sense, art therapy objectives are similar to those that we encounter in psychotherapy: strengthened self-confidence, experience of actively shaping one's life, and an acceptance of one's own personality. In view of the fact that most paraplegic patients refuse psychotherapy in early rehabilitation, and that art therapies pursue comparable objectives, the offer of art therapy would enhance early rehabilitation considerably and would help to reduce complications. We see in the chapter from Wolfgang Schmid that anxiety and depression scores are positively influenced by music therapy and we could transfer those results to this patient population. Art therapy should therefore become an integral part of early rehabilitation.

This is also relevant in cost–benefit analyses since art therapies may help to reduce the need for further hospitalization because of complications. With this in mind, art therapies might be an alternative to the 'coping effectiveness training' offered in other paraplegia centres.

Is there a way to make a cost–benefit analysis?

If art therapies during the learning and consolidation phases support progress towards acceptance, then the costs incurred are justified in any case. This study has revealed that there are patients who experienced exactly this beneficial effect so that subsequent costs were considerably lower and social reintegration was possible. It was important to continue art therapy interventions for these patients during the entire rehabilitation period, since qualitatively necessary steps over a period of time had to be supported. Patients left when they had reached the acceptance phase, so that it was justified to end the art therapy sessions at that point.

Patients who left while in the consolidation phase would have profited from continued art therapies on an outpatient basis, but only a minority wanted this. The expenditure seemed too high and demand too low.

For a cost–benefit analysis, it is also important to develop skills in presenting differentiated indications. This, and interdisciplinary coordination, improve the effects of art therapies. The entire team was challenged to cooperate with the art therapists to find a common language in order to describe patients' developments and to use combined effects to the maximum. Such close communication also allows us to end ineffective therapies earlier and thus to fight the general cost explosion in health care.

Any cost analysis should also take the effects on other therapies into account. A certain desperation and lack of motivation was observed in patients as well as therapists during the consolidation phase; but this mood often changed to something like active expectation when reports from art therapy sessions documented developmental steps, so that art therapies obviously helped to fight the threat of burnout. Further studies will be required to translate such effects into figures, and comprehensive system analyses should be performed, which appear justified in view of the findings of this study.

CHAPTER 11

Coda

David Aldridge

We have seen from the chapters in this book that music therapy is active as an intervention in neurological rehabilitation. Or rather music therapies are active in settings where neurological intervention takes place. Some of these interventions are specific for the problem being solved. In aphasia, for example, it is specific musical elements of articulation, repetition and prosody that are used through improvised singing. This method is not taught directly on training courses. The problem is that this book may well be read and practitioners will immediately conclude that music therapy works generically. Not so. It only works, from these results, using a particular method. Therapists from other approaches will have to apply a similarly structured study to comparable patients.

The same goes for the multiple sclerosis study. We have built upon the work of music therapy pioneers and related our study to their work. Indeed, the non-specificity of earlier studies helped us to be specific in this study.

What we have done for both studies is to provide an effect size statistic, and it is hoped that we can begin to develop a basis for comparability. This cannot be achieved by the adoption of statistical understanding alone. We need a collaborative culture of research endeavour.

Two chapters have told us how we need to be both specific and precise in our reporting. If we are to consolidate the advances made in practice, then we have to be thorough in our documentation and reporting if we are to offer evidence of therapeutic effect.

Thoroughly reported cases, with comparable data sets and meticulous small-scale studies, will provide the basis for efficacy studies that can be built into effectiveness studies. We can achieve this if we work together. Jobs will depend upon it and thereby the survival of music therapy practice.

We also see that human activity is a performance. Consciousness, or knowing with (from the Latin *con* for 'with' and *scire* for 'knowing'), is a dialogical activity.

We can speak of the ecology of communication as a mutual dynamic performance. The same can be said of cognition: it is a dynamic state that we achieve with others. Rhythm is the substrate of this ecology – not fixed but dynamic and flowing.

To return to the fear of non-communication that I expressed in the opening paragraphs of Chapter 1, this fear can be resolved by the hope that, through singing, people will come to the aid of my consciousness. Indeed, the danger that many of us face is isolation, as I have written elsewhere, in that we 'fall out' of the world. That world is a universe of others, a milieu of performances in which we partake. For those people we call 'other', or 'deviant', even if this is labelled as illness or handicap, we deny them the mutuality of performance with us. The way of return is through performance.

The performative metaphor was developed because I wanted to get away from the mechanical concept of chronological time and a body that could be repaired like a mechanism. We are more like works of art, and composed improvised pieces of work at that. Indeed, by extending the metaphor we can regard ourselves as works in progress, if not working in progress. This has implications for the performance of our development. Development is not simply a process that takes place in babies and small children: we develop throughout our lives.

When we think about development, we often consider this as a linear progression like climbing a ladder upwards for most of our lives with a rapid decline at the end. However, maybe our lives are not so simply performed. Sometimes we regress, but then make leaps forward. If we release ourselves from the idea of a developmental ladder of progress, then we can open ourselves to a constellation of stages through which we move during our life course. And, stages are those places where performances can take place.

Such participative performances were traditionally the basis for healing rituals that included music. One of the difficulties in writing about traditional approaches is that they are located in a past that has its own validity, so how can they be transposed in time to the present and to other cultures? Comparisons between classical Sufi descriptions of mystical states and mystical stations demand considerable reinterpretation even if we want to integrate them with modern and post-modern concerns about the mysticism of everyday life. The Sufi path is marked by a number of different stages or stations (maqam/maqamat) which the Sufi traveller passes through as he advances on the path. On his way the Sufi also experiences various psychological and emotional states. States differ from the stations through which the Sufi passes in that the states are transitory experiences granted to him by God and over which he has no control, whereas the stations are permanent stages on the path which he has achieved through his own individual effort.

One of the difficulties in studying Sufi writings is that authors differ in their categorization of states and stations. One reason for this is that the knowledge of such states is gained through interior experiences rather than through the external senses. A second, but related, reason is that each teacher will pass on that experience according to the time, place and students he or she is teaching. We can see the same things in the teaching that Gerhard Tucek writes about. These teachings were specific for a particular time, place and persons, like all schools of therapy. Transferring them directly to a modern-day context is rather like trying to turn us into fourteenth-century musicians or eleventh-century patients in a particular location in Turkey. Traditions have to live anew and that is through the direct understanding of making music today.

In trying to understand healing musics we must locate them within cultures that are relevant to their performance. We have not only performers but also listeners. When we consider musics that heal, we also have rituals that are located within particular communities with clearly defined roles and expectations. In some countries, musicians playing this music were from a particular caste and had a specific hierarchical relationship with the Sufi teacher and with their patrons. The principal function of the music was not in terms of healing but religious, in terms of spiritual attainment, although some musical modes were considered to be healing. Some of these musics are no longer applicable to health care delivery because they have been superseded by practices that are more effective; the nature of illness has changed relevant to time and culture, and our expectations of the process of sickness and recovery are different.

The use of the term 'maqam' (see Chapter 9) may be at first confusing. Maqam is literally a station *in terms* of a spiritual station or developmental level, as distinct from a state of consciousness. It is also a 'scale' or 'mode' in Arabic, Indic and Near-Eastern music. The maqam (plural *maqamat*) is a musical theme or style that defines the pitches, patterns and development of a piece of music. The Western term that comes closest to describing the maqam is the 'mode'. A mode, in music, is an ordered series of musical intervals, which along with the key, or tonic, define the pitches. In the world of Arab musics, maqam refers to specific tone scales, of which there is an enormous variety, and these include a vast range of 'microtones'. The Arabic scales, from which maqamat are built, are not even-tempered, unlike the chromatic scale used in Western classical music. Instead, fifth notes are tuned based on the third harmonic. The tuning of the remaining notes entirely depends on the maqam. The reasons for this tuning are probably historically based on string instruments like the oud. A side-effect of not having even-tempered tuning is that the same note (by name) may have a slightly different pitch depending on which maqam it is played in.

Many maqamat include notes that can be approximated with quarter tones, although they rarely are precise quarters falling exactly halfway between two semitones and depend upon microtonal subtleties. Each maqam must be learned by ear. This aural tradition is taught by a teacher and protected by that teacher. We also see this in terms of Sufi teachings that are passed on from teacher to seeker, where the teacher encourages the seeker to have experiences that lead to knowledge. Hence, each teacher will emphasize that it is his or her way that must be followed, and his or her way alone. This causes particular problems in modern systems of learning where students are encouraged to learn in modern settings but with a traditional, and sometimes fossilized, attitude.

Music as healing agent, music in healing rituals and music therapy in cultures of care are all vibrant activities that we can be involved in. We have resources of knowledge that can be shared and pooled. There is no one singular way of understanding this multiplicity of knowledge. Fortunately we are developing research cultures of tolerance that see human knowledge as being many-sided. Together we can orchestrate our knowings into a symphony of wisdom. In this sense health is a performance that can be achieved. Health is not simply a singular performance; it is performed with others. A woman that Wolfgang Schmid worked with said she was no longer a patient but a musician. Here lies an element of healing, the change in self-awareness from a stigmatized person with a degenerating future to the emergence of a proud creative artist. To achieve this performance she needed the mutuality of the relationship in a context that we defined as healing.

References

Abad, V. (2002) 'Reaching the Socially Isolated Person with Alzheimer's Disease Through Group Music Therapy – A Case Report.' Available at www.voices.no/mainissues/Voices2(3)abad.html.

Albert, M.L., Sparks, R.W. and Helm, N. (1973) 'MIT for aphasia'. *Archives of Neurology 29*, 130–131.

Alcock, G. Chambers, B., Christopheson, J., Heiser, D. and Groetzinger, D. (2001) 'Complementary and alternative therapies for Multiple Sclerosis.' In J. Halper (ed) *Advanced concepts in multiple sclerosis nursing care* (pp.239–266). New York: Demos Medical Publishing.

Aldridge, D. (1987) *One Body: A Guide to Healing in the Church*. London: SPCK.

Aldridge, D. (1989a) 'A phenomenological comparison of the organization of music and the self.' *The Arts in Psychotherapy 16*, 2, 91–97.

Aldridge, D. (1989b) 'Music, communication and medicine: discussion paper.' *Journal of the Royal Society of Medicine 82*, 12, 743–746.

Aldridge, D. (1991a) 'Aesthetics and the individual in the practice of medical research.' *Journal of the Royal Society of Medicine 84*, 3.

Aldridge, D. (1991b) 'Creativity and consciousness: Music therapy in intensive care.' *The Arts in Psychotherapy 18*, 4, 359–362.

Aldridge, D. (1993a) 'The music of the body: Music therapy in medical settings.' *Advances 9*, 1, 17–35.

Aldridge, D. (1993b) 'Music and Alzheimer's disease – assessment and therapy: Discussion paper.' *Journal of the Royal Society of Medicine 86*, 2, 93–95.

Aldridge, D. (1993c) 'Music therapy research: II. Research methods suitable for music therapy.' *The Arts in Psychotherapy 20*, 2, 117–131.

Aldridge, D. (1994) 'Alzheimer's disease: Rhythm, timing and music as therapy.' *Biomedicine and Pharmacotherapy 48*, 7, 275–281.

Aldridge, D. (1996) *Music Therapy Research and Practice in Medicine*. London: Jessica Kingsley Publishers.

Aldridge, D. (1997) *Kairos: Beiträge zur Musiktherapie in der Medizin*. Band 1. Bern: Hans Huber.

Aldridge, D. (1998a) *Suicide: The Tragedy of Hopelessness*. London: Jessica Kingsley Publishers.

Aldridge, D. (1998b) 'Music therapy and the treatment of Alzheimer's disease.' *Journal of Clinical Geropsychology 4*, 1, 17–30.

Aldridge, D. (1999a) *Music Therapy in Palliative Care: New Voices*. London: Jessica Kingsley Publishers.

Aldridge, D. (1999b) *Musiktherapie in der Medizin: Forschungsstrategien und praktische Erfahrung*. Bern: Hans Huber.

Aldridge, D. (ed.) (1999c) *Kairos: Beiträge zur Musiktherapie in der Medizin*. Bern: Hans Huber.

Aldridge, D. (2000a) *Music Therapy in Dementia Care*. London: Jessica Kingsley Publishers.

Aldridge, D. (2000b) 'It's not what you do but the way that you do it.' In D. Aldridge (eds) *Music Therapy in Dementia Care*. London: Jessica Kingsley Publishers.

Aldridge, D. (2000c) *Spirituality, Healing and Medicine.* London: Jessica Kingsley Publishers.

Aldridge, D. (2001a) 'Music therapy and neurological rehabilitation: Recognition and the performed body in an ecological niche.' *Music Therapy Today (online).* Retrieved January 2003, available at www.musictherapyworld.net.

Aldridge, D. (2001b) 'Gesture and dialogue; an embodied hermeneutic.' Paper presented at the conference Music Therapy and Art Therapy in Neurodegenerative Diseases, Vitoria-Gasteiz, Spain.

Aldridge, D. (2002) 'Philosophical speculations on two therapeutic applications of breath.' *Subtle Energies & Energy Medicine 12,* 2, 107–124.

Aldridge, D. (2003) 'The therapeutic effects of music.' In W.B. Jonas and C. Crawford (eds) *Healing Intention and Energy Medicine: Science, Research Methods and Clinical Implications.* London: Churchill Livingstone.

Aldridge, D. (2004) 'Nah an der Praxis bleiben: Evidenz – für wen, von wem?' In G. Tucek (ed) *Konzepte der Musiktherapie und Musikmedizin.* Wien: Facultas Verlag.

Aldridge, D. (2005) *Case Study Designs in Music Therapy.* London: Jessica Kingsley Publishers.

Aldridge, D. and Aldridge, G. (1992) 'Two epistemologies: Music therapy and medicine in the treatment of dementia.' *The Arts in Psychotherapy 19,* 4, 243–255.

Aldridge, D. and Aldridge, G. (2002) 'Therapeutic narrative analysis: A methodological proposal for the interpretation of music therapy traces.' Available at www.musictherapyworld.de/modules/mmmagazin, December 2002.

Aldridge, D. and Brandt, G. (1991) 'Music therapy and Alzheimer's disease.' *Journal of British Music Therapy 5,* 2, 28–63.

Aldridge, D., Gilbertson, S. and Wentz, M. (2004) *Music Therapy World Database CD ROM.* Witten: Music Therapy World.

Aldridge, D., Gustorff, D. and Hannich, H.J. (1990) 'Where am I? Music therapy applied to coma patients.' *Journal of the Royal Society of Medicine 83,* 6, 345–346.

Aldridge, G. (1998) 'Die Entwicklung einer Melodie im Kontext improvisatorischer Musiktherapie.' Unpublished doctoral thesis, University of Aalborg, Denmark.

Aldridge, G. (2000) 'Improvisation as an assessment of potential in early Alzheimer's disease.' In D. Aldridge (ed) *Music Therapy in Dementia Care.* London: Jessica Kingsley Publishers.

Alibali, M., Heath, D. and Myers, H. (2001) 'Effects of visibility between speaker and listener on gesture production: Some gestures are meant to be seen.' *Journal of Memory and Language 44,* 169–188.

Alibali, M., Kita, S. and Young, A. (2000) 'Gesture and the process of speech production: We think, therefore we gesture.' *Language and Cognitive Processes 15,* 6, 593–613.

Altmeyer, S. and Tietze, U. (2003) 'Strukturierte Gruppentherapie bei PatientInnen mit Multipler Sklerose-Nachuntersuchung.' *Forum Psychosomatik. Zeitschrift für psychosomatische Multiple Sclerosis-Forschung 12. Jg.,* 1/2003, 13–22.

Altschuler, I. (1948/2001) 'A psychiatrist's experience with music as a therapeutic agent. The series of classical articles.' *Nordic Journal of Music Therapy 10,* 1, 69–76.

Andrews, K. (1996) 'International Working Party on the Management of the Vegetative State: Summary Report.' *Brain Injury 10,* 11, S797–806.

Ansdell, G. (1995) *Music for Life: Aspects of Creative Music Therapy with Adult Clients.* London: Jessica Kingsley Publishers.

Apel, A., Greim, B. and Zettl, U. (2003) 'Inanspruchnahme alternativer und komplementärer Therapien (AKT) von Patienten mit Multiple Sklerose unter Berücksichtigung der Krankheitsbewältigung' Poster presentation at 76 Kongreß der Deutschen Gesellschaft für Neurologie, Hamburg, 3–6 September 2003. Supplement 30, p.110.

As-Sarrag and Abu Nasr (1990) *Schlaglichter über das Sufitum. Abu Nasr al Sarrags Kitab al-Luma.* Stuttgart: Gramlich.

Ashida, S. (2000) 'The effect of reminiscence music therapy sessions on changes in depressive symptoms in elderly persons with dementia.' *Journal of Music Therapy 37*, 3, 170–182.

Baker, F. (2001) 'The effects of live, tapes, and no music on people experiencing posttraumatic amnesia.' *Journal of Music Therapy 38*, 3, 170–192.

Barker, V.L. and Brunk, B. (1991) 'The role of a creative arts group in the treatment of clients with traumatic brain injury.' *Music Therapy Perspectives 9*, 26–31.

Basso, A., Capitani, E. and Vignolo, L.A. (1979) 'Influence of rehabilitation on language skills in aphasic patients.' *Archives of Neurology 36*, 190–196.

Baumgartner, G. (1997) 'Bewegungsfundierte Musiktherapie in der Gerontopsychiatrie: Ein Beispiel für die Anwendung der RES-diagnostik in der Praxis.' *Musik-, Tanz- und Kunsttherapie 8*, 105–114.

Bavastro, P., Britsch, M., Hönigschwid, J., Homann, K., Kohn, R. and Stehle, A. (1998) *Ethik-Charta.* www.fuente.de/fuente/bioethik/ethkch12.htm

Bayne, T. (2001) 'Co-consciousness: Review of Barry Dainton's "Stream of Consciousness".' *Journal of Consciousness Studies 8*, 3, S79–92.

Beatty, W., Testa, J., English, S. and Winn, P. (1997a) Influences of clustering and switching on the verbal fluency performance of patients with Alzheimer's disease.' *Aging Neuropsychology and Cognition 4*, 4, 273–279.

Beatty, W., Brumback, R. and von Sattel, J. (1997b) 'Autopsy-proven Alzheimer disease in a patient with dementia who retained musical skill in life.' *Archives of Neurology 54*, 12, 1448.

Beatty, W., Zavadil, D. and Bailly, R.C. (1988) 'Preserved musical skill in a severely demented patient.' *International Journal of Clinical Neuropsychology 10*, 4, 158–164.

Beatty, W.W., Winn, P., Adams, R.L., Allen, E.W., Wilson, D.A., Prince, J.R., Olson, K.A., Dean, K. and Littleford, D. (1994) 'Preserved cognitive skills in dementia of the Alzheimer type.' *Archives of Neurology 51*, 1040–1046.

Beck, C. (1998) 'Psychosocial and behavioral interventions for Alzheimer's disease patients and their families.' *American Journal of Geriatric Psychiatry 6*, 2, S41–48.

Becker-Glauch, W. (1997) *Das Reich Gottes als Leitbild in der Künstlerischen Therapie.* Münster: Paroli.

Beckermann, A. (1996) 'Können mentale Phänomene neurobiologisch erklärt werden?' In G. Roth and W. Prinz (eds) *Kopf-Arbeit: Gehirnfunktion und kognitive Leistungen.* Heidelberg: Spektrum Akademischer Verlag.

Belin, P. and Van Eckhout, P. (1996) 'Recovery from nonfluent aphasia after MIT: A PET-study.' *Neurology 47*, 6, 1504–1511.

Bender, M. and Cheston, R. (1997) 'Inhabitants of a lost kingdom: A model of the subjective experiences of dementia.' *Ageing and Society 17*, 513–532.

Benke, T., Bosch, S. and Andree, B. (1998) 'A study of emotional processing in Parkinson's disease.' *Brain and Cognition 38*, 1, 36–52.

Berger, G., Bernhardt, T., Schramm, U., Muller, R., Landsiedel-Anders, S. and Peters, J. (2004) 'No effects of a combination of caregivers support group and memory training/music therapy in dementia patients from a memory clinic population.' *International Journal of Geriatric Psychiatry 19*, 223–231.

Berman, I. (1981) 'Musical functioning, speech lateralization and the amusias.' *South African Medical Journal 59*, 78–81.

Berthold, H. (1983) 'Musik und Hemisphärendominanz: Untersuchung der Ausfälle von musikalischen Hirnfunktionen bei Patienten mit umschriebenen Hirnläsionen anhand standardisierter Musiktests.' Manuscript, Albert-Ludwigs-Universität.

Besson, M. and Friederici, A.D. (1998) 'Language and music: A comparative view.' *Music Perception 16*, 1, 1–9.

Bielefeld, J. (1986) *Körpererfahrung*. Göttingen: Hogrefe.

Bielefeld, J. (1991) *Körpererfahrung: Grundlagen menschlichen Bewegungsverhaltens*. Göttingen: Hogrefe.

Bischof, S. (2001) 'Musiktherapie mit apallischen Kindern'. In D. Aldridge (ed.) *Kairos V: Musiktherapie mit Kindern*. Bern: Huber Verlag.

Blackmore, S.J. (2001) 'There is no stream of consciousness.' *Journal of Consciousness Studies 9*, 5–6, S95–99.

Bolger, E.P. and Judson, M.A. (1984) 'The therapeutic value of singing.' *New England Journal of Medicine 311*, 1704.

Bond, J. and Corner, L. (2001) 'Researching dementia: Are there unique methodological challenges for health services research.' *Ageing and Society 21*, 95–116.

Bonder, B. (1994) 'Psychotherapy for individuals with Alzheimer disease.' *Alzheimer Disease and Associated Disorders 8*, Suppl. 3, 75–81.

Bonin, D. V., Giger, A., Stöcklin, C. and Moser, M. (1999) 'Rhythmologische Untersuchungen zur Sprachtherapie' In P. Heusser (ed) *Akademische Forschung in der Anthroposophischen Medizin*. Bern: Peter Lang.

Braben, L. (1992) 'A song for Mrs Smith.' *Nursing Times 88*, 41, 54.

Bradshaw, J.L. (1989) *Hemispheric Specialization and Psychological Function*. Chichester: John Wiley.

Breckinridge Church, R. (1999) 'Using gesture and speech to capture transitions in learning.' *Cognitive Development 14*, 2, 313–342.

Brendel, B. and Ziegler, W. (2001) 'Articulatory synchronization in the treatment of apraxia of speech.' Fourth International Speech Motor Conference, 13–16 June 2001, Nijmegen. Chapter 43, 175–177.

Brendel, B., Ziegler, W. and Deger, K. (2000) 'The synchronization paradigm in the treatment of apraxia of speech.' *Journal of Neurolinguistics 13*, 254–257.

Bright, R. (1986) 'The use of music therapy and activities with demented patients who are deemed "difficult to manage".' *Clinical Gerontologist 6*, 2, 131–144.

Bright, R. (1997) *Music Therapy and the Dementias: Improving the Quality of Life*. Washington: MMB Music, Inc.

Bright, R. and Signorelli, R. (1999) 'Improving quality of life for profoundly brain-impaired clients: The role of music therapy.' In R. Rebollo Pratt and D. Erdonmez Grocke (eds) *Music Medicine 3*. Parkville: University of Melbourne.

Brod, M., Mendelsohn, G. and Roberts, B. (1998) 'Patients' experiences of Parkinson's disease.' *Journal of Gerontology 53*, 4, 213–222.

Brookmeyer, R., Gray, S. and Kawas, C. (1998) 'Projections of Alzheimer's disease in the United States and the public health impact of delaying disease onset.' *American Journal of Public Health 88*, 1337–1342.

Brotons, M. (2000) 'An overview of the music therapy literature relating to elderly people.' In D. Aldridge (ed) *Music Therapy in Dementia Care*. London: Jessica Kingsley Publishers.

Brotons, M. and Koger, S.M. (2000) 'The impact of music therapy on language functioning in dementia.' *Journal of Music Therapy 37*, 3, 183–195.

Brotons, M., Koger, S. and Pickett-Cooper, P. (1997) 'Music and dementias: A review of literature.' *Journal of Music Therapy 34*, 4, 204–245.

Brotons, M. and Marti, P. (2003) 'Music therapy with Alzheimer's patients and their family caregivers: A pilot project.' *Journal of Music Therapy 40*, 2, 138–150.

Brotons, M. and Pickett-Cooper, P. (1994) 'Preferences of Alzheimer's disease patients for music activities: Singing, instruments, dance/movement, games, and composition/ improvisation.' *Journal of Music Therapy 31*, 3, 220–233.

Brotons, M. and Pickett-Cooper, P. (1996) 'The effects of music therapy intervention on agitation behaviors of Alzheimer's disease patients.' *Journal of Music Therapy 33*, 1, 2–18.

Brown, S., Götell, E. and Ekman, S. (2001) 'Singing as a therapeutic intervention in dementia care.' *Journal of Dementia Care*, July/August, 33–37.

Brück, W. (2002) 'Pathologie und Pathophysiologie.' In R.M. Schmidt and F. Hoffmann (eds) *Multiple Sklerose*. München: Urban & Fischer.

Bruijn, M. de and Hurkmans, J. (2002) *Speech–Music Therapy for Aphasia*. Groningen: SMTA Centrum voor Revalidatie.

Bruscia, K.E. (1995) 'The process of doing qualitative research. Part I: Introduction.' In B.L. Wheeler (ed) *Music Therapy Research: Quantitative and Qualitative Perspectives*. Phoenixville: Barcelona Publishers.

Brust, J.C.M. (1980) 'Music and Language: Musical Alexia and Agraphia.' *Brain 103*, 357–392.

Brustrom, J.E. and Ober, B.A. (1996) 'Source memory for actions in Alzheimer's disease.' *Aging Neuropsychology and Cognition 3*, 1, 56–66.

Buber, M. (1962) *Das dialogische Prinzip*. Heidelberg: Verlag Lambert Schneider GmbH. (Aufl. 1997 bei Lambert Schneider im Bleicher Verlag GmbH, Gerlingen.)

Buck, M. and Beckers, D (1993) *Rehabilitation bei Querschnittlähmung*. Berlin: Springer.

Bunne, S. (1986) *Musik i äldringsvård – et hjälpmedel i arbetet*. Sweden: Musikverksta'n HB.

Burke, D., Alexander, K., Baxter, M., Baker, F., Connel, K., Diggles, S., Feldman, K., Horny, A., Kokinos, M., Moloney, D. and Withers, J. (2000) 'Rehabilitation of a person with severe traumatic brain injury.' *Brain Injury 14*, 463–471.

Calvin, W.H. (1998) *Wie das Gehirn denkt: Die Evolution der Intelligenz*. Heidelberg: Spektrum Akademischer Verlag.

Carlisle, B.J. (2000) 'The effects of music-assisted relaxation therapy on anxiety in brain injury patients.' Unpublished masters thesis, Michigan State University, Michigan.

Carr, T. (1996) *Newman & Gadamer: Towards a Hermeneutics of Religious Knowledge*. Atlanta: Scholar's Press.

Carruth, E. (1997) 'The effects of singing and the spaced retrieval technique on improving face–name recognition in nursing home residents with memory loss.' *Journal of Music Therapy 34*, 165–186.

Casby, J.A. and Holm, M.B. (1994) 'The effect of music on repetitive disruptive vocalizations of persons with dementia.' *American Journal of Occupational Therapy 48*, 10, 883–899.

Chenery, H.J. (1996) 'Semantic priming in Alzheimer's dementia.' *Aphasiology 10*, 1, 1–20.

Cheston, R. (1998) 'Psychotherapeutic work with people with dementia: A review of the literature.' *British Journal of Medical Psychology 71*, 211–231.

Christie, M. (1992) 'Music therapy applications in a skilled and intermediate care nursing home facility: A clinical study.' *Activities, Adaptation and Aging 16*, 4, 69–87.

Christie, M. (1995) 'The influence of a highly participatory peer on motivation group behaviours of lower functioning persons who have probable Alzheimer's type dementia: A feasibility study.' *Music Therapy Perspectives 13*, 2, 91–96.

Claeys, M.S., Miller, A.C., Dalloul-Rampersad, R. and Kollar, M. (1989) 'The role of music and music therapy in the rehabilitation of traumatically brain injured clients.' *Music Therapy Perspectives 6*, 71–77.

Clair, A. (1991) 'Music therapy for a severely regressed person with a probable diagnosis of Alzheimer's disease.' In K.E. Bruscia (ed) *Case Studies in Music Therapy*. Phoenixville, PA: Barcelona Publishers.

Clair, A. (1996a) 'The effect of singing on alert responses in persons with late stage dementia.' *Journal of Music Therapy 33*, 4, 234–247.

Clair, A. (1996b) *Therapeutic Uses of Music with Older Adults*. Baltimore, MD: Health Professions Press.

Clair, A. (2002) 'The effects of music therapy on engagement in family caregiver and care receiver couples with dementia.' *American Journal of Alzheimer's Disease and Other Dementias 17*, 5, 286–290.

Clair, A. and Bernstein, B. (1990a) 'A preliminary study of music therapy programming for severely regressed persons with Alzheimer's-type dementia.' *Journal of Applied Gerontology 9*, 3, 299–311.

Clair, A. and Bernstein, B. (1990b) 'A comparison of singing, vibrotactile and nonvibrotactile instrumental playing responses in severely regressed persons with dementia of the Alzheimer's type.' *Journal of Music Therapy 27*, 3, 119–125.

Clair, A. and Bernstein, B. (1993) 'The preference for vibrotactile versus auditory stimuli in severely regressed persons with dementia of the Alzheimer's type compared to those with dementia due to alcohol abuse.' *Music Therapy Perspectives 11*, 24–27.

Clair, A. and Bernstein, B. (1994) The effect of no music, stimulative background music and sedative background music on agitated behaviors in persons with severe dementia. *Activities, Adaptation and Aging 19*, 1, 61–70.

Clair, A., Bernstein, B. and Johnson, G. (1995) 'Rhythm playing characteristics in persons with severe dementia including those with probable Alzheimer's type.' *Journal of Music Therapy 32*, 2, 113--131.

Clair, A. and Ebberts, A. (1997) 'The effects of music therapy on interactions between family caregivers and their care receivers with late stage dementia.' *Journal of Music Therapy 34*, 148–164.

Clark, M.E., Lipe, A.W. and Bilbrey, M. (1998) 'Use of music to decrease aggressive behaviors in people with dementia.' *Journal of Gerontological Nursing*, July, 10–17.

Clarke, M. and Oxman, A. (2002) *Cochrane Reviewer's Handbook 4.1.5* (updated April 2002). Oxford: Update Software.

Cohen, J. (1988) *Statistical Power Analysis for the Behavioural Sciences* (second edition). Hillsdale, NJ: Lawrence Earlbaum Associates.

Cohen, N.S. (1992) 'The effect of singing instruction on the speech production of neurologically impaired persons.' *Journal of Music Therapy*, 29, 2, 87–102.

Cohen, N.S. and Ford, J. (1995) 'The effect of musical cues on the nonpurposive speech of persons with aphasia.' *Journal of Music Therapy 32*, 46–57.

Cohen, N.S. and Masse, R. (1993) 'The application of singing and rhythmic instructions as a therapeutic intervention for persons with neurogenic communication disorders.' *Journal of Music Therapy 30*, 81–99.

Cohen-Mansfield, J. (2000) 'Use of patient characteristics to determine non-pharmacologic interventions for behavioral and psychological symptoms of dementia.' *International Psychogeriatrics 12*, Suppl. 1, 373–380.

Collette, F., VanderLinden, M., Bechet, S., Belleville, S. and Salmon, E. (1998) 'Working memory deficits in Alzheimer's disease.' *Brain Cognition 37*, 1, 147–149.

Conn, V.S., Isaramalai, S., Rath, S., Jantarakupt, P., Wadhawan, R. and Dash, J. (2003) 'Beyond MEDLINE for literature searches.' *Journal of Nursing Scholarship 35*, 2, 177–182.

Cooper, J.K., Mungas, D. and Weiler, P.G. (1990) 'Relation of cognitive status and abnormal behaviors in Alzheimer's disease.' *Journal of the American Geriatric Society 38*, 8, 867–870.

Corballis, M.C. (2003) 'From mouth to hand: gesture, speech, and the evolution of right-handedness.' *Behaviour and Brain Sciences 26*, 2, 199–208.

Crossley, M. (2000) 'Narrative psychology, trauma and the study of self/identity.' *Theory & Psychology 10*, 4, 527–546.

Crowder, R.G., Serafine, M.L. and Repp, B. (1990) 'Physical interaction and association by contiguity in memory for words and melodies of songs.' *Memory and Cognition 18*, 469–476.

Crystal, H.A., Grober, E. and Masur, D. (1989) 'Preservation of musical memory in Alzheimer's disease.' *Journal of Neurology, Neurosurgery, and Psychiatry 52*, 1415–1416.

Cutler, A., Dahan, D. and van Donselaar, W. (1997) 'Prosody in the comprehension of spoken language: a literature review.' *Language and Speech 40*, 2, 141–201.

Decker-Voigt, H.H., Knill, P.J., and Weymann, E. (ed) (1996) *Lexikon Musiktherapie*. Göttingen: Hogrefe Verlag.

Deikman, A.J. (1996) '"I"=Awareness.' *Journal of Consciousness Studies 3*, 4, S350–356.

Dennett, D.C. (1994) *Philosophie des menschlichen Bewußtseins*. Hamburg: Hoffmann und Campe.

Dennett, D.C. (1996) 'Facing backwards on the problem of consciousness.' *Journal of Consciousness Studies 3*, 1, S4–6.

Denney, A. (1997) 'Quiet music: An intervention for mealtime agitation?' *Journal of Gerontological Nursing 23*, 7, 16–23.

Diebel, E. (1981) 'Identität unter dem Einfluß chronischer Krankheit am Beispiel der Multiplen Sklerose.' Unpublished doctoral thesis, Georg-August University of Göttingen, Germany.

Dienstfrey, H. (1999) 'Disclosure and health: An interview with James W. Pennebaker.' *Advances in Mind–Body Medicine 15*, 161–195.

Drachman, D., O'Donnell, B., Lew, R. and Swearer, J. (1990) 'The prognosis in Alzheimer's disease.' *Archives of Neurology 47*, 851–856.

Dykstra, K., Gandour, J. and Stark, R. (1995) 'Disruption of prosody after frontal lobe seizures in the nondominant hemisphere.' *Aphasiology 9*, 453–476.

Edelman, G.M. and Tononi, G. (1997) 'Neuronaler Darwinismus: Eine selektionistische Betrachtungsweise des Gehirns.' In H. Meier and D. Ploog (eds) *Der Mensch und sein Gehirn: Die Folgen der Evolution*. München: Piper Verlag.

Edwards, J. (2002) 'Using the evidence based medicine framework to support music therapy posts in healthcare settings.' *British Journal of Music Therapy 16*, 1, 29–34

Edwards, J. (2004) 'Can music therapy in medical contexts ever be evidenced-based?' *Music Therapy Today (online)*. Retrieved August 2004, available from www.musictherapyworld.net.

Eeg, S. (2001) *Musikprojektet på Betania: Om musik og demente*. Århus: Lokalcenter Betania.

Eimer, M. (1996) 'Kognitive Psychologie, Neurobiologie und das "Gehirn-Bewußtsein-Problem".' In G. Roth and W. Prinz (eds) *Kopf-Arbeit: Gehirnfunktion und kognitive Leistungen*. Heidelberg: Spektrum Akademischer Verlag.

Ellis, D.G. (1996) 'Coherence patterns in Alzheimer's discourse.' *Communication Research 23*, 4, 472–495.

Emich, I.F. (1980) 'Rehabilitative potentialities and successes of aphasia therapy in children and young people after cerebrotraumatic lesions.' *Rehabilitation 19*, 3, 151–159.

Engel, A. and Singer, W. (2001) 'Temporal binding and the neural correlates of sensory awareness.' *Trends in Cognitive Sciences 5*, 1, 16–25.

Erber, R. and Erber, M. (2000) 'Mysteries of mood regulation. II: The case of the happy thermostat.' *Psychological Inquiry 11*, 3, 210–213.

Erdfelder, E. (1984) 'Zur Bedeutung und Kontrolle des β-Fehlers bei der inferenzstatistischen Prüfung log-linearer Modelle.' *Zeitschrift für Sozialpsychologie 15*, 18–32.

Erickson, R.J. and Goldinger, S.D. (1996) 'Auditory vigilance in aphasic individuals: Detecting nonlinguistic stimuli with full or divided attention.' *Brain and Cognition 30*, 2, 244–253.

Ettlin, Th. M. (1978) 'Körpererleben, insbesondere Lageerlebnisse nach akut traumatischer, kompletter Querschnittlähmung.' Promotion Universität Basel.

Fachner, J. (1994) 'Die Kunsttherapeutisch orientierte Nordoff/Robbins Musiktherapie in Herdecke.' Diplomarbeit, Universität Dortmund.

Feinberg, T.E. (2002) *Gehirn und Persönlichkeit: Wie das Erleben eines stabilen Selbst hervorgebracht wird*. Kirchzarten bei Freiburg VAK-Verlags GmbH.

Filipp, S.-H. and Aymanns, P. (1996) 'Bewältigungsstrategien [Coping].' In R.H. Adler, J.M. Herrmann and T.V. Uexküll (eds) *Psychosomatische Medizin*. München: Urban & Schwarzenberg.

Fitzgerald-Cloutier, M.L. (1993) 'The use of music therapy to decrease wandering: An alternative to restraints.' *Music Therapy Perspectives 11*, 32–36.

Folstein, M.F., Folstein, S.E. and McHugh. P.R. (1975) 'Mini-Mental State: A practical method for grading the state of patients for the clinician,' *Journal of Psychiatric Research 12*, 189–198.

Folstein, S. (1989) *Huntington's Disease: A Disorder of Families*. London: Johns Hopkins University Press.

Forsell, Y., Jorm, A.F. and Winblad, B. (1998) 'The outcome of depression and dysthymia in a very elderly population: Results from a three-year follow-up study.' *Aging and Mental Health 2*, 2, 100–104.

Foster, N.A. (1998a) 'An examination of the facilitatory effect of music on recall, with special reference to dementia sufferers. Study 1.' Unpublished PhD dissertation, University of London.

Foster, N.A. (1998b) 'An examination of the facilitatory effect of music on recall, with special reference to dementia sufferers. Study 3.' Unpublished PhD dissertation, University of London.

Foster, N.A. (1998c) 'An examination of the facilitatory effect of music on recall, with special reference to dementia sufferers. Study 4.' Unpublished PhD dissertation, University of London.

Foster, N.A. and Valentine, E.R. (2001) 'The effect of auditory stimulation on autobiographical recall in dementia.' *Experimental Aging Research 27*, 215–228.

Friis, S. (1987) *Musik i ældreplejen*. København: Munksgaard.

Frommer, J. (1995) 'Wie sollen wir seelische Krisen diagnostizieren?' *Zeitschrift für Klinische Psychologie, Psychopathologie und Psychotherapie 2*, 43, 101–184.

Frommer, J. (1997) 'Qualitative Diagnostikforschung bei Neurosen und Persönlichkeitsstörungen.' *Psychotherapeut 42*, 163–169.

Fuchs-Heinritz, W., Lautmann, R., Rammstedt, O. and Wienold, H. (eds) (1994) *Lexikon zur Soziologie*. Opladen: Westdeutscher Verlag.

Fujiwara, S. Nakasato, N., Ogasawara, K. *et al.* (1993) 'Evaluation of the severity of prolonged consciousness disturbances after head injury: A scoring system developed in our department.' *Proceedings of the 2nd Annual Meeting of the Society for the Treatment of Coma* (pp.121–126). Tokyo: Society for Treatment of Coma.

Gadomski, M. and Jochims, S. (1986) 'Musiktherapie bei schweren Schädel-Hirn-Traumen.' *Musiktherapeutische Umschau 7*, 2, 103–110.

Gaertner, M. (1999) 'The sound of music in the dimming, anguished world of Alzheimer's disease.' In T. Wigram and J. De Backer (ed) *Clinical Applications of Music Therapy in Psychiatry.* London: Jessica Kingsley Publishers.

Gallese, V. (2003) 'The roots of empathy: The shared manifold hypothesis and the neural basis of intersubjectivity.' *Psychopathology 36*, 4, 171–180.

Garbarini, F. and Adenzato, M. (2004) 'At the root of embodied cognition: Cognitive science meets neurophysiology.' *Brain and Cognition 56*, 1, 100–106.

Gardiner, J.C., Furios, M., Tansley, D. and Morgan, B. (2000) 'Music therapy and reading as intervention strategies for disruptive behavior in dementia.' *Clinical Gerontologist 22*, 1, 31–46.

Gates, A. and Bradshaw, J. (1977) 'The role of the cerebral hemispheres in music.' *Brain and Language 4*, 403–431.

Gates, G.A., Cobb, J.L., Linn, R.T., Rees, T., Wolf, P.A. and Dagostino, R.B. (1996) 'Central auditory dysfunction, cognitive dysfunction, and dementia in older people.' *Archives of Otolaryngology – Head and Neck Surgery 122*, 2, 161–167.

Gerdner, L.A. (1997) 'An individualized music intervention for agitation.' *Journal of the American Psychiatric Nurses Association 3*, 177–184.

Gerdner, L.A. (2000) 'Music, art, and recreational therapies in the treatment of behavioral and psychological symptoms of dementia.' *International Psychogeriatrics 12*, 1, 359–366.

Gerdner, L.A. and Swanson, E.A. (1993) 'Effects of individualized music on confused and agitated elderly patients.' *Archives of Psychiatric Nursing 7*, 5, 284–291.

Gerken, L. (1996) 'Prosody's role in language acquisition and adult parsing.' *Journal of Psycholinguistic Research 25*, 2, 345–376.

Gerner, H.J. (1992) *Die Querschnittlähmung, Erstversorgung, Behandlungsstrategie, Rehabilitation.* Berlin: Blackwell Wissenschaft.

Gerstenbrand, F. (1967) *Das traumatische apallische Syndrom: Klinik, Morphologie, Pathophysiologie und Behandlung.* New York: Springer.

Gervin, A.P. (1991) 'Music therapy compensatory technique utilizing song lyrics during dressing to promote independence in the patient with a brain injury.' *Music Therapy Perspectives 9*, 87–90.

Gilbertson, S. (1999) 'Music therapy in neurosurgical rehabilitation.' In T. Wigram and J. De Backer (eds) *The Application of Music Therapy in Development Disability, Paediatrics and Neurology.* London: Jessica Kingsley Publishers.

Gilbertson, S. (2002) *Light on a Dark Night.* Music Therapy World Information CD ROM IV. Witten: Music Therapy World.

Gilbertson, S. (2004) 'Improvisation in der Musiktherapie mit Menschen mit traumatischen Schädel-Hirn-Verletzungen: Eine Literaturbersicht aus dem "Structured Review Project".' *Musiktherapeutische Umschau 25*, 1, 63–69.

Gilbertson, S. and Aldridge, D. (2003a) 'Strategies for searching electronic databases.' *Music Therapy Today (online).* Retrieved November 2003, available from www.musictherapyworld.net.

Gilbertson, S. and Aldridge, D. (2003b) 'Searching PubMed/MEDLINE, Ingenta and the Music Therapy World Journal Index for articles published in the *Journal of Music Therapy*.' *Journal of Music Therapy, 40*, 4, 324–344.

Glanville, H.J. (1982) 'What is Rehabilitation?' In L. Illis (ed) *Neurological Rehabilitation*. Oxford: Blackwell Scientific Publications.

Glaser, B. and Strauss, A. (1967) *The Discovery of Grounded Theory*. Chicago, IL: Aldine.

Glassman, L.R. (1991) 'Music therapy and bibliotherapy in the rehabilitation of traumatic brain injury: A case study.' *Arts in Psychotherapy 18*, 2, 149–156.

Glenn, S.M. and Cunningham, C.C. (1984) 'Nursery rhymes and early language acquisition by mentally handicapped children.' *Exceptional Child 51*, 1, 72–74.

Glentzer, U. (1995) 'Specialna Uloha Muzikoterapie pri Reahilitacii Pacientov po Mozgovomiesnych Poraneniach.' *Rehabilitácia 28*, 2, 93–96.

Glosser, G., Wiley, M.J. and Barnoski, E.J. (1998) 'Gestural communication in Alzheimer's disease.' *Journal of Clinical and Experimental Neuropsychology 20*, 1, 1–13.

Glynn, N.J. (1992) 'The music therapy assessment tool in Alzheimer's patients.' *Journal of Gerontological Nursing 18*, 1, 3–9.

Goddaer, J. and Abraham, I. (1994) 'Effects of relaxing music on agitation during meals among nursing home residents with severe cognitive impairment.' *Archives of Psychiatric Nursing 8*, 3, 150–158.

Goldberg, E. (2002) *Die Regie im Gehirn: Wo wir Pläne schmieden und Entscheidungen treffen*. Kirchzarten bei Freiburg: VAK Verlags GmbH.

Goldin-Meadow, S. (1997) 'When gestures and words speak differently.' *Current Directions in Psychological Science 6*, 5, 138–143.

Goldin-Meadow, S. (1999) 'The role of gesture in communication and thinking.' *Trends in Cognitive Sciences 3*, 11, 419–429.

Goldin-Meadow, S. (2000) 'Beyond words: The importance of gesture to researchers and learners.' *Child Development 71*, 1, 231–239.

Görres, H.-J., Ziegeler, G., Friedrich, H. and Lücke, G. (1988) 'Formen psychosozialer Bewältigung der Multiplen Sklerose.' *Zeitschrift für Psychosomatische Medizin 34*, 274–290.

Götell, E., Brown, S. and Ekman, S.L. (2000) 'Caregiver-assisted music events in psychogeriatric care.' *Journal of Psychiatric Mental Health and Nursing 7*, 2, 119–125.

Götell, E., Brown, S. and Ekman, S.L. (2002) 'Caregiver singing and background music in dementia care.' *Western Journal of Nursing Research 24*, 2, 195–216.

Götell, E., Brown, S. and Ekman, S.L. (2003) 'Influence of caregiver singing and background music on posture, movement, and sensory awareness in dementia care.' *International Psychogeriatrics 15*, 4, 411–430.

Griesehop, H. (2002) 'Multiple Sklerose: Prozesse biographischer Aneignung und Lebensgestaltung im Kontext einer chronischen Erkrankung.' Unpublished doctoral thesis, University of Bremen, Germany.

Groene, R.W. (1993) 'Effectiveness of music therapy 1:1 intervention with individuals having senile dementia of the Alzheimer's type.' *Journal of Music Therapy 30*, 3, 138–157.

Groene, R.W. (2001) 'The effect of presentation and accompaniment styles on attentional and responsive behaviors of participants with dementia diagnoses.' *Journal of Music Therapy 38*, 36–50.

Groene, R.W., Zapchenk, S., Marble, G. and Kantar, S. (1998) 'The effect of therapist and activity characteristics on the purposeful responses of probable Alzheimer's disease participants.' *Journal of Music Therapy 35*, 2, 119–136.

Grün, M., Dill-Schmölders, C. and Greulich, W. (1999) 'Schöpferische Musiktherapie und Parkinson.' In D. Aldridge (ed) *Kairos III: Beiträge zur Musiktherapie in der Medizin.* Bern: Verlag Hans Huber.

Grüninger, W. and Klassen, G. (1985) *Psychologische Aspekte: Querschnittlähmungen.* Berlin: Springer Verlag.

Gurevitch, Z. (2000) 'Plurality in dialogue: A comment on Bakhtin.' *Sociology 34*, 2, 243–263.

Gurevitch, Z. (2001) 'Dialectical dialogue: The struggle for speech, repressive silence, and the shift to multiplicity.' *British Journal of Sociology 52*, 1, 87–104.

Gutzmann, H. (1901) 'Über die Behandlung der Aphasie.' *Berliner Klinische Wochenschrift 38*, 739–744.

Gwyther, L.P. and Strulowitz, S.Y. (1998) 'Care-giver stress.' *Current Opinion in Psychiatry 11*, 4, 431–434.

Häcker, H. and Stapf, K.H. (eds) (1998) *Dorsch Psychologisches Wörterbuch.* Bern: Hans Huber.

Haggard, P. (2001) 'The psychology of action.' *British Journal of Psychology 92*, 113–128.

Hannich, H.-J. (1994) 'Beziehung und Interaktion mit Bewußtlosen.' In C. Bienstein and A. Fröhlich (eds) *Bewußtlos.* Dsseldorf: Verlag Selbstbestimmtes Leben.

Hannich, H.-J. (1999) 'Der musiktherapeutische Dialog als Zugang zum bewusstseins-veränderten Patienten auf der Intensivstation.' In K.-D. Neander (ed) *Musik und Pflege.* München: Urban & Fischer.

Hannich, H.-J. (2003) 'Was ist wirklich? Verborgenes in der Wahrnehmung apallischer Patienten.' Vortrag zur Jahrestagung der Österreichischen Wachkoma Gesellschaft Wien (ÖWG), 24 October.

Hannich, H.-J. and Dierkes, B. (1996) 'Ist Erleben im Koma möglich? *Zeitschrift Intensiv 4*, 4–7.

Hanser, S. and Clair, A.A. (1996) 'Retrieving the losses of Alzheimer's disease for patients and caregivers with the aid of music.' In T. Wigram, B. Saperston and R. West (eds) *The Art and Science of Music Therapy: A Handbook.* Amsterdam: Harwood Academic Publishers.

Hanson, N., Gfeller, K., Woodworth, G., Swanson, E. and Garand, L. (1996) 'A comparison of the effectiveness of differing types and difficulty of music activities in programming for older adults with Alzheimer's disease and related disorders.' *Journal of Music Therapy 33*, 2, 93–123.

Harlan, J. (1993) 'The therapeutic value of art for persons with Alzheimer's disease and related disorders.' *Loss, Grief and Care 6*, 4, 99–106.

Harper, P. (1991) *Huntington's Disease.* London: WB Saunders.

Harris, P.B. (1998) 'Listening to caregiving sons: Misunderstood realities.' *Gerontologist 38*, 3, 342–352.

Hartje, W. and Poeck, K. (2002) *Klinische Neuropsychologie.* Stuttgart: Thieme Verlag.

Hatfield, K. and McClune, N. (2002) 'Principles of person-centered care in music therapy.' In A. Innes and K. Hatfield (eds) *Healing Arts Therapies and Person-centered Dementia Care.* London: Jessica Kingsley Publishers.

Haupts, M. and Smala, A. (2002) 'Multiple sclerosis und Lebensqualität-gesundheitsökonomische Aspekte.' In R.M. Schmidt and F. Hoffmann (eds) *Multiple Sklerose.* München: Urban and Fischer.

Haus Königsborn (2002) *Konzept.* Unpublished.

Heal, H.C. and Husband, H.J. (1998) 'Disclosing a diagnosis of dementia: is age a factor?' *Aging and Mental Health 2*, 2, 144–150.

Heck, S. (2004) 'Mythische, historische und spirituelle Wurzeln der Altorientalischen Musiktherapie.' Diploma thesis in Altorientalischer Musiktherapie, 1997–2002, Rosenau, Austria.

Heesen, C. (2003) 'Leib, Seele und Sprache.' *Forum Psychosomatik. Zeitschrift für psychosomatische Multiple sclerosis-Forschung 12. Jg.*, 2/2003, 6–9.

Hendrie, H. (1998) 'Epidemiology of dementia and Alzheimer's disease.' *American Journal of Geriatric Psychiatry 6*, 2, S3–18.

Herkenrath, A. (2002) 'Musiktherapie und Wahrnehmung: Ein Beitrag der Musiktherapie zur Evalierung der Wahrnehmungsfähigkeit bei Patienten mit schweren Hirnverletzungen.' In D. Aldridge and M. Dembski (eds) *Music Therapy World: Musiktherapie, Diagnostik und Wahrnehmung*. Witten: University of Witten-Herdecke.

Herkenrath, A. (2004) 'Begegnung mit dem Bewusst-Sein von Menschen im Wachkoma: Darstellung und Untersuchung von Beobachtungen zu Bewusstsein und Entwicklung kognitiver Gehirnleistung von Menschen im Wachkoma am Beispiel der Begegnung in der Musiktherapie.' Unpublished doctoral thesis, Faculty of Medicine, University of Witten-Herdecke.

Hiller, P.U. (1989) 'Song story: A potent tool for cognitive and affective relearning in head injury.' *Cognitive Rehabilitation 7*, 2, 20–23.

Hinterhuber, H. (2001) *Die Seele. Natur- und Kulturgeschichte von Psyche, Geist und Bewusstsein.* Wien: Springer Verlag.

Hintz, M. (2000) 'Geriatric music therapy clinical assessment: Assessment of music skills and related behaviours.' *Music Therapy Perspectives 18*, 1, 31–40.

Hohmann, W. (1997) 'Erfahrungen in der Auditiven Musiktherapie mit Hirngeschaedigten.' *Musiktherapeutische-Umschau 18*, 3, 178–192.

Hurt, C.P., Rice, R.R., McIntosh, G.C. and Thaut, M.H. (1998) 'Rhythmic auditory stimulation in gait training for patients with traumatic brain injury.' *Journal of Music Therapy 35*, 4, 228–241.

Hüther, G. (1998) *Biologie der Angst.* Göttingen: Sammlung Vandenhoeck.

Iljine, V.N. (1990) 'Kokreation–die leibliche Dimension des Schöpferischen: Aufzeichnungen aus gemeinsamen Gedankengängen.' In H. Petzold and I. Orth (eds) *Die neuen Kreativitätstherapien. Handbuch der Kunsttherapie, 1.* Paderborn: Junfermann Verlag.

Ingarden, R. (ed) (1968) *Vom Erkennen des literarischen Kunstwerks.* Tübingen: Niemayer.

Jack, A.I. and Roepstorff, A. (2003) 'Why trust the subject.' *Journal of Conscious Studies 10*, 9/10, v–xx.

Jacome, D. (1984) 'Aphasia with elation, hypermusia, musicophilia and compulsive whistling.' *Journal of Neurological and Neurosurgical Psychiatry 47*, 3, 308–310.

Jennett, B. and Plum, F. (1972) 'Persistent vegetative state after brain damage: A syndrome in search of a name.' *The Lancet 1*, 7753, 734–737.

Jochims, S. (1990) 'Coping with illness in the early phase of severe neurologic diseases: A contribution of music therapy to psychological management in selected neurologic disease pictures.' *Psychotherapie, Psychosomatik, Medizinische Psychologie 40*, 3/4, 115–122.

Jochims, S. (1992) 'Emotionale Krankheitsverarbeitungsprozesse in der Frühphase erworbener zerebraler Läsionen'. *Musik-, Tanz- und -Kunsttherapie 3*, 3, 129–136.

Jochims, S. (1994) 'Kontaktaufnahme im Frühstadium schwerer Schädel-Hirn-Traumen: Klang als Brücke zum verstummten Menschen.' *Krankengymnastik: Zeitschrift für Physiotherapeuten 46*, 10, 1316–1324.

Jochims, S. (1995) 'Emotional processes of coping with disease in the early stages of acquired cerebral lesions.' *The Arts in Psychotherapy 22*, 1, 21–30.

Johnson, C., Lahey, P. and Shore, A. (1992) 'An exploration of creative arts therapeutic group work on an Alzheimer's unit.' *The Arts in Psychotherapy 19*, 4, 269–277.

Johnson, J.K., Cotman, C.W., Tasaki, C.S., and Shaw, G.L. (1998) 'Enhancement of spatial–temporal reasoning after a Mozart listening condition in Alzheimer's disease: A case study.' *Neurologic Research 20*, December, 666–672.

Jones, C.P. (1990) 'Spark of life.' *Geriatric Nursing 11*, 4, 194–196.

Jones, R., Hux, K., Morton-Anderson, K.A. and Knepper, L. (1994) 'Auditory stimulation effect on a comatose survivor of traumatic brain injury.' *Archives of Physical Medicine and Rehabilitation 75*, 2, 164–171.

Joseph, R. (1988) 'The right cerebral hemisphere: Emotion, music, visual–spatial skills, body image, dreams and awareness.' *Journal of Clinical Psychology 44*, 5, 630–673.

Jossmann, P. (1927) 'Die Beziehungen der motorischen Amusie zu den apraktischen Störungen.' *Monatsschrift für Psychiatrie und Neurologie 63*, 239–274.

Jungblut, M. (2003) 'Rhythmisch-melodisches Stimmtraining auf musiktherapeutischer Grundlage mit Broca- und Globalaphasikern in der Langzeitrehabilitation.' Unpublished doctoral thesis, Institute of Music Therapy, University of Witten-Herdecke.

Jungblut, M. and Aldridge, D. (2004) 'Musik als Brücke zur Sprache: Die musiktherapeutische Behandlungsmethode SIPARI bei Langzeitaphasikern.' *Neurologie & Rehabilitation 10*, 2, 69–78.

Kalayam, B. and Shamoian, C. (1990) 'Geriatric psychiatry: An update.' *Journal of Clinical Psychiatry 51*, 5, 177–183.

Kamar, O. (1997) 'Light and death: Art therapy with a patient with Alzheimer's disease.' *American Journal of Art Therapy 35*, 4, 118–124.

Karanth, P. and Rangamani, G.N. (1988) 'Crossed aphasia in multilinguals.' *Brain and Language 34*, 1, 169–180.

Karbe, H. and Thiel, A. (1998) 'Brain plasticity in poststroke aphasia: What is the contribution of the right hemisphere?' *Brain and Language 64*, 2, 215–231.

Keijzer, F. (1998) 'Doing without representations which specify what to do.' *Philosophical Psychology 11*, 3, 269–302.

Kelly, G.A. (ed) (1955) *The Psychology of Personal Constructs, I and II*. New York: W.W. Norton & Co.

Kennelly, J. and Edwards, J. (1997) 'Providing music therapy to the unconscious child in the paediatric intensive care unit.' *Australian Journal of Music Therapy 8*, 18–29.

Kennelly, J., Hamilton, L. and Cross, J. (2001) 'The interface of music therapy and speech pathology in the rehabilitation of children with acquired brain injury.' *Australian Journal of Music Therapy 12*, 13–20.

Kermani, N. (2003) *Gott ist schön: Das ästhetische Erleben des Koran*, 2nd edn. München: CH Beck.

Kiene, H. (2001) *Komplementäre Methodenlehre der klinischen Forschung*. Berlin: Springer Verlag.

Kimelman, M.D. and McNeil, M.R. (1987) 'An investigation of emphatic stress comprehension in adult aphasia: A replication.' *Journal of Speech and Hearing Research 30*, 3, 295–300.

Kirshner, H.S. (1995) *Handbook of Neurological Speech and Language Disorders*. New York: Marcel Dekker.

Kitwood, T. (1997) *Dementia reconsidered: The Person Comes First*. Buckingham: Open University Press.

Klaasen, R. (1994) *Lebenslügen: Langzeitverläufe und Spätresultate bei Querschnittlähmung*. Berlin: Springer Verlag.

Klauer, T. and Filipp, S.-H. (1987) 'Der "Fragebogen zur Erfassung der Krankheitsbewältigung" (FEKB). Kurzbeschreibung des Verfahrens. (Forschungsberichte aus dem Projekt "Psychologie der Krankheitsbewältigung" No.13).' Department of Psychology, University of Trier, Germany.

Knott, R., Patterson, K. and Hodges, J.R. (1997) 'Lexical and semantic binding effects in short-term memory: Evidence from semantic dementia.' *Cognitive Neuropsychology 14*, 1165–1218.

Knox, R. and Jutai, J. (1996) 'Music-based rehabilitation of attention following brain injury.' *Canadian Journal of Rehabilitation 9*, 3, 169–181.

Koger, S.M. and Brotons, M. (2000) 'Music therapy for dementia symptoms (Cochrane review).' *Cochrane Database Systematic Review 2000*, 3, CD001121.

Koplas, P., Gans, H., Wisely, M., Kuchibhatla, M., Cutson, T., Gold, D., Taylor, C. and Schenkman, M. (1999) 'Quality of life and Parkinson's disease.' *Journal of Gerontology 54*, 4, Suppl. M197–M202.

Korb, C. (1997a) 'The influence of music therapy on patients with a diagnosed dementia. Part 1.' *Canadian Journal of Music Therapy 5*, 1, 26–36.

Korb, C. (1997b) 'The influence of music therapy on patients with a diagnosed dementia. Part 2.' *Canadian Journal of Music Therapy 5*, 1, 36–54.

Kotchoubey, B., Lang, S., Bostanov, V. and Birbaumer, N. (2002) 'Is there a mind? Electrophysiology of unconscious patients.' *News in Physiological Sciences 17*, 1, S38–42.

Kremer, J. and Starkstein, S. (2000) 'Affective disorders in Parkinson's disease.' *International Review of Psychiatry 12*, 290–297.

Kretschmer, E. (1940) 'Das apallische Syndrom.' *Zeitschrift für die gesamte Neurologie und Psychiatrie 169*, S576–579.

Kriz, J. (ed) (1994) *Grundk–onzepte der Psychotherapie.* Weinheim: Psychologie Verlags Union.

Kurtzke, J.F. (1983) 'Rating neurologic impairment in multiple sclerosis: An Expanded Disability Status Scale (EDSS).' *Neurology 33*, 1444–1452.

Kusatz, M. (2002) *Das Krefelder Moidell (KM). Stellenwert der Musiktherapie in einem multimodalen Behandlungskonzept bei subakutem und chronishem Tinnitus im ambulanten Setting.* Witten: Faculty of Medicine, University of Witten-Herdeck.

Kydd, P. (2001) 'Using music therapy to help a client with Alzheimer's disease adapt to long-term care.' *American Journal of Alzheimer's Disease and Other Dementias 16*, 2, 103–108.

Langenmayr, A. (1997) *Sprachpsychologie.* Göttingen: Hogrefe-Verlag.

Larsen, R. (2000) 'Towards a science of mood regulation.' *Psychological Inquiry 11*, 3, 129–141.

Larson, E.B. (1998) 'Management of Alzheimer's disease in a primary care setting.' *American Journal of Geriatric Psychiatry 6*, 2, S34–40.

Lazarus, R.S. (1995) 'Stress und Stressbewältigung: Ein Paradigma.' In S.-H. Filipp (ed) *Kritische Lebensereignisse.* Weinheim: Psychologie Verlags Union.

Lee, K. and Baker, F. (1997) 'Towards integrating a holistic rehabilitation system: The implications for music therapy.' *Australian Journal of Music Therapy 8*, 30–37.

Leischner, A. (1987) *Aphasien und Sprachentwicklungsstörungen.* Stuttgart: Thieme Verlag.

Leischner, A. (1998) 'Die ältere deutsche Hirnpathologie unter besonderer Berücksichtigung der Aphasieforschung.' *Fortschritte der Neurologie-Psychiatrie 8*, 66, 345–356.

Lemkuhl, L.D. (1992) *The Brain Injury Glossary.* Retrieved March 2002, available from www.neuroskills.com/tbi/hgi/glossary.shtml.

Lengdobler, H. and Kießling, W.R. (1989) 'Gruppenmusiktherapie bei Multipler Sklerose: ein erster Erfahrungsbericht.' *Psychotherapie medizinische Psychologie 39*, 9/10, 369–373.

Levelt, W.J.M. (1989) *Speaking: From Intention to Articulation.* Cambridge, MA: MIT Press.

Lichtenberger, H. (1993) 'Musiktherapie im Rahmen der Rehabilitation von Querschnittpatienten.' *Praxis Ergotherapie 6*, August, 218–222.

Lindenmuth, G.F., Patel, M. and Chang, P.K. (1992) 'Effects of music on sleep in healthy elderly and subjects with senile dementia of the Alzheimer type.' *American Journal of Alzheimers Disease and Related Disorders and Research 2*, 13–20.

Lindfield, K.C., Winfield, A. and Goodglass, H. (1999) 'The role of prosody in the mental lexicon.' *Brain and Language 68*, 1–2, 312–317.

Lindenmuth, G.F., Patel, M. and Chang, P.K. (1992) 'Effects of music on sleep in healthy elderly and subjects with senile dementia of the Alzheimer type.' *American Journal of Alzheimers Disease and Related Disorders and Research 2*, 13–20.

Lipe, A. (1991) 'Using music therapy to enhance the quality of life in a client with Alzheimer's dementia: A case study.' *Music Therapy Perspectives 9*, 102–105.

Lipe, A. (1995) 'The use of music performance tasks in the assessment of cognitive functioning among older adults with dementia.' *Journal of Music Therapy 32*, 3, 137–151.

Lippe, zur, R. (1987) *Sinnesbewusstsein. Grundlegung einer anthropologischen Ästhetik.* Hamburg: Rowohlt.

Lipsey, M.W. and Wilson, D.B. (1993) 'The efficacy of psychological, educational, and behavioural treatment: Confirmation from meta-analysis.' *American Psychologist 48*, 1181–1209.

Littig, E., Schmidt, R.M. and Hoffmann, F. (2002) 'Differentialdiagnose, Sonderformen, Diagnosesicherung.' In R.M. Schmidt and F. Hoffmann (eds) *Multiple Sklerose.* München: Urban and Fischer.

Livingston, F. (1996) '"Can rock music really be therapy?" Music therapy programs for the rehabilitation of clients with acquired brain injury.' *Australasian Journal of Neuroscience 9*, 1, 12–14.

Lord, R.R. and Garner, J.E. (1993) 'Effects of music on Alzheimer patients.' *Perceptual and Motor Skills 76*, 2, 451–455.

Lou, M.-F. (2001) 'The use of music to decrease agitated behaviour of the demented elderly: The state of the science.' *Scandinavian Journal of Caring Science 15*, 165–173.

Lucia, C.M. (1987) 'Toward developing a model of music therapy intervention in the rehabilitation of head trauma patients.' *Music Therapy Perspectives 4*, 34–39.

Ludwig-Körner, C. (ed) (1992) *Der Selbstbegriff in Psychologie und Psychotherapie.* Wiesbaden: Deutscher Universitäts-Verlag.

Lysaker, P. and Lysaker, J. (2001) 'Psychosis and the disintegration of dialogical self-structure: Problems posed by schizophrenia for the maintenance of dialogue.' *British Journal of Medical Psychology 74*, 23–33.

Magee, W. (1998) 'A comparative study of familiar pre-composed music and unfamiliar improvised music in clinical music therapy with adults with Multiple Sclerosis.' Doctoral, Royal Hospital for Neuro-disability, London.

Magee, W. (1999a) 'Music therapy in chronic degenerative illness: Reflecting the dynamic sense of self.' In D. Aldridge (ed) *Music Therapy in Palliative Care: New voices.* pp.82–94. London: Jessica Kingsley Publishers.

Magee, W. (1999b) 'Music therapy within brain injury rehabilitation: To what extent is our clinical practice influenced by the search for outcomes?' *Music Therapy Perspectives 17*, 1, 20–26.

Magee, W. and Davidson, J. (2002) 'The effect of music therapy on mood states in neurological patients: A pilot study.' *Journal of Music Therapy 39*, 1, 20–29.

Mahler, M. and Benson, D. (1990) 'Cognitive dysfunction in multiple sclerosis: A subcortical dementia?' In S. Rao (ed) *Neurobehavioural Aspects of Multiple Sclerosis.* Oxford: Oxford University Press.

Mango, C. (1992) 'Emma: Art therapy illustrating personal and universal images of loss.' *Omega Journal of Death and Dying 25,* 4, 259–269.

Marsh, L. (2000a) 'Anxiety disorders in Parkinson's disease.' *International Review of Psychiatry 12,* 307–318.

Marsh, L. (2000b) 'Parkinson's disease and its neuropsychiatric features.' *International Review of Psychiatry 12,* 261–262.

Martin, A. and Drees, V. (eds) (1999) *Vertrackte Beziehungen: Die versteckte Logik sozialen Verhaltens.* Darmstadt: Wissenschaftliche Buchgesellschaft.

Mastnak, W. (1994) *Sinne- Künste- Lebenswelten-polyästhetische Erziehung und Therapie durch mehrsinnliches Wahrnehmen und gesamtkünstlerisches Gestalten.* Presov Slowakei: Matus Verlag.

Mastnak, W. and Tucek, G. (2005) *Systematik der Musiktherapie.* (in preparation)

Mathews, R.M., Clair, A.A. and Kosloski, K. (2001) 'Keeping the beat: Use of rhythmic music during exercise activities for the elderly with dementia.' *American Journal of Alzheimer's Disease and Other Dementias 16,* 6, 377–380.

Mathews, R.M., Clair, A. and Kosloski, K. (2000) 'Brief in-service training in music therapy for activity aides: Increasing engagement of persons with dementia in rhythm activities.' *Activities, Adaptation & Ageing 24,* 4, 41–49.

Mayberry, R. and Jacques, J. (2000) 'Gesture production during stuttered speech: Insights into the nature of gesture–speech integration. In D. McNeill (ed) *Language and Gesture.* Cambridge: Cambridge University Press.

Mayberry, R. and Nicoladis, E. (2000) 'Gesture reflects language develoment: Evidence from bilingual children.' *Current Directions in Psychological Research 9,* 6, 192–196.

McCloskey, L. (1990) 'The silent heart sings. Special issue: Counseling and therapy for elders.' *Generations 14,* 1, 63–65.

Mees-Christeller, E., Altmeier, M. and Frieling, E. (2000) *Therapeutisches Zeichnen und Malen aus Anthroposophische Kunsttherapien.* Stuttgart: Urachhaus.

Meinefeld, W. (1997) 'Ex-ante Hypothese in der qualitativen Sozialforschung: Zwischen "fehl am Platz" und "unverzichtbar".' *Zeitschrift für Soziologie 26,* 1, 22–34.

Menke, C. (1999) 'Wozu Ästhetik?' Available at www.information-philosophie.de/philosophie/aesthetik03.html.

Miles, M.B. and Huberman, A.M. (1994) *Qualitative Data Analysis. An Expanded Sourcebook,* 2nd edn. Thousand Oaks, CA: Sage Publications.

Mills, M.A. (1997) 'Narrative identity and dementia: A study of emotion and narrative in older people with dementia.' *Ageing and Society 17,* 673–698.

Mohr, D. and Goodkin, D. (1999) 'Treatment of depression in multiple sclerosis: Review and meta-analysis.' *Clinical Psychology: Science and Practice 6,* 1, 1–9.

Moore, R.S., Staum, M.J. and Brotons, M. (1992) 'Music preferences of the elderly: Repertoire, vocal ranges, tempos, and accompaniments for singing.' *Journal of Music Therapy 29,* 4, 236–252.

Morgan, O. and Tillduckdharry, R. (1982) 'Preservation of singing function in severe aphasia.' *West Indian Medical Journal 31,* 159–161.

Morris, M. (1991) 'Psychiatric aspects of Huntington's disease.' In P. Harper (ed) *Huntington's Disease.* London: WB Saunders.

Müllges, W. and Stoll, G. (2002) 'Hypoxisch-ischämische Enzephalopathie.' *Aktuelle Neurologie 29*, 431–446.

Mummenthaler, M. and Mattle, H. (2002) *Neurologie.* Stuttgart: Thieme-Verlag.

Munk-Madsen, N.M. (2001a) *Musikterapi til demente med adfærdsforstyrrelser.* Gentofte Kommune: Plejehjemmet Kridthuset.

Munk-Madsen, N.M. (2001b) 'Assessment in music therapy with clients suffering from dementia.' *Nordic Journal of Music Therapy 10*, 2, 205–208.

Murray, C. and Lopez, A. (1997) 'Global mortality, disability, and the contribution of risk factors: Global Burden of Disease Study.' *The Lancet 349*, 1436–1442.

Murray, G.D., Teasdale, G.M., Braakman, R., Cohadon, F., Dearden, M., Iannotti, F. *et al.* (1999) 'The European Brain Injury Consortium Survey of Head Injuries.' *Acta Neurochirurgica 141*, 3, 223–236.

Murray, L. and Trevarthen, C. (1986) 'The infant's role in mother–infant communications.' *Journal of Child Language 13*, 15–29.

Muthny, F.-A. (1992) 'Krankheitsverarbeitung im Vergleich von Herzinfarkt-, Dialyse- und Multiple sklerose-Patienten.' *Zeitschrift für Klinische Psychologie 21*, 4, 372–391.

Naeser, M.A. and Helm-Estabrooks, N. (1985) 'CT scan lesion localization and response to melodic intonation therapy with nonfluent aphasia cases.' *Cortex 21*, 2, 203–223.

Naeser, M.A. and Palumbo, C.L. (1998) 'Visible changes in lesion borders on CT-scan after five years poststroke and long-term recovery in aphasia.' *Brain and Language 62*, 1, 1–28.

National Institutes of Health Consensus Development Panel on Rehabilitation of Persons with Traumatic Brain Injury (1999) 'Rehabilitation of persons with traumatic brain injury.' *Journal of the American Medical Association 282*, 10, 974–983.

Nayak, S., Wheeler, B.L., Shiflett, S.C. and Agostinelli, S. (2000) 'Effect of music therapy on mood and social interaction among individuals with acute traumatic brain injury and stroke.' *Rehabilitation Psychology 45*, 3, 274–283.

Neubauer, E. (1990) *Arabische Anleitungen zur Musiktherapie. Sonderdruck der Zeitschrift für Geschichte der arabisch-islamischen Wissenschaften.* Band 6. Institut für Geschichte der Arabisch-Islamischen Wissenschaften an der Johann Wolfgang Goethe Universisität Frankfurt-Main.

Neumann, R. and Strack, F. (2000) "Mood contagion": The automatic transfer of mood between persons.' *Journal of Personality and Social Psychology 79*, 2, 211–223.

Newman, S. and Ward, C. (1993) 'An observational study of intergenerational activities and behaviour change in dementing elders at adult day care centers.' *International Journal of Aging and Human Development 36*, 4, 321–333.

Noda, R., Moriya, T., Ebihara, T., Hayashi, N., Sato, Y., Kobayashi, Y., Matsuzuki, M., Nishikawa, E. and Yamamoto, K. (2003) 'Clinical evaluation of musico-kinetic therapy for patients with brain injury during the subacute phases.' In M. Shigemori and T. Kanno (eds) *Proceedings of the 12th Annual Meeting of the Society for Treatment of Coma.* Tokyo: Society for Treatment of Coma.

Norberg, A., Melin, E. and Asplund, K. (1986) 'Reactions to music, touch, and object presentation in the final stage of dementia: An exploratory study.' *International Journal of Nursing Studies 23*, 4, 315–323.

Nordoff, P. and Robbins, C. (1977) *Creative Music Therapy*, 2nd edn. New York: John Day.

O'Boyle, M. and Sandford, M. (1988) 'Hemispheric asymmetry in the matching of melodies to rhythm sequences tapped in the right and left palms.' *Cortex 24*, 211–221.

O'Callaghan, C. (1994) 'Song writing in palliative care.' Unpublished masters thesis, University of Melbourne, Australia.

O'Callaghan, C. (1999) 'Lyrical themes in songs written by palliative care patients.' In D. Aldridge (ed) *Music Therapy in Palliative Care: New Voices.* London: Jessica Kingsley Publishers.

Odell-Miller, H. (1996) 'Approaches to music therapy in psychiatry with specific emphasis upon a research project with the elderly mentally ill.' In T. Wigram, B. Saperston and R. West (eds) *The Art and Science of Music Therapy: A Handbook.* Amsterdam: Harwood Academic Publishers.

Oepen, G. and Berthold, H. (1983) 'Rhythm as an essential part of music and speech abilities: Conclusions of a clinical experimental study in 34 patients.' *Revue Roumaine de Neurologie et de Psychiatrie 21,* 3, 168–172.

Ojakangas, C. (1984) 'Courage residence: A unique transitional brain injury program.' *Cognitive Rehabilitation 2,* 6, 4–10.

Olderog-Millard, K.A. and Smith, J.M. (1989) 'The influence of group singing therapy on the behavior of Alzheimer's disease patients.' *Journal of Music Therapy 26,* 2, 58–70.

Orange, J.B. and Colton-Hudson, A. (1998) 'Enhancing communication in dementia of the Alzheimer's type.' *Topics in Geriatric Rehabilitation 14,* 2, 56–75.

Orange, J., VanGennep, K., Miller, L. and Johnson, A. (1998) 'Resolution of communication breakdown in dementia of the Alzheimer's type: A longitudinal study.' *Journal of Applied Communication Research 26,* 1, 120–138.

Oyama, A., Arawaka, Y., Oikawa, A., Owada, H., Oimatsu, H., Obonai, T., Nakasato, N., Nagamine, Y., Fujiwara, S. and Noda, R. (2003) 'Trial of musicokinetic therapy for traumatic patients with prolonged disturbance of consciousness: Two case reports.' In M. Shigemori and T. Kanno (eds) *Proceedings of the 12th Annual Meeting of the Society for Treatment of Coma.* Tokyo: Society for Treatment of Coma.

Pacchetti, C., Mancini, F., Aglieri, R., Fundaro, C., Martignoni, E. and Nappi, G. (2000) 'Active music therapy in Parkinson's disease: An integrative method for motor and emotional rehabilitation.' *Psychosomatic Medicine 62,* 3, 386–393.

Palo-Bengtsson, L., Winblad, B. and Ekman, S.L. (1998) 'Social dancing: A way to support intellectual, emotional and motor functions in persons with dementia.' *Journal of Psychiatric and Mental Health Nursing 5,* 6, 545–554.

Paul, S. and Ramsey, D. (2000) 'Music therapy in physical medicine and rehabilitation.' *Australian Occupational Therapy Journal 47,* 3, 111–118.

Paulus, P. (ed) (1986) *Körpererfahrung und Selbsterfahrung in Persönlichkeits-psychologischer Sicht.* Göttingen: Verlag für Psychologie Dr C.J. Hogrefe.

Pell, M. (1997) 'An acoustic characterization of speech prosody in right-hemisphere-damaged patients: Interactive effects of focus distribution, sentence modality, and emotional context. Dissertation, Quebec McGill University.

Pennebaker, J., Kiecolt-Glaser, J. and Glaser, R. (1988) 'Disclosure of traumas and immune function: Health implications for psychotherapy.' *Journal of Consulting and Clinical Psychology 56,* 239–245.

Peretz, I. (1990) 'Processing of local and global musical information by unilateral brain-damaged patients.' *Brain 113,* 1185–1205.

Peters, U.H. (ed) (1990) *Wörterbuch der Psychiatrie und medizinischen Psychologie.* München: Urban und Schwarzenberg.

Petersen, P. (2000) *Der Therapeut als Künstler: Ein integrales Konzept von Psychotherapie und Kunsttherapie.* Stuttgart: Mayer.

Pfeifer, W. (ed) (1993) *Etymologisches Wörterbuch des Deutschen.* München: Deutscher Taschenbuch Verlag.

Pickenhain, L. (1998) *Basale Stimulation: Neurowissenschaftliche Grundlagen.* Düsseldorf: Verlag Selbstbestimmtes Leben.

Pilz, W. (ed) (1999) *Widerstand: Konstruktion eines Begriffes für die improvisatorische Musiktherapie nach Nordoff/Robbins mit psychiatrischen Patienten.* Frankfurt am Main: Lang.

Pirsig, R. (1992) *Leila: oder ein Versuch über Moral.* Frankfurt: Fischer.

Poeck, K. and Hacke, W. (1998) *Neurologie,* 10th edn. Berlin: Springer Verlag.

Polk, M. and Kertesz, A. (1993) 'Music and language in degenerative disease of the brain.' *Brain and Cognition 22,* 98–117.

Pollack, N.J. and Namazi, N.H. (1992) 'The effect of music participation on the social behavior of Alzheimer's disease patients.' *Journal of Music Therapy 29,* 1, 54–67.

Poser, S. and Schäfer, U. (2002) 'Betreuung und Rehabilitation von Multiple sklerose-Patienten.' In R.M. Schmidt and F. Hoffmann (eds) *Multiple Sklerose.* München: Urban und Fischer.

Pot, A., Deeg, D. and VanDyck, R. (1997) 'Psychological well-being of informal caregivers of elderly people with dementia: Changes over time.' *Aging and Mental Health 1,* 3, 261–268.

Price-Lackey, P. and Cashman, J. (1996) 'Jenny's story: Reinventing oneself through occupation and narrative configuration.' *American Journal of Occupational Therapy 50,* 4, 306–314.

Prickett, C.A. and Moore, R.S. (1991) 'The use of music to aid memory of Alzheimer's patients.' *Journal of Music Therapy 28,* 2, 101–110.

Pring, T. (2004) 'Ask a silly question: Two decades of troublesome trials.' *International Journal of Language and Communication Disorders 39,* 3, 285–302.

Prinz, W. (1996) 'Bewusstsein und Ich-Konstitution.' In G. Roth and W. Prinz (1996) *Kopf-Arbeit: Gehirnfunktion und kognitive Leistungen.* Heidelberg: Spektrum Akademischer Verlag.

Prosser, L.A., Kuntz, K.M., Bar-Or, A. and Weinstein, M.C. (2003) 'Patients and community preferences for treatments and health states in multiple sclerosis.' *Multiple Sclerosis 9,* 3, 311–319.

Purdie, H. (1997) 'Music therapy with adults who have traumatic brain injury and stroke.' *British Journal of Music Therapy 11,* 2, 45–50.

Quester, R., Schmitt, E.W. and Lippert-Günner, M. (eds) (1997) *Stufen zum Licht: Hoffnungen für Schädel-Hirnpatienten.* Leimersheim: Fachverlag hw-studioweber.

Ragneskog, H., Kihlgren, Karlsson, and Norberg (1996) 'Dinner music for demented patients: Analysis of video-recorded observations.' *Clinical Nursing Research 5,* 3, 262–282.

Ragneskog, H. and Kihlgren, M. (1997) 'Music and other strategies to improve the care of agitated patients with dementia.' *Scandinavian Journal of Caring Science 11,* 176–182.

Randall, C. (1982) 'The medical social worker in the rehabilitation team.' In R. Capildeo and A. Maxwell (eds) *Progress in Rehabilitation: Multiple Sclerosis.* London: Macmillan Press.

Raskind, M.A. (1998) 'The clinical interface of depression and dementia.' *Journal of Clinical Psychiatry 59,* 9–12.

Reiter, A. (2003) 'Einführung in die humanistische Psychologie.' Available at www.sbg.ac.at/psy/people/reiter/vorlesungen/humanistische_psychologie/humanistische%20psychologie.doc

Remington, R. (2002) 'Calming music and hand massage with agitated elderly.' *Nursing Research 51,* 5, 317–323.

Richarz, B. (1997) 'Considerations to the psychosomatics of Alzheimer's disease.' *Dynamische Psychiatrie 30,* 5/6, 340–355.

Rickert, E., Duke, L., Putzke, J., Marson, D. and Graham, K. (1998) 'Early stage Alzheimer's disease disrupts encoding of contextual information.' *Aging Neuropsychology and Cognition 5*, 1, 73–81.

Ridder, H.M. (2001) 'Musikterapi med ældre.' In L.O. Bonde, I.N. Pedersen and T. Wigram (eds) *Musikterapi: når ord ikke slår til.* Århus: KLIM.

Ridder, H.M. (2003) 'Singing dialogue: Music therapy with persons in advanced stages of dementia. A case study research design.' Unpublished PhD thesis, Aalborg University.

Ridder, H.M. (2005a) 'Music therapy with the elderly: Complementary data as a rich approach to understanding communication.' In D. Aldridge (ed) *Case Study Design in Music Therapy.* London: Jessica Kingsley Publishers.

Ridder, H.M. (2005b) *Musik & Demens. Musikaktiviteter og musikterapie med demenstramte. 2. reviderede udgave.* Århus: Forlaget KLIM.

Rider, M. (1997) *The Rhythmic Language of Health and Disease.* St Louis, MO: MMB Music Inc.

Riegler, J. (1980) 'Comparison of a reality orientation program for geriatric patients with and without music.' *Journal of Music Therapy 17*, 26–33.

Rimpau, W. (2000) 'Ärztliche Anamnese.' *Forum Psychosomatik. Zeitschrift für psychosomatische Multiple sklerose-Forschung 9*, 1, 54–57.

Risse, G.L. and Gates, J.R. (1997) A reconsideration of bilateral language representation based on the intracarotid amobarbital procedure. *Brain and Cognition 33*, 118–132.

Rittner, S. (1990) 'Zur Rolle der Vokalimprovisation in der Musiktherapie.' *Musiktherapeutische Umschau 11*, 104–119.

Robb, S.L. (1996) 'Techniques in song writing: Restoring emotional and physical well-being in adolescents who have been traumatically injured.' *Music Therapy Perspectives 14*, 1, 30–37.

Roberts, B.L. and Algase, D.L. (1988) 'Victims of Alzheimer's disease and the environment.' *Nursing Clinics of North America 23*, 1, 88–93.

Robinson, G. (2001) 'An investigation of immediate and short-term influences of music, as a therapeutic medium, on brain-injured patient's communication and social interaction skills.' *British Journal of Occupational Therapy 64*, 6, 304.

Robinson, G. and Solomon, D.J. (1974) 'Rhythm is processed by the speech hemisphere.' *Journal of Experimental Psychology 102*, 508–511.

Robson, C. (1993) *Real World Research: A resource for social scientists and practitioner-researchers.* Oxford: Blackwell.

Rogers, C.R. (1959) 'A theory of therapy, personality, and interpersonal relationships, as developed in the client-centered framework.' In S. Koch (ed) *Psychology: A study of a science.* New York: McGraw-Hill.

Rohde, H. and Burges, S. (eds) (1993) *Feldstudie zur Wirksamkeit der Feldenkrais-Methode bei Multiple sklerose-Betroffenen.* Saarbrîcken: Deutsche Multiple Sklerose Gesellschaft, Landesverband Saar.

Rolvsjord, R. (1998) 'Når musikken minner om livet: Musikalsk samhandling som reminisens. En infallsvinkel til musikkterapi i geriatrien.' *Nordic Journal of Music Therapy 7*, 1, 4–13.

Rosenfeld, J.V. and Dun, B. (1999) 'Music therapy with children with severe traumatic brain injury.' In R. Rebollo Pratt and D. Erdonmez Grocke (eds) *Music Medicine 3.* Parkville: University of Melbourne.

Rosnow, R.L. and Rosenthal, R. (1996) 'Computing controls, effects sizes, and counternulls on other people's published data: General procedures for research consumers.' *Psychological Methods 1*, 331–340.

Ross, J.A. (2003) 'The self: From soul to brain.' *Journal of Consciousness Studies 10*, 2, 67–85.

Roth, G. and Prinz, W. (1996) *Kopf-Arbeit: Gehirnfunktion und kognitive Leistungen.* Heidelberg: Spektrum Akademischer Verlag.

Rothwell, P.M., McDowell, Z., Wong, C.K. and Dorman, P.J. (1997) 'Doctors and patients don't agree: Cross-sectional study of patients' and doctors' perceptions and assessments of disability in multiple sclerosis.' *British Medical Journal 314,* 1580–1583.

Rudolf, J. (2000) 'Beitrag der Positronen-Emissionstomographie zur diagnostischen Zuordnung und prognostischen Einschätzung postanoxischer Hirnschäden.' *Fortschritt Neurologischer Psychiatrie 68.* Stuttgart: Thieme.

Rusted, J., Marsh, R., Bledski, L. and Sheppard, L. (1997) 'Alzheimer patients' use of auditory and olfactory cues to aid verbal memory.' *Aging and Mental Health 1,* 4, 364–371.

Sacks, O. (1990) *Der Mann, der seine Frau mit einem Hut verwechselte.* Rheinbek: Verlag Rowohlt.

Salmon, D.P., Thal, L.J., Butters, N. and Heindel, W.C. (1990) 'Longitudinal evaluation of dementia of the Alzheimer type: A comparison of three standardized mental status examinations.' *Neurology 40,* 8, 1225–1230.

Sambandham, M. and Schirm, V. (1995) 'Music as a nursing intervention for residents with Alzheimer's disease in long-term care.' *Geriatric Nursing 16,* 2, 79–83.

Samson, S. and Zatorre, R.J. (1991) 'Recognition memory of songs after unilateral temporal-lobe lesion: Evidence for dual encoding.' *Journal of Experimental Psychology 17,* 793–804.

Schifferdecker, M. (2002) 'Psychische Veränderungen-Krankheitsbewältigung-Patientenführung.' In R.M. Schmidt and F. Hoffmann (eds) *Multiple Sklerose.* München: Urban & Fischer.

Schilder, P. (1950) *The Image and the Appearance of the Human Body.* New York: John Wiley.

Schinner, K.M., Chisolm, A.H., Grap, M.J., Siva, P., Hallinan, M. and LaVoice-Hawkins, A.M. (1995) 'Effects of auditory stimuli on intercranial pressure and cerebral perfusion pressure in traumatic brain injury.' *Journal of Neuroscience Nursing 27,* 6, 349–354.

Schipperges, H. (1987) *Eine 'Summa Medicinae' bei Avicenna. Zur Krankheitslehre und Heilkunde des Ibn Sina (980–1037).* Stuttgart: Springer Verlag.

Schlenck, K.J. (1990) 'Rehabilitation aphasischer Patienten nach Schlaganfall.' *Prävention und Rehabilitation 2,* 56–63.

Schmid, W. and Aldridge, D. (2004) 'Active music therapy in the treatment of multiple sclerosis patients: A matched control study.' *Journal of Music Therapy 41,* 3, 225–240.

Schmid, W., Aldridge, D., Kaeder, M., Schmidt, C. and Ostermann, T. (2003) 'Gesundheit und kreativer Prozess: eine Pilotstudie zur musiktherapeutischen Betreuung von MS-Patienten.' *Pflegemagazin 4,* 5, 14–23.

Schmidt, H.U. and Hennings, U. (1998) 'Gruppenmusiktherapie bei Patienten mit Multiple sklerose.' Unpublished documentation of the 10th Ulmer Workshop 1998.

Schrag, A., Jahanshahi, M. and Quinn, N. (2001) 'What contributes to depression in Parkinson's disease?' *Psychological Medicine 31,* 65–73.

Schüßler, G. (ed) (1993) *Bewältigung chronischer Krankheiten.* Gîttingen: Vandenhoeck & Ruprecht.

Scruton, R. (ed) (1999) *The Aesthetics of Music.* Oxford: Oxford University Press.

Searle, J.R. (1997) 'Die wissenschaftliche Erforschung des Bewußtseins.' In H. Meier and D. Ploog (eds) *Der Mensch und sein Gehirn: Die Folgen der Evolution,* 2nd edn. München Piper Verlag.

Sherrat, K., Thornton, A. and Hatton, C. (2004a) 'Music interventions for people with dementia: A review of the literature.' *Aging and Mental Health 8,* 1, 3–12.

Sherrat, K., Thornton, A. and Hatton, C. (2004b) Emotional and behavioural responses to music in people with dementia: An observational study.' *Aging and Mental Health 8*, 3, 233–241.

Shiloah, A. (2002) 'Die Islamische Musik.' In B. Lewis (ed) *Welt des Islam*. München : Orbis Verlag.

Shoulson, I. (1990) 'Huntington's disease: Cognitive and psychiatric features.' *Neuropsychiatry, Neuropsychology, and Behavioural Neurology 3*, 15–22.

Silber, F. (1999) 'The influence of background music on the performance of the MMSE with patients diagnosed with Alzheimer's disease.' *Journal of Music Therapy 36*, 3, 196–206.

Silber, F. and Hes, J. (1995) 'The use of songwriting with patients diagnosed with Alzheimer's disease. Special Issue: International music therapy.' *Music Therapy Perspectives 13*, 1, 31–34.

Silvestrini, M. and Troisi, E. (1995) 'Involvement of the healthy hemisphere in recovery from aphasia and motor deficit in patients with cortical ischemic infarction: A trancranial Doppler study.' *Neurology 45*, 1815–1820.

Simpson, F. (2000) 'Creative music therapy: A last resort?' In D. Aldridge (ed) *Music Therapy in Dementia Care*. London: Jessica Kingsley Publishers.

Smeijsters, H. (1997) 'Musiktherapie bei Alzheimerpatienten: Eine Meta-Analyse von Forschungsergebnissen.' *Musiktherapeutische Umschau 4*, 268–283.

Smith, D. (1999) 'The civilizing process and the history of sexuality: Comparing Norbert Elias and Michael Foucault.' *Theory and Society 28*, 79–100.

Smith, S. (2000) 'Performing the (sound)world.' *Environment and Planning D: Society and Space 18*, 615–637.

Smith-Marchese, K. (1994) 'The effects of participatory music on the reality orientation and sociability of Alzheimer's residents in a long-term care setting.' *Activities, Adaptation, and Aging 18*, 2, 41–55.

Smythies, J. (2003) 'Space, time and consciousness.' *Journal of Consciousness Studies 10*, 3, 47–56.

Sparks, R., Helm, N. and Albert, M. (1974) 'Aphasia rehabilitation resulting from melodic intonation therapy.' *Cortex 10*, 4, 303–316.

Sparks, R. and Holland, A.L. (1976) 'Method: Melodic intonation therapy.' *Journal of Speech and Hearing Disorders 41*, 287–297.

Sparks, R.W., Deck, M.S. and Deck, J.W. (1986) 'Melodic intonation therapy.' In R. Chapey (ed) *Language Intervention Strategies in Adult Aphasia*. Baltimore, MD: Williams & Wilkins.

Speer, S.R., Kjelgaard, M.M. and Dobroth, K.M. (1996) 'The influence of prosodic structure on the resolution of temporary syntactic closure ambiguities.' *Journal of Psycholinguistic Research 25*, 2, 249–271.

Spering, M. (2000) *Das Problem des Bewusstseins: neurophysiologische Grundlagen*. Summer Academy, St Johann. Heidelberg: Kognitive Neurowissenschaft, Univ. Heidelberg.

Springer, A., Clark, S., Price, E. and Weldon, P. (2001) 'Psychosocial implications of multiple sclerosis.' In J. Halper (ed) *Advanced Concepts in Mulitple Sclerosis Nursing Care*. New York: Demos Medical Publishing.

Stein, D.G., Brailowsky, S. and Will, B. (2000) *Brain-Repair: Das Selbstheilungspotential des Gehirns oder wie das Gehirn sich selbst hilft*. Stuttgart: Thieme.

Strauss, A. and Corbin, J. (1996) *Grundlagen Qualitativer Sozialforschung*. Weinheim: Beltz.

Street, R.L.J. and Cappella, J.N. (1989) 'Social and linguistic factors influencing adaptation in children's speech.' *Journal of Psycholinguisic Research 18*, 5, 497–519.

Sturm, E. (1979) *Rehabilitation von Querschnittgelähmten: Eine medizinpsychologische Studie*. Bern: Huber Verlag.

Sullivan, M., Mikail, S. and Weinshenker, B. (1997) 'Coping with a diagnosis of multiple sclerosis.' *Canadian Journal of Behavioural Science 29*, 4, 249–257.

Sullivan, M., Weinshenker, B., Mikail, S. and Edgley, K. (1995) 'Depression before and after diagnosis of multiple sclerosis.' *Multiple Sclerosis 1*, 104–108.

Sutherland, K. (2001) 'Consciousness and emotion.' *Journal of Consciousness Studies 8*, 12, 79–82.

Suzuki, M., Kanamori, M. and Watanabe, M. (2004) 'Behavioral and endocrinological evaluation of music therapy for elderly patients with dementia.' *Nursing and Health Sciences 6*, 11–18.

Svenaeus, F. (2000) 'The body uncanny: Further steps towards a phenomenology of illness.' *Medicine, Health Care and Philosophy 3*, 125–137.

Swartz, K., Walton, J., Crummer, G., Hantz, E. and Frisina, R. (1992) 'P3 event-related potentials and performance of healthy older and Alzheimer's dementia subjects for music perception tasks.' *Psychomusicology 11*, 96–118.

Synder Smith, S. and Winkler, P. (1990) 'Traumatic head injuries.' In D.A. Umphred (ed) *Neurological Rehabilitation*. St Louis, MO: CV Mosby.

Tabboni, S. (2001) 'The idea of social time in Norbert Elias.' *Time and Society 10*, 1, 5–27.

Tabloski, P., McKinnon-Howe, L. and Remington, R. (1995) 'Effects of calming music on the level of agitation in cognitively impaired nursing home residents.' *American Journal of Alzheimer's Care and Related Disorders and Research*, Jan./Feb., 10–15.

Tamplin, J. (2000) 'Improvisational music therapy approaches to coma arousal.' *Australian Journal of Music Therapy 11*, 38–51.

Taylor Sarno, M. (1991) *Acquired Aphasia*. New York: Academic Press.

Thaut, M. and McIntosh, G. (1999) 'Music therapy in mobility training with the elderly: A review of current research.' *Care Management Journal 1*, 1, 71–74.

Thaut, M., Mcintosh, G., Rice, R., Miller, R., Rathbun, J. and Brault, J. (1996) 'Rhythmic auditory stimulation in gait training for Parkinson's disease patients.' *Movement Disorders 11*, 2, 193–200.

Thaut, M. and Miltner, R. (1996) 'Rhythmisch-akustische Stimulation (RAS in der Gangrehabilitation: Zusammenfassung bisheriger Befunde und Hinweise zur praktischen Durchführung).' *Neurologische Rehabilitation 2*, 81–86.

Thaut, M., Miltner, R., Lange, H., Hurt, C. and Hoemberg, V. (1999) 'Velocity modulation and rhythmic synchronization of gait in Huntington's disease.' *Movement Disorders 14*, 5, 808–819.

Thomas, D., Heitman, R. and Alexander, T. (1997) 'The effects of music on bathing cooperation for residents with dementia.' *Journal of Music Therapy 34*, 246–259.

Thompson, C.K. (2000) Neuroplasticity: Evidence from aphasia. *Journal of Communication Disorders 33*, 4, 357–366.

Thorne, S., Paterson, B., Russell, C. and Schultz, A. (2002) 'Complementary/alternative medicine in chronic illness.' *International Journal of Nursing Studies 39*, 671–683.

Tierney, M.C., Szalai, J.P., Snow, W. and Fisher, R. (1996) 'The prediction of Alzheimer disease: The role of patient and informant perceptions of cognitive deficits.' *Archives of Neurology 53*, 5, 423–427.

Tomaino, C. (ed) (1998) *Clinical Applications of Music in Neurologic Rehabilitation*. St Louis, MO: MMB Music Inc.

Tomaino, C.M. (2000) 'Working with images and recollection with elderly patients.' In D. Aldridge (ed) *Music Therapy in Dementia Care*. London: Jessica Kingsley Publishers.

Tucek, G. (1995) 'Orientalische Musik- und Tanztherapie.' *Musik-, Tanz- und Kunsttherapie 6*, 3, 149–166.

Tucek, G. (1997) 'Musiktherapie in der islamischen Heilkunde: Ein historischer Rückblick? *Musik-, Tanz- und Kunsttherapie 8*, 1, 69–72.

Tucek, G. (2000) 'Altorientalische Musik- und Tanztherapie.' In Hörmann (ed), *Jahrbuch für Transkulturelle Medizin und Psychotherapie 1996/97. Tanztherapie: Transkulturelle Perspektiven.* Berlin: VWB-Verlag für Wissenschaft und Bildung.

Tucek, G. (2003) 'Altorientalische Musiktherapie im interkulturellen Dialog: Kulturimmanente und kulturtranszendente Aspekte im Menschenbild. In H. Egner (ed) *Heilung und Heil: Begegnung – Verantwortung Interkultureller Dialog.* Düsseldorf: Patmos Verlag.

Tucek, G., Auer-Pekarsky, A.-M. and Stepansky, R. (2001) '"Altorientalische Musiktherapie" bei Schädel-Hirn-Trauma.' *Musik-, Tanz- und Kunsttherapie 12*, 1, 1–12.

Uexküll, T.V., Fuchs, M., Müller-Braunschweig, H. and Johnen, R. (eds) (1997) *Subjektive Anatomie: Theorie und Praxis körperbezogener Psychotherapie.* Stuttgart: Schattauer.

Usher, J. (1998) 'Lighting up the mind: Evolving a model of consciousness and its application to improvisation in music therapy.' *British Journal of Music Therapy 12*, 1, 4–19.

Usita, P., Hyman, I. and Herman, K. (1998) 'Narrative intentions: Listening to life stories in Alzheimer's disease.' *Journal of Aging Studies 12*, 2, 185–197.

Ustvedt, H.J. (1937) 'Über die Untersuchung der musikalischen Funktionen bei Patienten mit Gehirnleiden, besonders bei Patienten mit Aphasie.' *Acta Medica Scandinavica*, Suppl. 86.

Valarino, E.E. (1995) *Erfahrungen an der Schwelle des Todes.* Genf: Ariston Verlag.

Van de Winckel, A., Feys, H. and De Weerdt, W. (2004) 'Cognitive and behavioural effects of music-based exercises in patients with dementia.' *Clinical Rehabilitation 18*, 253–260.

Vasterling, J., Seltzer, B., Carpenter, B. and Thompson, K. (1997) 'Unawareness of social interaction and emotional control deficits in Alzheimer's disease.' *Aging Neuropsychology and Cognition 4*, 4, 280–289.

Vertes, L. (1996) 'Nurses and midwives through the artist's eyes.' *Nover 9*, 4, 25–26.

Vieth-Fleischhauer, H. and Petzold, H. (1999) 'Ausdruck und Erstehen in der musikalischen Improvisation als kokreative Fluktualisierung–Perspektiven Integrativer Musiktherapie.' *Integrative Therapie 2–3*, 139–168.

Vincent, C. and Furnham, A. (1996) 'Why do patients turn to complementary medicine? An empirical study.' *British Journal of Clinical Psychology 35*, 37–48.

Vink, A. (2000) The problem of agitation in elderly people and the potential benefit of music therapy. In D. Aldridge (ed) *Music Therapy in Dementia Care.* London: Jessica Kingsley Publishers.

Vink, A.C., Birks, J. S., Bruinsma, M.S. and Scholten, R.J. (2004) 'Music therapy for people with dementia (Cochrane Review).' In *The Cochrane Library 3.* Chichester: John Wiley.

Volicer, L., Harper, D., Manning, B., Goldstein, R. and Satlin, A. (2001) 'Sundowning and circadian rhythms in Alzheimer's disease.' *American Journal of Psychiatry 158*, 5, 704–711.

Wade, D.T. and Johnston, C. (1999) 'The permanent vegetative state: Practical guidance on diagnosis and management.' *British Medical Journal 319*, 841–844.

Walsh, J.S., Welch, H.G. and Larson, E.B. (1990) 'Survival of outpatients with Alzheimer-type dementia.' *Annals of Internal Medicine 113*, 6, 429–434.

Wang, J., Reimer, M.A., Metz, L. and Patten, S. (2000) 'Major depression and quality of life in individuals with multiple sclerosis.' *International Journal of Psychiatry in Medicine 30*, 4, 309–317.

Watzlawick, P., Beavin, J.H. and Jackson, D.D. (1990) *Menschliche Kommunikation. Formen, Störungen, Paradoxien* (8th edition). Berne: Verlag Hans Huber.

Weed, L. (1968) 'Medical records that guide and teach.' *New England Journal of Medicine 278*, 598–600.

Wellendorf, B. (1991) 'Musik som en bro mellem fortid og nutid.' *Sygeplejersken 50*, 22–23.

Welter, F. and Schönle, P. (1997) *Neurologische Rehabiliation.* Stuttgart: Fischer Verlag.

Westerman, G. and Reck Miranda, E. (2004) 'A new model of sensorimotor coupling in the development of speech.' *Brain and Language 89*, 2, 393–400.

Wheeler, B. (ed) (1995) *Music Therapy Research: Quantitative and Qualitative Perspectives.* Phoenixville, USA: Barcelona Publishers.

Wheeler, B., Shiflett, S. and Nayak, N. (2003) 'Effects of number of sessions and group or individual music therapy on the mood and behaviour of people who have had strokes or traumatic brain injury.' *Nordic Journal of Music Therapy 12*, 2, 139–151.

White, D. and Murphy, C. (1998) 'Working memory for nonverbal auditory information in dementia of the Alzheimer type.' *Archives of Clinical Neuropsychology 13*, 4, 339–347.

Widmer, R. (1997) 'Therapie mit hirnverletzten Menschen: Die Möglichkeiten der Kunsttherapie.' *Psychoscope 18*, 4, 16–18.

Wiens, M.E., Reimer, M.A. and Guyn, H.L. (1999) 'Music therapy as a treatment method for improving respiratory muscle strength in patients with advanced Multiple Sclerosis: A pilot study.' *Rehabilitation Nursing 24*, 2, 74–80.

Wiesmann, U., Machtems, W. and Hannich, H.-J. (2000) 'Multiple Sklerose und Arbeitsmotivation – eine quantitative Studie.' *Zeitschrift für Gesundheitswissenschaften 8*, 1, 26–37.

Wiesmann, U., Machtems, W. and Hannich, H.-J. (2000) 'Multiple Sklerose und Kognitive Anpassung.' *Zeitschrift für Gesundheitpsychologie 9*, 3, 99–111.

Wigram, T., Nygaard Pedersen, I. and Bonde, L.O. (2002) *A Comprehensive Guide to Music Therapy.* London: Jessica Kingsley Publishers.

Wilber, K. (1997) 'An integral theory of consciousness.' *Journal of Consciousness Studies 4*, 1, 71–92.

Wilson, B.A. (1999) *Case Studies in Neuropsychological Rehabilitation.* Oxford: Oxford University Press.

Wingruber, M. (1995) 'Mutabor: Intensive home treatment and ambulatory promotion for persons with acquired brain damage.' *Rehabilitation 34*, 2, 101–105.

Wit, V., Knox, R., Jutai, J. and Loveszy, R. (1994) 'Music therapy and rehabilitation of attention in brain injury: A pilot study.' *Canadian Journal of Music Therapy 2*, 1, 72–89.

World Health Organization (1969) *Technical Report 419*, 1.2.1. Geneva: World Health Organization.

World Health Organization (2004) *World Report on Road Traffic Injury Prevention.* Retrieved May 2004, available at www.who.int/world-health-day/2004/infomaterials/world_report/en/.

Wötzel, C., Wehner, C., Pöllman, W. and König, N. (1997) *Therapie der Multiplen Sklerose.* München: Pflaum Verlag.

Yamamoto, K., Osora, M., Noda, R. and Maeda, Y. (2003) 'The importance of effective music selection for synchronized musico-kinetic therapy in patients with disturbances of consciousness.' In M. Shigemori and T. Kanno (eds) *Proceedings of the 12th Annual Meeting of the Society for Treatment of Coma.* Tokyo: Society for Treatment of Coma.

York, E. (1994) 'The development of a quantitative music skills test for patients with Alzheimer's disease.' *Journal of Music Therapy 31*, 4, 280–296.

Zatorre, R.J. (1984) 'Music perception and cerebral function: A critical review.' *Music Perception 2*, 196–221.

Zieger, A. (1996) 'Musik als Vermittlerin neuen Lebens.' *Zeitschrift für Heilpädagogik 47*, S310–317.

Zieger, A. (1998) 'Grenzbereiche der Wahrnehmung: Über die ungewöhnliche Lebensform von Menschen im Wachkoma.' *Behinderte in Familie, Schule und Gesellschaft 6.* Graz: Reha Druck.

Zieger, A. (1999) 'Wieviel Gehirn braucht der Mensch? Dialogaufbau mit Menschen im Koma und apallischen Syndrom.' In K.-D. Neander (ed) *Musik und Pflege.* München: Urban & Fischer.

Zieger, A. (2003) 'Traumatisiert an Leib und Seele: Konsequenzen für den Umgang mit Wachkoma-Patienten aus beziehungsmedizinischer Sicht.' *Vortrag zur Jahrestagung der Österreichischen Wachkoma Gesellschaft Wien* (ÖWG), 24 October 2003.

Zillmer, E.A. and Spiers, M.V. (2001) *Principles of Neuropsychology.* London: Wadsworth.

Znoj, H.-J., Lude, P. and Lude, Y. (1999) *Zur Lage der Querschnittgelähmten und ihrer Angehörigen in der Schweiz.* Bern: Institut für Psychologie der Universität Bern.

The Contributors

David Aldridge is Chair for Qualitative Research in Medicine at the Faculty of Medicine, University of Witten-Herdecke. He specializes in developing research methods for various therapeutic initiatives including creative arts therapies, complementary medicine and nursing. He teaches and supervises research in medicine, music therapy, creative arts and nursing.

He initially trained in Fine Arts, and his interests have since extended to photography and large format print media, with a focus on landscape photography. He is currently working on "Stations of the Cross"; a series based upon Australian landscapes.

With the aim of broadening the audience for creative arts therapies, David has created a website, www.musictherapyworld.net, which includes an electronic journal, free access to a variety of complementary medicine databases and information about music therapy worldwide.

Simon K. Gilbertson was born in New Mills, England. After his childhood in Bermuda, he returned to England where he completed his studies in ethnomusicology and composition at King's College, London. Simon moved to Germany in 1994 and is currently working as a research assistant on a structured literature review project at the Department for Qualitative Research in Medicine at the University of Witten-Herdecke. His clinical expertise is in the field of neurorehabilitation, and in March 2005 he completed his doctoral thesis on music therapy in early rehabilitation with people who have experienced traumatic brain injury.

Ansgar Herkenrath was born in Duisburg, Germany. He studied at Folkwang College of Music in Essen, and was organist and conductor of various Roman Catholic choirs. He later trained as a male nurse, working in a psychiatric clinic, before going on to study music therapy at the University of Witten-Herdecke. Ansgar has worked as a music therapist since 1997, and in 2004 received a doctorate in qualitative research in medicine.

Monika Jungblut is a freelance music therapist practising at the University of Witten-Herdecke, where she received a doctorate in qualitative research in medicine in 2003. She worked as an opera and concert singer for many years, and taught singing at the Hamburg and Essen Academies of Music before going on to study music therapy in Hamburg. Her work involves clinical practice in the fields of psychotherapy and psychiatry, as well as neurological rehabilitation treatment for aphasia outpatients.

Anke Scheel-Sailer was born in Dortmund, Germany. She studied medicine at the University of Witten-Herdecke, and received the Guttman Prize for fundamental research in paraplegic science. She worked as a surgeon, psychiatrist and practitioner at various hospitals between 1994 and 2000, later becoming a specialist in primary care. She currently works as a specialist in physical medicine, rehabilitation and psychosomatic illness at Reha Rheinfelden, Switzerland.

Wolfgang Schmid studied piano in Augsburg and Munich, before joining the music therapy course at the University of Witten-Herdecke, where he later became a lecturer in group work. His clinical practice has included work with developmentally challenged children, adults with Multiple Sclerosis (MS) and Parkinson's Disease, and those recovering from a stroke or a coma. His dissertation focused on creative music therapy for people living with MS.

Hanne Mette Ridder is Associated Professor at the Institute of Music and Music Therapy at the University of Aalborg, where she completed her music therapy training in 1989. She has since worked with children, adolescents and elderly people. In 2003 she completed her PhD dissertation entitled "Singing Dialogue. Music therapy with persons in advanced stages of dementia." Her clinical work and research focuses on music therapy for people with different degrees of neurodegeneration.

Gerhard Tucek was born in Vienna, where he studied ethnology, applied cultural sciences and traditional oriental music therapy. He is Scientific Director for music and the creative arts therapies at the Vienna International Academy of Holistic Medicine (GAMED), where he is also Director of Studies for the training course in traditional oriental music therapy. He directs a series of lectures and teaching seminars in "Music and Medicine" at the Karayan Centre in Vienna, and lectures in medical anthropology and music psychology at various universities. His clinical work is in the fields of neurological rehabilitation, child cancer, cardiological rehabilitation, handicap and psychiatric rehabilitation.

Subject Index

Author Index

299